MW00776317

A WELL *of* WONDER

ESSAYS ON C. S. LEWIS, J. R. R. TOLKIEN, AND THE INKLINGS

Clyde S. Kilby

Edited by Loren Wilkinson and Keith Call

PARACLETE PRESS
BREWSTER, MASSACHUSETTS
BARGA, ITALY

For Clyde S. Kilby, with gratitude

2016 First Printing

A Well of Wonder: Essays on C. S. Lewis, J. R. R. Tolkien, and The Inklings

ISBN 978-1-61261-862-3

Library of Congress Cataloging-in-Publication Data
Names: Kilby, Clyde S., author. | Wilkinson, Loren, editor.
Title: A well of wonder : essays on C.S. Lewis, J.R.R. Tolkien, and the Inklings / Clyde S. Kilby ; edited by Loren Wilkinson and Keith Call.
Description: Brewster MA : Paraclete Press Inc., 2016.
Identifiers: LCCN 2016035753 | ISBN 9781612618623 (volume 1 : hard cover)
Subjects: LCSH: Christianity. | Theology. | Christian literature. | Christianity and literature. | Lewis, C. S. (Clive Staples), 1898-1963. | Tolkien, J. R. R. (John Ronald Reuel), 1892-1973. | Inklings (Group of writers)
Classification: LCC BR96 .K43 2016 | DDC 230.092/241—dc23
LC record available at https://lccn.loc.gov/2016035753

10 9 8 7 6 5 4 3 2 1

Published by Paraclete Press
Brewster, Massachusetts, and Barga, Italy
www.paracletepress.com

Printed in the United States of America

CONTENTS

Section 3
THE INKLINGS AS SHAPERS OF A NEW CHRISTIAN IMAGINATION

A Tribute to Clyde S. Kilby

It is a time when apples ripen,
friendships thicken,
maples kindle a fall fire
west of Blanchard. Through the halls
scholars and students quicken
at a familiar voice,
and on the corner of Washington and Jefferson
squirrels and sparrows rejoice
because you're home. Like a hobbit
come back to the Shire
you're home again, our friend,
bringing Martha with you, and sunflower
seeds, a sackful of nuts, three score
years and ten worth of wisdom, under
your arm—letters and Lewis-lore—
your mind a well of wonder.

It was your mind, your inner eye, that
saw it long before it happened—
the hierarchy of shelves
dusted obliquely by the late sun
behind old glass in the narrow room once occupied
by a minority of one
and now inhabited by Inklings and Elves.
Like a gardener raking grass,
piling the bright and varied leaves,
from far you gathered treasure, sheaves
of manuscripts, papers ornamented
with the rich, crabbed, English script,

searched out the volumes
burnished and precious with
scholarship and age—
"fact shrunk to truth" speaking
from every page.

Then you swung open for us all
the wardrobe door,
pushed us farther up and farther in
(accompanied by some favorite talking beast)
to Middle-earth, Narnia, and the Utter East.
In there, for us to re-explore,
is perfect Perelandra.
Treebeard is growing up the cornered wall.
In the Deep Space behind the rows of books
eldila elude us; Curdie
encounters Mr. Bultitude the bear.
There in that room
we smell the past, untainted by decay or death
but fragrant, for in there
the mallorns bloom
and all the blessed air
is warm with Aslan's breath.

—*Luci Shaw*

Introduction

CLYDE S. KILBY: THE MAN WHO REOPENED THE DOORS TO WONDER

LOREN WILKINSON

In the poem to Clyde Kilby that stands as an epigraph to this collection of his writings, Luci Shaw—one of many writers and scholars who received early encouragement from Dr. Kilby—uses two metaphors to describe the kind of experience this remarkable scholar and teacher provided for many of his students. The first is of a doorkeeper, an allusion to the imaginative entrance to the world C. S. Lewis created in *The Chronicles of Narnia.*

Then you swung open for us all
the wardrobe door,
pushed us farther up and farther in.

The second picture is of the man as a deep well, returning with his wife, Martha, after a summer in England, bringing

three score
years and ten worth of wisdom, under
your arm—letters and Lewis-lore—
your mind a well of wonder.

As we prepared this book and its companion volume, *The Arts and the Christian Imagination: Essays on Art, Literature, and Aesthetics*, which includes Kilby's writings on these topics, we invited many of his former students to write of his influence on them. Many of them responded with similar language. Mark Noll also sees Kilby as a doorkeeper. For a whole generation of American evangelicals, says Noll, "Kilby opened a wardrobe onto a land of wonder where the Lion stalked." Tom Howard continues the metaphor in describing the effect of taking Kilby's class in Romantic poetry: "He threw open the shutters. . . . He pointed to the things that troubled the very marrow in one's bones, but for which one never had the vocabulary to summon into visibility."

In the dedication of his first book, *Christ the Tiger*, Howard uses the language of seeing: "For Dr. Kilby, who took my arm and said, 'Look.'" Leanne Payne continues the metaphor. Speaking of the blindness resulting from a common kind of reductive modern analysis, Payne says, "He came against this blindness in all of his courses, and his bright students, heavy into analysis and sorely introspective, dropped their blinders, looked up, and began to see." The poet Jeanne Murray Walker uses a different picture: "I praise him for being a liberator." Dick Taylor, a historian with the Illinois State Historical Society, sums up Kilby's effect on him in a seminar in life writing: "I can't remember a thing he taught me about writing biography, but my experience in that class changed my life forever."

As this small sampling of comments makes plain, Clyde S. Kilby was, for many students, an extraordinary teacher. It is with that fact, rather than with his early, long, and effective championing of writers like Lewis and Tolkien, that I must begin in introducing this collection of his writings on those makers of "modern mythology" (as he called it). Kilby's greatness was not simply the result of his influence from, or defense of, Lewis, Tolkien, and friends; rather he turned to them (and turned many others to them) *because* they expressed a truth about God and creation that he had already come to know.

That truth—which kept filling and refilling that "well of wonder" which was Dr. Kilby's life—was the fact that the whole of created reality is the miraculous gift of a loving, personal, and ever-present Creator. And this was not just a propositional truth intellectually known: it was lived, experienced, and shared. Often it was experienced—and expressed—through the apparently trivial or insignificant. Several of his former students, for example, mention Dr. Kilby's love for the dandelion, and Marilee Melvin recalls his bringing a drooping dandelion to class and asking, "in a voice filled with awe, how many of you believe that the Lord God made *this* dandelion for our pleasure on *this* day."

Now it is not easy for a college student of any generation, let alone a sober faculty colleague, to take seriously someone who publicly shares his awe over a dandelion; there were many who were themselves mystified by the life-changing effect Dr. Kilby had on people. Since I, too, am one of those whose life was changed by the man, I want to try to express something of the mystery of how and why that change was effected.

The dandelion incident calls to mind G. K. Chesterton's words in *Orthodoxy* (one of the many books that I read first through Dr. Kilby's recommendation).

> Because children have abounding vitality, because they are in spirit fierce and free, they want things repeated and unchanged. They always say "Do it again"; and the grown-up person does it again until he is nearly dead. For grown-up people are not strong enough to exult in monotony. But perhaps God is strong enough to exult

> in monotony. It is possible that God says every morning "Do it again" to the sun, and every evening "Do it again" to the moon. It may not be automatic necessity that makes all daisies alike; it may be that God makes every daisy separately, but has never got tired of making them. It may be that he has the eternal appetite of infancy; for we have sinned and grown old, and our Father is younger than we.[1]

Almost every recollection of Kilby mentions something of this quite unselfconscious, childlike delight in creaturely being. Chesterton traces that childlike delight in the commonplace back to its divine source, and all of the writers whose works, letters, and manuscripts Kilby was to assemble in what became the "Wade Collection" express something of that joyful wonder at the gift of Being. Writers like George MacDonald, Chesterton, Lewis, and Tolkien helped Kilby understand and express that awareness of Being as a divine gift—but he responded to the vision in them because it was first in him. Their springs flowed from the same source.

This connection between wonder at the world, on the one hand, and trying to be a faithful Christian, on the other, was one that evangelical Christians like myself, growing up in mid-twentieth-century America, desperately needed to make. My own initial encounter with Kilby was in registration week at Wheaton in September 1961. Still somewhat groggy from a three-day bus trip across the continent (I had never been east of Oregon before), I recall a genial little man (speaking, I realize now, in his capacity as chairman of the English department) telling a group of us assembled for a freshman writing exemption test, "You've already been selected; now we're going to select you some more." But it was not

1 G. K. Chesterton, *Orthodoxy* (London: John Lane, 1936), 60.

till the next fall, when I took Kilby's Romantic poetry class, that my world began to change—or perhaps it would be more accurate to say that a deep wound in my world began to heal.

I had, sometime in high school, already fallen in love with the Romantic poets, especially Keats and Shelley. The intensity of their response to the beauty of the world articulated something I too had felt deeply. I grew up on a forested farm along an Oregon river, had hiked and climbed the Cascade Mountains, and was deeply homesick for that wild landscape (about as different from the plains and suburbs of northern Illinois as can be imagined). But I had no place, in my understanding of what it meant to be a Christian, to put this intensity of my response to creation. I had chosen Wheaton almost by accident—mainly because it was Jim Elliot's school, and I assumed that being a missionary like him, preferably a martyr, was the only way to follow Christ in a world doomed to damnation anyhow. I was an anthropology major (as a preparation for being a missionary), and the Romantic poetry course was a luxury I felt a bit guilty about.

We read Wordsworth early in the course. "Tintern Abbey," in Kilby's hands, bowled me over. To begin with, it seemed to describe my own solitary, unreflective boyhood.

> . . . The sounding cataract
> Haunted me like a passion: the tall rock,
> The mountain and the deep and gloomy wood,
> Their colours and their forms, were then to me
> An appetite; a feeling and a love.

But it also seemed to describe what I was feeling now, far removed from those places.

> . . . I have learned
> To look on nature, not as in the hour
> Of thoughtless youth; but hearing oftentimes

> The still, sad music of humanity. . . .
> . . . And I have felt
> A presence that disturbs me with the joy
> Of elevated thoughts; a sense sublime
> Of something far more deeply interfused,
> Whose dwelling is the light of setting suns,
> And the round ocean and the living air,
> And the blue sky, and in the mind of man;
> A motion and a spirit, that impels
> All thinking things, all objects of all thought,
> And rolls through all things.

It would have been easy enough for this experience to degenerate into a kind of pantheism. What Kilby managed to convey, however—not usually by explanation or analysis, but mainly by simply reading the poems and stammering his appreciation of them—was that the sort of experience Wordsworth was describing could be fully appreciated and comprehended best within the circle of Christian faith, a circle that grew steadily bigger for me as the course progressed.

The door Kilby opened for me in that fall semester course in the Romantic poets allowed creation itself, and the full range of human feelings, to pour through, and by Christmas a door back into the world had been flung open. It has taken a lifetime to work out some of the implications of that Christian Romanticism. But the door was opened then.

A year later, with my new fiancée, Mary Ruth Kantzer, we joined a crowd of other students who climbed one evening a week the stairs of the house on Washington Street to read and discuss the works of Lewis, MacDonald, Tolkien, and Williams in the Kilbys' crowded living room. In that setting I began to explore the resources that enabled me later to begin to connect "Romantic" experience with Christian faith. The two of us learned another lesson there, helped along by Martha's incomparable cherry cheesecake: that the best learning is apt to happen not in a classroom but in a home, helped along by food and drink. The hospitality we began to learn from the Kilbys has enriched our own teaching for more than fifty years.

I have lingered on my own experience of Kilby's teaching because I think it illustrates in one particular instance (the one I know best) the sort of door-opening that Kilby accomplished—directly, for generations of students at Wheaton, and indirectly, for the wider public of his work on behalf of Lewis, Tolkien, and the others of the "seven" that formed the focus of the Wade Collection (now known as the Marion E. Wade Center). Clyde Kilby was fundamentally a teacher, but what he had to teach was not a collection of facts; rather, he taught an awed, thankful, and joyful stance toward creation and Creator. From the time he first came to Wheaton—as assistant dean of men and professor of English, in 1935—he was able to embrace the bigness of vision that the Christian liberal arts college embodied, and that is well expressed in words from Jonathan Blanchard, Wheaton's first president and the subject of a biography by Kilby, *Minority of One*: "Every truth is religious because all truth belongs to God."

But Blanchard wrote those words early in the nineteenth century, when evangelical Christianity was still in a place of power, and the perfectibility of society still seemed a possible end to the great American Christian experiment. But—as many have documented—by the early decades of the twentieth century this robust Christianity had been marginalized, and Christian faith became defensive. All intensities of feeling were suspect, except the intensity of need to turn people back from the wrath to come. Though Wheaton College never completely gave in to that withdrawal from engagement with the world and the life of the mind, the culture that supported it had increasingly withdrawn to a small, closed room, characterized by a premillennial eschatology that tended to devalue both creation and culture, a gospel that preached the good news of salvation *from*, but with no sense of salvation *for*, and personal piety that stressed relationship between the soul and God—but not how to appreciate the sanctity of the world around. So Mark Noll, long a history professor at Wheaton—and a former student of Dr. Kilby—was able to write with some lament of "the scandal of the evangelical mind," the scandal being that it doesn't have much of a mind.

But it was not just the life of the mind to which we had closed the door: we were also walled up in a Christianity that had little room for intensities of feeling, especially toward the created world. It was that door—the door opening on *beauty*, and what it implied about ourselves and our God—that Kilby opened for many of us. And he didn't just open the doors. He put us in the hands of a whole set of wise, holy, and imaginative guides. Kilby knew a great deal already of the country he helped us to explore, and one of the marks of his own saintliness is the eagerness with which he stepped aside and let these guides lead us on out through the door he had opened.

Here Luci Shaw's other metaphor is apt. Kilby didn't just open a door; he opened a floodgate, and what poured out was a stream of truth that was gloriously refreshing because it flowed not from "evangelical" or "Protestant" or even "Christian" sources, but from a wonder at creation itself, which is the source of all true myth. The writers for whom Kilby became a channel were certainly Christian, but what they gave us enlarged our understanding of what "Christian" meant: they helped us understand what *water* meant, along with the whole torrent of created reality that flows everywhere. Lewis's great mentor, George MacDonald, put it beautifully: "There is no water in oxygen, no water in hydrogen;

it comes bubbling fresh from the imagination of the living God, rushing from under the great white throne of the glacier."[2] Water must be understood as water before it can be understood as "the water of life," and these great mythmakers enabled us to understand both. I recall a chapel talk Kilby delivered based on Jesus's words from the cross, in which he spoke of the immense and gracious irony that caused the maker of water to cry, "I thirst." Such a recognition helped make Kilby such an effective conduit for the work of these writers whose imaginations has deepened our understanding of both Christianity and creation. The essays that follow, taken from lectures, reviews, interviews, and scholarly articles, provide a good, deep drink from Kilby's "well of wonder."

---

2 *George MacDonald: An Anthology*, ed. C. S. Lewis (New York: Macmillan, 1960), 81.

SECTION 1

C. S. LEWIS ON THEOLOGY AND THE WITNESS OF LITERATURE

Chapter 1

LOGIC AND FANTASY: THE WORLD OF C. S. LEWIS

Here, in an article first published in Christian Action, *January 1969, Kilby presents a brief survey of Lewis's life and work, chronicling the beloved writer's life from childhood to his death in 1963. He stresses the importance of his early education, particularly in the discipline of logic, received under the tutelage of the formidable W. T. Kirkpatrick. Kilby's insistence on the powerful combination of logic and imagination in Lewis is echoed by another British Christian, the theologian J. I. Packer, who has often remarked that Lewis's strength lies in the fact that "all his arguments are pictures, and all his pictures are arguments."*

If you continue to love Jesus, nothing much can go wrong with you, and I hope you may always do so." That remark may sound like a fond old grandmother's, but it was written to a little girl by one of the most brilliant men of our time. The man was Clive Staples Lewis, distinguished professor at Oxford and Cambridge Universities and author of more than forty books. It was written less than a month before his death on November 22, 1963, the same afternoon President John F. Kennedy was assassinated.

C. S. Lewis did not easily come to so simple and straightforward a faith. Born in Ireland, he learned simple goodness from his first nursemaid; but afterward, through the influence of a well-meaning but wrongheaded school matron, he turned atheist. His father was a successful but eccentric Irish solicitor, and his mother was a cheerful and wise woman who early started her son off in the study of French and Latin. But neither parent was noteworthy for the sort of deep faith that eventually was to characterize their son.

Nor had the parents two other deep strains that came to mark their son's outlook. The first was a romantic strain of longing for an indefinable but intense thing called joy. The second was just the opposite—a mind trained razor-sharp in logic. In the course of time the British *Guardian* said that following the train of an argument by Lewis was "like watching a master chess player who makes a seemingly trivial and unimportant move which ten minutes later turns out to be a stroke of genius." The *New York Times* spoke of one of his books as possessing "a brevity comparable to St. Paul's" and an argument "distilled to the unanswerable."

The romantic strain in Lewis was associated with the green Castlereagh Hills, which Lewis and his brother Warren could see from their nursery window, and with a toy garden of moss, twigs, and arid flowers made by Warren on the lid of a can. Later this tendency came to include a profound love of Norse legend, the "Ring" cycle of Richard Wagner's operas, and the entire world of Norse mythology. The logician strain is best seen in Lewis the lecturer and biblical apologist. For instance, at the beginning of his book *The Problem of Pain* he makes out a better, or at least a more succinct, case for atheism than Bertrand Russell ever did, and then he proceeds to demolish that case. But it should be said that nearly always the romantic and the logical are combined both in his books and in his whole way of thought.

The big house to which his family moved when he was seven years old helped to shape Lewis's love of solitude. It was a place of "long corridors, empty sunlit rooms, upstair indoor silences, attics explored in solitude, distant noises of gurgling cisterns and pipes, and the noise of wind under the tiles." There on long rainy afternoons he and his brother read among the hundreds of books with which every room downstairs was filled. Clive began early to write stories of animals, including chivalrous mice, and finally set out to do a full, fanciful history of Animal-land complete with maps and drawings.

This happy childhood experience was cruelly broken by the death of his mother when he was ten years old. Her illness marked the first real religious experience he had. He prayed that she would be healed. But at this time he thought of God as a magician who would heal his mother's cancer and then go away.

Afterward he was taught a more substantial notion of God in the English boarding school to which, dressed in uncomfortable shoes, bowler hat, and tight, unyielding shoes, he was sent by his father. At first he fervently hated both England and the bad food, cold beds, and horrid sanitation of the school. He described his teacher, called Oldie by the boys, as likely to come in after breakfast and, looking over the little group, say, "Oh, there you are, Rees, you horrid boy. If I'm not too tired I shall give you a good drubbing this afternoon." Yet here he did find people talking about Christianity as though they believed it, and the little boy struggled, yet unsuccessfully, to gain a realization of God. The best thing about his school life was the anticipation of the holidays—the trip home to Ireland and the long days full of play, good reading, cycling, and solitude.

Later in other English schools he learned a love of that country's beautiful landscape and the raw and brutal tyranny of older boys over younger ones, of rampant homosexuality, of a brash and silly sophistication in ideas, clothes, and women. In short, he learned a system of education calculated, as he put it, to make genuinely uneducated prigs and highbrows. For the rest of his life he never missed an opportunity to satirize this sort of school system as one calculated to fill the country with "a bitter, truculent, skeptical, debunking and cynical *intelligentsia*" rather than to make good citizens.

In these days Lewis, as college students often do, was living in many different worlds. His private world was still that of "Northerness" and joy. At the same time he was now an atheist and was trying to incorporate his ideas around that pole of conviction. "I maintained that God did not exist. I was also very angry with God for not existing. I was equally angry with Him for creating a world."[1]

Increasingly sick of college life, Lewis persuaded his father to let him prepare for the university under the tutelage of W. T. Kirkpatrick in Surrey. Almost from the minute he first met this man Lewis's intellectual life underwent a sharp change. The tall, shabbily dressed man with Franz Joseph whiskers met the boy at the railway station, took his hand in an iron grip, and as they walked away promptly pounced upon Lewis for a passing remark about the unexpected "wildness" of the Surrey landscape. "Stop!" he shouted at the fifteen-year-old boy. "What do you mean by wildness and what ground had you for not expecting it?" After further questions, he asked, "Do you not see, then, that you had no right to have any opinion whatever on the subject?"

This was the beginning of a training in logical thought the like of which had not often occurred before. The "Old Knock," as he was called, was the very personification of reason and trained his increasingly adept student in the practice of a relentlessly logical handling of ideas. Finally the time came when the pupil could stand up to the master. Lewis found that Kirkpatrick was an atheist and was glad to have his own atheism bolstered by that of his tutor, but the time came when the Old Knock's ubiquitous logic actually put Lewis on the road to God.

1 C. S. Lewis, *Surprised by Joy* (New York: Harcourt, Brace and Company, 1956), 115.

Lewis tells how on the first school day the Old Knock sat down with his pupil and without a word of introduction read aloud in Greek the first twenty lines or so of Homer's *Iliad* and translated with very few explanations about a hundred lines. He told his understudy to dig in, and it was not long until Lewis was beginning to think in Greek. And so it was with Latin and other languages. Years later Lewis looked back at this time as one of the happiest periods of his life.

His childhood love of nature was continued in the intimate landscape of Surrey with its dingles, copses, and little valleys and with quiet saunters under great trees. He had a happiness that seemed of another world.

By the age of sixteen he had already begun to feel a deep-seated antipathy to the shallow "getting and spending" that occupied people's lives, to ideas of collectivism, of modern education, of inflated desires caused by false advertising, of slanted news, of built-in obsolescence in manufacturing, and of the whole scheme of "getting ahead" in the world. Even more he began to be alarmed about modern movements such as logical positivism, Freudianism, relativism, scientism, sexual frankness that resulted only in more and worse sexual deviation, "modernism," in religion and the contradictory idea of inevitable improvement from natural causes, and the increasing feeling of hopelessness in society. He felt that even democracy itself was taking the impossible road of trying to make men equal rather than providing a way for men clearly unequal to live together in peace.

Lewis had hardly passed his examinations for admission to Oxford when he was called into the war then raging. He enlisted as a second lieutenant in the Somerset light infantry, and on his nineteenth birthday he found himself in the frontline trenches of France. Five months later, in April 1918, he was wounded in battle and sent back to London for recuperation. But even earlier

Lewis had heard the distant baying of the Hound of Heaven, and now, in a long period given almost wholly to wide reading, he had the opportunity to learn more about writers such as G. K. Chesterton and George MacDonald. Through them the Hound drew nearer and made it clear enough that Lewis was his prey.

Early in 1919 Lewis was back at University College, Oxford. There he met men of high intelligence who were Christians, or at least theistic, in their thinking. One of them, Owen Barfield, was destined to be his lifelong friend. Barfield had read, said Lewis, all the right books but had got the wrong things out of them. Lengthy and warm debates with Barfield and others forced him to a careful reexamination of the foundations of his atheism. Meanwhile Lewis went on to highest honors, taught for a year at University College, and then was chosen a fellow of Magdalen College, a position he was to hold for thirty years.

Lewis continued to be troubled by what looked like the finger of God pointing directly at him. On the one side were Christian colleagues and on the other side one shattering experience with "the hardest boiled of all the atheists" he had known. This man sat in Lewis's room before the fire and finally blurted out, "Rum thing. . . . All that stuff of Frazer's about the Dying God. Rum thing. It almost looks as if it had really happened once." So a second atheist was added to the Old Knock in the process of turning Lewis toward God.

Lewis's account of how God finally came to him must be read just as he puts it:

> You must picture me alone in that room in Magdalen, night after night, feeling, whenever my mind lifted even for a second from my work, the steady, unrelenting approach of Him whom I so earnestly desired not to meet. That which

> I greatly feared had at last come upon me. . . . I gave in, and admitted that God was God, and knelt and prayed: perhaps, that night, the most dejected and reluctant convert in all England. I did not then see what is now the most shining and obvious thing; the Divine humility which will accept a convert even on such terms.[2]

The rest of his life was to consist of teaching and writing. If that seems a dull business, remember that Lewis's adventures among ideas were as exciting as the exploits of a big-game hunter or an Alpine climber. He became one of the great teachers of his time. His lectures were always crowded. One of his students said that he had at his fingertips more knowledge than he had ever known in any other scholar, and another said that Lewis had "the most exact and penetrating mind" he had ever encountered.

Lewis's conversion brought to him the long-sought joy, and soon he was writing books about Christianity. Millions of copies of them have been sold. Though many of his books treat their subjects directly, such as *Miracles*, *The Problem of Pain*, and *Mere Christianity*, perhaps his best-loved books are of the creative variety. Would you like to make a trip to hell and examine its fondest hopes and its strategy for winning souls? Would you care to know the subtleties of Satan that surround you and are intent at this moment on destroying you? Would you care to learn what happens to a particular imp who lets a soul slip through his fingers into the hands of the "Enemy"? If so, you can go to Lewis's most popular (though he himself did not at all feel his best) book, *The Screwtape Letters*.

Or would you like to take a bus trip with people going from hell to heaven and hear the earnest appeal of celestial beings for them to come in, as well as listen to the excuses for not doing so? You

2 Lewis, *Surprised by Joy*, 228.

can hear the claims of people who do not believe in heaven, even one famous preacher, while they are looking at a part of its glory. You can meet the man who has "done his best" all his life and now wants what he thinks is due him. Or you can meet the man who thinks heaven is just another trick of "the Management." Or you can meet the woman who on earth hounded her husband literally to death in her efforts to promote him in business and society and refuses heaven unless she will be allowed there to take charge of him again. If you would like to observe that, as Lewis insists, people in hell really choose that malign place, you can read it all in *The Great Divorce*.

Or if you would rather take a space journey, you can go to an unfallen planet and there see another Eve undergoing the temptation to disobey. There a very evil man and a good one meet this lady in her own glorious surroundings and each endeavors to persuade her to his viewpoint. The reader has an intimate and startling experience of what Eden and the temptation might have been like, as well as an insight into the far-reaching and subtle grounds of that temptation. All this is in *Perelandra*.

Or one may go to Lewis's seven much-loved stories for children and discover not only charming adventures but also little episodes that put the gospel clearer than many a sermon. In one of them, for instance, a little girl wants a drink of water but finds the lion Aslan (Christ) between her and the water.

> "Are you not thirsty?" said the Lion.
>
> "I'm *dying* of thirst," said Jill.
>
> "Then drink," said the Lion.
>
> "May I—could I—would you mind going away while I do?" said Jill.
>
> The Lion answered this only by a look and a very low growl. . . .

> "I daren't come and drink," said Jill.
> "Then you will die of thirst," said the Lion.
> "Oh dear!" said Jill, coming another step nearer. "I suppose I must go and look for another stream then."
> "There is no other stream," said the Lion.[3]

In another of the books the idea that a Christian lives in daily contact with God is suggested when the youngsters, voyaging into a far-off country, come upon a place where a sumptuous table is set. They inquire and learn that it is Aslan's table.

> "Why is it called Aslan's table?" asked Lucy presently.
> "It is set here by his bidding."
> "But how does the food keep?" asked the practical Eustace.
> "It is eaten, and renewed, every day," said the girl.[4]

And we could hardly imagine a finer depiction of the necessity for divine salvation than that in another of the children's books. A boy called Eustace Scrubb had accidentally gone along on the voyage of the *Dawn Treader*. He hated the other children and made all the trouble he could. When they came to an uninhabited island far away, he ran off from the group and in the course of events was turned into a dragon. Shocked through and through to realize his terrible condition, he longed to be a boy again (and a good one). In his terror, he remembered that snakes cast off their skins and thought it might also be true of dragons. He got a rent made and managed to slip off his entire skin.

He was happy until he looked in a well of water and found another skin on his body that was just as ugly and knobbly as the

3 C. S. Lewis, *The Silver Chair* (The Macmillan Company, 1953).
4 C. S. Lewis, *The Voyage of the Dawn Treader* (The Macmillan Company, 1952), 169–70.

first. Again he managed to pull off this skin, but again underneath was another that was no better. Finally Aslan said, "You will have to let me undress you." Eustace was afraid of Asian's claws, but being desperate now for relief, he lay down and let Asian take over.

> This is how Eustace told the story to his friends later:
>
> The very first tear he made was so deep that I thought it had gone right into my heart. And when he began pulling the skin off, it hurt worse than anything I've ever felt.
>
> Well, he pulled the beastly stuff right off—just as I thought I'd done it myself the other three times, only they hadn't hurt—and there it was lying on the grass only ever so much thicker, and darker, and more knobbly looking than the others had been."[5]

Afterward Aslan bathed him in the water (baptism) and dressed him in clothes, and Eustace never again was the cantankerous child he had been.

A truly fresh air blows through Lewis's books. Though his ideas are profound, his words are as simple as can be. One American who visited Lewis summarized him well. "You find yourself using his ideas and forgetting that they are his. His mind seems a colossal picture-making machine, and each picture reduces a great and terrible theological abstraction to the clarity of a Gospel parable. He moves in on you, and possesses the stray ends of your imagination, not by the color and fire of his intellectual pyrotechnics, as his enemies assert, but rather by the simple reality of his service to your spirit." Like the greatest writers, he knew how to take simple things and make them illustrate profound things.

5 C. S. Lewis, *Voyage of the Dawn Treader*, 89–90.

He was anything but a solemn, long-faced saint. In fact, he once said, "I'm not the religious type." He once went to address a congregation wearing a lounge coat, slacks, and tennis shoes. He had little use for hymns and hated organ music. He usually attended the early service in his little parish church in order to have a minimum of music and sermon. He so ardently loved the outdoors that on one particularly beautiful day he stood outside and dictated to his secretary through the open window. He loved sitting with friends and swapping jokes. It was his "unsaintly" attitude, together with his unanswerable logic, that made him, as Chad Walsh says, the apostle to the skeptics. One of them said, "His books exposed the shallowness of our atheist prejudices; his vision illumined the Mystery which lay behind the appearances of daily life."

In a BBC address, Lewis said, "All I'm doing is to get people to face the facts—to understand the questions which Christianity claims to answer."

C. E. M. Joad, professor of philosophy at the University of London, said of Lewis, "He had the rare gift of being able to make righteousness readable." Like St. Augustine, Lewis was deeply convinced that no man will ever find rest until he rests in God, indeed that a man will never really be a man until he recognizes God's rights to him. The only real face is the face turned in contrition and gratitude to God.

Perhaps his greatest fear had to do with the ease and subtlety with which even a man's best acts become tinged with selfishness. Though always perhaps a bit more decent than the average man, Lewis says that when he examined himself before God about the time of his conversion, he found within what appalled him, "a zoo of lusts, a bedlam of ambitions, a nursery of fears, a harem of fondled hatreds." He saw the necessity for a Christian to commit himself anew every morning to God and really to live the life commanded. "Nothing you have not given away will ever be yours," he said. Also, "Until you have given yourself up to Him you will never have any real self." He believed that God calls Christians to perfection and that the whole of life is a preparation for even further training in the next until God fulfills quite literally his promise of perfection.

What Lewis genuinely believed in and attempted to practice was a life of holiness. He saw true holiness not as a dull and negative sort of thing but as something irresistible, and he believed that if even 10 percent of Christians had holiness the world speedily would be converted. One close friend said that he saw in Lewis what he had never seen in any other man—"In Lewis the natural and the supernatural seemed to be one, to flow one into the other." Lewis did not have many enemies, but some of those he had simply could not understand a man, and especially a man as lively as he, seriously intent on holiness.

The wide range of interest in Lewis is suggested by two letters I happened to receive in the same mail. One was from a Boston wool merchant who said, "I am frank to admit no Christian writer has made the contribution to my own faith and my ability to defend the Christian position that Lewis has." He said he had given away many of Lewis's books to people in spiritual need.

The other letter was from a teacher in New Jersey who was reading Lewis's *The Lion, the Witch and the Wardrobe* to her third-graders. She had come to the point where the lion Aslan allowed himself to be killed by his enemies to save a bad boy's life. "The attitude of the room," said this teacher, "was worship, holiness. The rare impression of that moment will never leave me. When I had finished the chapter about Aslan's death the room was in stunned disbelief. Aslan dead! And then a child who had read further said, 'Don't give up—something wonderful is going to happen.' It crept through the room and sighs issued. The little people had caught glimpses of the very real, the miracle of spiritual understanding."

During the last eight years of his life Lewis moved from Oxford to Cambridge, but he never gave up his beloved house four miles east of Oxford. During this period, when he was fifty-eight, he married Helen Joy Gresham and had a little more than three blissful years before his wife died of cancer. His own physical troubles steadily increased, and on July 15, 1963, about three months before his actual death, he went into a coma during which he had such a glimpse of the glory ahead that he was disappointed to awaken on earth. Afterward he wrote a friend that he thought Lazarus was really the first martyr because of being brought back and having his "dying to do again." No one can read Lewis's numerous accounts of the glories and joys of heaven without anticipating the abundant entrance this great and good man had into that realm. He was buried in the churchyard of his small parish church a half mile from his home.

One of the world's greatest scholars in his chosen field and great-minded in all his thoughts, he was nevertheless a man who rejoiced in the simple things of earth and who from the heart believed that God was alive and really meant what he had said to men.

Chapter 2

MY FIRST (AND ONLY) VISIT WITH MR. LEWIS

Kilby met C. S. Lewis only once, in the summer of 1953. Of the several accounts of that meeting, this one, published later that year in Kodon, *the Wheaton College literary magazine, is the freshest.*

At noon on July first, I went by appointment to the office of C. S. Lewis in Magdalen College, Oxford. Thinking that Mrs. Kilby would enjoy the visit with me, I had inquired earlier at the college gate whether there was anything to the report that Mr. Lewis disliked women and had been told that there was "some truth in it." Consequently, she went shopping and I climbed the stairs to his office alone. When I knocked, he immediately answered and invited me in, coming around his desk to greet me warmly at the door.

He is about fifty-four years old and of average height. He has a pleasant, almost jolly face, full though not fat, with a double chin. He has a high forehead and thinning hair. Actually, he is a much better looking man than the published picture of him. He was dressed well, though in ordinary clothes. His office is large, with used but comfortable furniture.

He invited me to sit down on a sofa, and he remained in his working chair. He was busy on the bibliography of his history of sixteenth-century literature, one volume of the Oxford Dictionary of English Literature. He spoke of the making of a bibliography as just plain labor and laughed about the idea of the scholar's life as a sedentary one, saying that the physical labor of pulling the big folios from the shelves of the Bodleian was all the exercise he needed. Later he told me that apart from the last twenty years of the sixteenth century, there was relatively little of value in the literature of that time. He said also that he felt the Renaissance was not nearly so much of a "rebirth" as some scholars declare it to be. (Since my visit Mr. Lewis has written me giving his exact definition: "an imaginary entity responsible for everything the modern reader likes in the fifteenth and sixteenth centuries.") I told him I had the feeling that literary periods are doubtfully described by our neat classifications, and he agreed heartily.

We talked at some length about Palestine and my recent visit there. He was much interested and spoke of the pleasure it would give him to go to the Holy Land. He talked of a book on Sumerian archaeology in which an ancient expressed his surprise at the antiquities before his own day. Mr. Lewis said that he asked a Jew if it was the intention of the Israeli to set up the biblical temple and sacrifices. The Jew answered that he did not know and that he had no explanation as to why his nation had stopped the ancient sacrifices. I suggested that a Jew lecturing at Wheaton College had laid the blame on St. Paul. Mr. Lewis demonstrated his shrewdness by promptly pointing out the Jewish claim not to have followed Paul and therefore the Jews could not have been led astray by someone they refused to follow.

One of the main questions I wished to ask Mr. Lewis concerned the relation of Christianity and art. He said the same relation existed between Christianity and art as between Christianity and carpentry, and he suggested that he had discussed the problem to some extent in his essay called "Transposition." I mentioned Jonathan Blanchard's assertion that a novel is at best a "well-told lie." As I expected, he disagreed completely with this claim, saying that one is far more likely to find the truth in a novel than in a newspaper. In fact, he said he had quit reading newspapers because they were so untruthful.

One of the men I had hoped to see in England was C. E. M. Joad, professor of philosophy at the University of London, but he had died while I was in Palestine. I asked Mr. Lewis his opinion of Joad, and he said that after he had sat up and talked with Joad most of the night on two occasions, he had changed his mind about him, having found him vain, but sincerely and consciously so, and not hiding his vanity under a mask as most of us do while practicing our own brand of self-righteousness. Mr. Lewis had not yet read Joad's account of his turn from agnosticism to Christianity (*The Recovery of Belief*). He declared that Joad was definitely not a charlatan, as some people have described him. I asked Mr. Lewis if he knows the critic D. S. Savage. He said he had never heard of him and asked naively, "Should I know him?" I told him something of the Christian viewpoint of that writer.

I told Mr. Lewis that one of the questions frequently asked in America was when he intended to come over here and lecture. In fact, while I was in Palestine, I had received a letter from a man at the University of Redlands asking me in the name of several California institutions to urge Lewis to come and offering to pay him liberally. He said definitely that he had no intention of coming to America until he retired. When I suggested the possibility of his coming during the summer, he said he had to get some vacation then, and a trip to this country would be anything but a vacation. He expressed sincere gratitude for the invitations and in that connection pointed out that his books sell somewhat better over here than in England. On the day before my visit I had bought a copy of one of his books in order to have him autograph it. When I pulled the book out of my pocket, he readily agreed to my request but added that he "saw no sense in it." Both from reading his books and talking with him, I get the impression that he is far more fearful than most of us of the subtle sin of pride and tries in every way to escape it: thus his reticence to give an autograph.

I asked him if I would have an opportunity while in Oxford of hearing him lecture, either in the university or on the outside. He said he had no lectures scheduled and bantered me as a college professor wanting to hear a lecture while on vacation. In fact, in all his talk there is an incipient good humor and genuineness that makes a conversation with him a real pleasure. (I noticed the same genuineness in Chad Walsh when he was at Wheaton.)

I mentioned his remark in one of his books that the study of the metaphor would be a lifetime affair. I added that as far as I could judge, the secret of literature is bound up in the metaphor. He repeated his idea concerning the significance of metaphor and urged me to undertake the study. When I told him I was too old for that, he laughed and asked if I thought he was any younger than myself.

He had shown no sign whatever of wishing to get back to his work, but I felt that I had no right to impose upon him and therefore excused myself. He followed me to the door and gave me a warm handshake and greeting as I left.

Chapter 3

ON SCRIPTURE, MYTH, AND THEOLOGY

Summarizing four Lewis titles, Kilby discusses the Oxford professor's rare ability to encapsulate profound and sometimes complex theological ideas in simple, figurative language. Kilby is very aware that he is introducing Lewis to an American evangelical Christian audience for whom a belief in the divine inspiration of Scripture is foundational. Thus he goes to some pains to defend Lewis's high view of Scripture, and especially the idea that divine truth can—indeed must—be conveyed in myth, metaphor, and symbol. Thus, like much of Kilby's writing, this essay is as much a defense of literature as it is of C. S. Lewis's view of Scripture.

In what follows I should like to outline some of C. S. Lewis's theological beliefs, particularly as they are expressed in *Reflections on the Psalms*, *Miracles*, *Mere Christianity*, and *Letters to Malcolm: Chiefly on Prayer*. It is not correct to say that Lewis has a "theology" if by that term is meant a systematic, all-embracing complex like that of John Calvin or Karl Barth. He repeatedly declared that he was not a theologian. Perhaps his chief aim in attempting to retain amateur status is that he may be "one person talking to another." Yet anyone who writes a score or more of books on Christian topics inevitably will possess, in some sense, a theology. Perhaps the big difference between Lewis and the "professional" theologian is less abstraction and more particular instance and creativity. I am especially interested here in Lewis's view of the Scripture itself as the source of theological truth.

REFLECTIONS ON THE PSALMS

One of the important ideas in *Reflections on the Psalms* is that the Bible itself has a creative rather than an abstractive quality. The Psalms are poems rather than doctrinal treatises or even sermons. The Bible is literature. Of course one must not read it merely as literature, thus missing the very thing it is about. On the other hand, unless such parts as the Psalms are read as poetry "we shall miss what is in them and think we see what is not." The Psalms, Lewis continues, are great poetry—some, such as Psalm 18 and 19, perfect poetry. At the same time the Bible is made up of a great variety of elements, some of which may seem inconsequential, crabbed, practical, or rhapsodic.

Lewis starts with those elements in the Psalms that trouble him. Most troubling for a modern reader, says Lewis, are the vindictive or cursing Psalms. Occasionally indeed we come upon a verse that is nothing short of devilish, as where the psalmist asks the Lord to slay his enemies or that extreme instance in which a blessing is offered to anyone who will crush a Babylonian baby against the pavement. Such maledictions, declares Lewis, are sinful, and when seen as such rather than minimized in any way, will suggest to the Christian reader similar sins in his or her own life, even if such sins are more cleverly disguised. Nor can Old Testament believers be excused, since they had plenty of Scripture against vengeance and grudges, in fact plenty of teaching very similar to that of Christ's. The truth is that Christ's teaching was anticipated by all teachers of truth, some even outside of Judaism. This, Lewis insists, is exactly what should be expected as a result of that Light which has lighted everyone from the beginning. All truth is from God.

Nevertheless, the Hebrews seem to have been even more vitriolic than their Pagan neighbors. Lewis thinks this might be based on the principle of "the higher the more in danger," that is, a person with greatness of soul and an abiding conception of right and wrong is more likely to show an ugly fanaticism than a smaller person who is not so much above temptation as below it. Under some circumstances the absence of indignation may be a worse sign than indignation itself. The very elevation of religion is bound to make a religious bad person the worst sort of bad person. Satan himself was once an angel in heaven. Shocking as the cursing Psalms may be, then, it is clear that their composers were people neither morally indifferent nor willing, like some today, to reduce wickedness to a neurosis.

With these difficulties out of the way, Lewis turns to the great positives of the Psalms. First is the robust, virile, spontaneous, and mirthful delight in God, displayed by the Hebrews. They often felt a genuine longing for the mere presence of God that shames Christians. They had an "appetite" for God that did not let a false sense of good manners preclude their enjoyment of him. They were ravished by their love of God's law, which they believed to be firmly rooted in his nature and as real as trees and clouds.

Lewis reminds us that the ancient Hebrews were not merchants and financiers at all but farmers and shepherds. Though their poetry says little about landscape, it does give us weather "enjoyed almost as a vegetable might be supposed to enjoy it": "Thou art good to the earth . . . thou waterest her furrows . . . thou makest it soft with the drops of rain . . . the little hills shall rejoice on every side . . . the valleys shall stand so thick with corn that they shall laugh and sing" (see Ps. 65:9ff.). The Jews understood better than their neighbors, and perhaps we also, a pristine doctrine of God as creator of nature, one that at once empties nature of anything like a pantheistic divinity and at the same time makes her a symbol or manifestation of the Divine.

Lewis confesses that when he first became a Christian he was disturbed by the continuous command in the Psalms to praise God. It sounded as if God were saying, "What I most want is to be told that I am good and great." Even the very quantity of the praise seemed important to the psalmists. Then he discovered the principle that praise is simply the sign of healthy understanding. To ascribe praise to whatever is truly praiseworthy reflects the character of both the thing praised and the one who praises. Praise likewise completes enjoyment, whether of God or a sunset or one's friend.

Lewis completes his reflections by three chapters devoted to what he calls "second meanings," that is, prophetic or allegorical meanings, and the doctrine of scriptural inspiration. Since both these topics are in Lewis's view related to myth, I should like to give special attention to them.

As to prophecy or allegory, he cites the famous passage from Virgil that describes a virgin, a golden age beginning, and a child sent down from heaven, also Plato's discussion of the fate of a perfect man in a wicked world, and says that a Christian reading either of these two non-Christian accounts will be struck by their similarity to the biblical accounts. Now Lewis holds that the similarity in Virgil was doubtless accidental but in Plato only partially so. Plato perhaps had in mind the recent death of his teacher Socrates, a great man who died at the hands of people who feared and despised justice. It was not mere luck but rather great wisdom that enabled Plato to extrapolate from the experience of Socrates the vision of the perfect man who dies as a sacrifice to evil, even though Plato probably had no intuition that such an instance would ever become history.

Mythology is replete with the dying god, with death and rebirth, and the idea that one must undergo death if he would truly live. The resemblance between such myths and Christian truth has the same relation as the sun and its reflection in a pond. It is not the same thing but neither is it a wholly different thing. The kernel of wheat is indeed, as Christ said, "reborn" after "death." Because God made wheat thus, it should occasion no total surprise if a Pagan sees there a symbol and puts it into the form of a myth. Because, like all men, the Pagans suffered longing for Joy, even when they were unable to identify its source, they incorporated their unsteady conceptions into myths and, because no myth was ever quite equivalent to the longing, created more and more myths. Myth arises from "gleams of celestial strength and beauty failing on a jungle of filth and imbecility," as he put it in *Perelandra.* A "pressure from God" lay upon the Pagan mythmakers. Yet they would have been as surprised as anyone else if they had learned that they were talking a better thing than they ever dreamed.

If Pagan sources did so well, what of sacred ones? We have two excellent reasons, says Lewis, for accepting the truth of the biblical second meanings. One is that they are holy and inspired, the other that our Lord himself taught it and indeed claimed to be the second meaning of many Old Testament passages such as Isaiah 53, the Sufferer in Psalm 22, the King in Psalms 2 and 72, and the Incarnation in Psalm 45. Lewis confesses that though he once believed the interpretation of the Bridegroom as Christ in the Song of Songs was "frigid and far-fetched," he later began to discover that even in this instance there might be second meanings that are not arbitrary and meanings indeed that spring from depths one would not suspect.

As to the inspiration of the Bible, he does not consider the Old Testament as "the Word of God" if by that we mean that each passage, in itself, gives us impeccable science or history.

Rather, the Old Testament "carries" the Word of God, and we should use it not as "an encyclopedia or an encyclical" but "by steeping ourselves in its tone or temper and so learning its overall message." He cites St. Jerome's remark that Moses described the creation "after the manner of a popular poet" and Calvin's doubt whether Job were actual history as his own views also. The fact that miracles are recorded in the Old Testament has nothing to do with his view on inspiration. Belief in God includes belief in his supernatural powers.

Lewis is even willing to accept the Genesis account of creation as derived from, though a great improvement upon, earlier Semitic stories, which were Pagan and mythical—provided "derived from" is interpreted to mean that the retellers were themselves guided by God. And so with the whole of the Old Testament. It consists of the same kind of material, says Lewis, as any other literature, yet "taken into the service of God's word." God of course does not condone the sin revealed in the cursing Psalms but causes his word to go forth even through the written account of sin and the sinner who wrote it. We must even suppose that the canonizing and the work of redactors and editors are under some kind of "Divine pressure."

One might be at first inclined, says Lewis, to think that God made a mistake in giving us such a Bible rather than a rigorously systematic statement of his truth in a form as unrefracted as that of the multiplication table. But even the teaching of Christ, "in which there is no imperfection," does not come to us in that manner and is not a thing for the intellect alone but rather something for the whole person. Understanding the true meaning of Christ is not learning a "subject" but rather "steeping ourselves in a Personality, acquiring a new outlook and temper, breathing a new atmosphere, suffering Him, in His own way, to rebuild in us the defaced image of Himself."

The seeming imperfection in the way the Bible is composed may be an illusion. "It may repel one use in order that we may be forced to use it in another way—to find the Word in it, not without repeated and leisurely reading nor without discriminations made by our conscience and our critical faculties, to re-live, while we read, the whole Jewish experience of God's gradual and graded self-revelation, to feel the very contentions between the Word and the human material through which it works. . . . Certainly it seems to me that from having had to reach what is really the Voice of God in the cursing Psalms through all the horrible distortions of the human medium, I have gained something I might not have gained from a flawless, ethical exposition." Even the "nihilism" of Ecclesiastes with its "clear, cold picture of life without God" is a part of God's Word.

In view of the importance of scriptural inspiration to many Christians, I take the liberty of submitting here an additional comment that Professor Lewis was kind enough to send me.

> I enclose what, at such short notice, I feel able to say on this question. If it is at all likely to upset anyone, throw it in the waste paper basket. Remember too that it is pretty tentative, much less an attempt to establish a view than a statement of the issue on which, whether rightly or wrongly, I have come to work. To me the curious thing is that neither in my own Bible-reading nor in my religious life as a whole does the question *in fact* ever assume that importance which it always gets in theological controversy. The difference between reading the story of Ruth and that of Antigone—both first class as literature—is to me unmistakable and even overwhelming. But the question 'Is Ruth historical?' (I've no reason to suppose it is not) doesn't really seem to arise till afterwards. It can still

> act on me as the Word of God if it weren't, so far as I can see. All Holy Scripture is written for our learning. But learning of what? I should have thought the value of some things (e.g., the Resurrection) depended on whether they really happened, but the value of others (e.g., the fate of Lot's wife) hardly at all. And the ones whose historicity matters are, as God's will, those where it is plain.

To Lewis the story of creation in Genesis is mythical, but that does not mean it is untrue. It means rather that it is truer than history itself. The account of Adam and Eve, God and an apple, symbolizes clearly a time long ago when catastrophe fell upon mankind. "For all I can see," says Lewis, "it might have concerned the literal eating of a fruit, but the question is of no consequence." Indeed, one might ask whether humanity and history are not actually as mysterious as myth. The great historians are quite agreed that to state the *facts* of history may be to leave out its essence, since history is made up both of objective, overt actions and also of the joys, agonies, and deep motives of the human soul. Christianity is the Christian creed, but it is also the glorious experience of God in the heart of a believer. We must not think we have a greater thing when we accept the "hypostasized abstract nouns" of a creed as more real than the myth which incorporates them and Reality itself. Melville once remarked that the true places are never down on any map. A myth is indeed to be defined by its very power to convey essence rather than outward fact, reality rather than semblance, the genuine rather than the accidental. It is the difference between the factual announcement of a wedding and the ineluctable joys actually incorporated in the event. Corbin S. Carnell says that for Lewis "the great myths of the Bible as well as of pagan literature refer not to the non-historical but rather to the non-describable. The historical correlative for something like the Genesis account of the creation and fall may be disputed. But the theological validity of the myth rests on its uniqueness as an account of real creation (out of nothing), on its psychological insight into the rebellious will, and on its clear statement that people have a special dignity by virtue of their being made in God's 'image.'"[6] The historical correlative is less significant than the thing it signifies. All facts are misleading in proportion to their divergence from Eternal Fact.

Perhaps Marjorie E. Wright stated it correctly when she says that for Lewis and certain other writers Christianity itself is the great central historical embodiment of myth. "It is the archetypal myth of which all others are more or less distorted images."[7] Christ is the great Reality that makes every other reality a jarring note and cracked vessel. The trouble, says Lewis, is that we are so inveterately given to factualizing Christian truth it is practically impossible for us to hear God when he says that one day he will give us the Morning Star and cause us to put on the splendor of the sun.

Only once did myth ever become fact, and that was when the Word became flesh, when God became man. "This is not 'a religion,' nor 'a philosophy.' It is the summing up and actuality of them all."

It would be a bad mistake to infer from what has been said in the last few paragraphs that Lewis regarded the Bible as simply another good book. He repeatedly calls it "Holy Scripture," assures us that it bears the authority of God, sharply distinguishes even between the canon and the apocrypha, presses the historical reliability of the New Testament in particular, and often assures us that we must "go back to our Bibles," even to the very words. The biblical account,

6 Corbin Carnell, *The Dialectic of Desire: C. S. Lewis' Interpretation of Sehnsucht*, PhD dissertation (Gainesville: University of Florida, 1960), 124.

7 Marjorie E. Wright, *The Cosmic Kingdom of Myth: A Study in the Myth-Philosophy of Charles Williams, C. S. Lewis, and J. R. R. Tolkien*, PhD dissertation (University of Illinois, 1961), 141.

says he, often turns out to be more accurate than our lengthy theological interpretations of it. It is all right to leave the words of the Bible for a moment to make some point clear. "But you must always go back. Naturally God knows how to describe Himself much better than we know how to describe Him."[8]

Doctrinally, Lewis accepted the Nicene, Athanasian, and Apostles' Creeds. He was never failing in his opposition to theological "modernism." Some of his most acerbic satire is employed against it in both his fiction and his expository works. It is as ridiculous, he declares, to believe that the earth is flat as to believe in the watered-down popular theology of modern England. In *The Screwtape Letters* a major employment of hell itself is in encouraging theologians to create a new "historical Jesus" in each generation. He repeatedly insists that, contrary to the opinion of many modern theologians, it was less St. Paul than Christ who taught the terrors of hell and other "fierce" doctrines rather than sweetness and vapid love.[9]

Though Lewis denied the doctrine of total depravity on the grounds that if we were totally depraved we should not know it and because we have the idea of good, the denial is more nearly theoretical than actual in his works. Everywhere we find him representing humanity as a horror to God and a "miserable offender." In "Religion and Rocketry"[10] he says that non-Christians often suppose that the Incarnation implies some special merit in humanity but that it implies "just the reverse: a particular demerit and depravity" because "no creature that deserved Redemption would need to be redeemed. . . . Christ died for men precisely because men are *not* worth dying for."

8 C. S. Lewis, *Mere Christianity* (New York: Macmillan, 1952), 135. Does this sentence contradict Lewis's charges against some of the vengeful psalmists?

9 It occurs to me that, following the same analogy, Lewis might well have controverted the idea of a vengeful deity in the Old Testament by showing how often the Psalms speak of his mercy.

10 In *The World's Last Night.*

The most vivid picture of what it means to be saved—and Lewis does not hesitate to use this word—is the transformation of Eustace from a dragon back into a person in *The Voyage of the Dawn Treader.* Eustace tells how he remembered that a dragon might be able to cast its skin like a snake and began to work on himself. At first the scales alone came off but as he went deeper he found his whole skin starting to peel off and finally was able to step right out of it altogether. This is the point at which a less orthodox writer might stop, but not Lewis. Eustace started to wash himself, but when he put his foot into the water he saw that it was as hard and rough and scaly as it had been before. So he began again to scratch and finally peeled off another entire dragon skin. But once again he found under it another. At this point Aslan said, "You will have to let me undress you." Though Eustace was deathly afraid of Aslan's claws, he lay down before him. His fears were justified, for the very first tear made by Aslan was so deep he felt it had gone clear down to his heart. When the skin was at last off, Eustace discovered it "ever so much thicker, and darker, and more knobbly-looking than the others had been." Afterward Aslan bathed him and dressed him in new clothes, the symbolism of which is clear enough.

In respect to the church, Lewis teaches that it has no beauty except that given it by Christ and that its primary purpose is to draw men to him, "the true Cure." The Christian's vocation, however, is not mainly to spread Christianity but rather to love Christ. The Christian is not so much to follow rules as to possess a Person and to wait upon the Holy Spirit for guidance. The Christian is not called to religion or even good works but to holiness before God. Christianity is not a "safe" vocation, for Christ is to be followed at all hazards.

Lewis believed that prayer must include confession and penitence, adoration, and fellowship with God as well as petition.

"Prayer," he says, "is either a sheer illusion or a personal contact between embryonic, incomplete persons (ourselves) and the utterly concrete Person." He believed that where Christianity and other religions differ, Christianity is correct. He held that conversion is necessary and that heaven and hell are final.

If in some of his beliefs Lewis stands somewhat to the left of orthodoxy, there are others in which he moves toward the right, at least as orthodoxy is normally practiced by most Christians. For instance, the speaking in tongues at Pentecost is not only accepted by Lewis but also explained in an ingenious manner that is worth describing. The holy phenomenon of talking in tongues bears the same relationship to the gibberish sometimes taken for it as a miraculous event to a natural one. Looking from below, one will always suppose a thing to be "nothing but" or "merely" this or that. The natural to which one is accustomed will so fill the eye that the supernatural does not appear. One sees clearly the facts but not their meaning. But from above one can see both the fact and the meaning, the supernatural and the natural. The supernatural must be transposed if sinners are to have any notion of it, yet the transposition is bound to be like that of a person required to translate from a language of twenty-two vowels into one of only five vowels—one must give each character more than one value. Hence St. Paul's admonition that spiritual things must be discerned not naturally but spiritually.

Again, Lewis believes firmly in prayer for the sick. I think he is talking about Mrs. Lewis when he tells of a woman suffering from incurable cancer who was apparently healed by the laying on of hands and prayer. Lewis defends the proposition that the devil is alive and active, and he goes further than most of us in his belief concerning the reality and work of angels. He believes one enters heaven immediately at death. He thinks the Bible teaches clearly the second coming of Christ, and he thinks this may be the next great event in history. Generally Lewis stands with St. Paul in upholding the man as head of the wife, though he does not forget the rest of St. Paul's analogy. Despite his conception that the early part of Genesis is mythical (in the sense I have described), Lewis's frequent discussions of the Garden of Eden make it apparent that it means a hundred times more to him as myth than it does to most Christians as history. And we can say also that Lewis's God is alive, not static and not in the least hazy and far away. Lewis is set apart from most Christians, says Chad Walsh, by the "vividness of the gold in his religious imagination."[11]

MIRACLES

Different from the meditative and devotional nature of *Reflections on the Psalms*, the book called *Miracles* is closely reasoned. It consists of three parts plus an epilogue and two very interesting appendixes. The first seven chapters, preliminary to the main theme, describe two basic types of thought about the universe. One is that of the Naturalist, one who believes that nature is "the whole show" and that nothing else exists. This person thinks of nature as being like a pond of an infinite depth with nothing but water. The other is the Supernaturalist, who believes that one Thing exists outside time and space and has produced nature. He believes that the pond is not merely water forever but has a bottom—mud, earth, rock, and finally the whole bulk of earth itself.

The Naturalist believes that nothing exists beyond some great process or "becoming," while the Supernaturalist believes nature may be only one "system" or choice among possibilities chosen by some Primary Thing. If Naturalism is true, then miracles

11 Chad Walsh, *C. S. Lewis: Apostle to the Skeptics*, (New York: MacMillan, 1949), 107.

are impossible, yet if Supernaturalism is true, it is still possible to inquire whether God does in fact perform miracles. But Naturalism contains a great self-contradiction: it assumes that the mind itself is also "nature" and hence irrational. It is nonsense when one uses the human mind to prove the irrationality of the human mind. "All arguments about the validity of thought make a tacit, and illegitimate, exception in favor of the bit of thought you are doing at that moment." Lewis insists that reason exists on its own and that nature is powerless to produce it. Nature can only "keep on keeping on."

Naturalism for Lewis is also faced with an insurmountable problem in the "oughtness" of things. If nature is all, then conscience is also a product of nature and there is no logical place for the notion that one ought to die for his country or practice any other moral action. Contrariwise, Lewis holds that the practices of conscience are a product of a reason derived from a greater Moral Wisdom which exists absolutely and could not possibly arise out of a theory that supposes blind nature as the basis of life and thought. In fact, human rationality is itself a miracle.

Lewis then proceeds to his main theme and begins with an instance of what he calls chronological snobbery, that is, the idea that people in older times could believe in miracles because they were unacquainted with the laws of nature. Joseph, he points out, was fully as wise as any modern gynecologist on the main point of Mary's situation—that a virgin birth is contrary to nature. In finally accepting the situation as a miracle, Joseph was affirming not only the miracle but, equally, the law of nature itself as it applies to childbirth. Joseph is by no means an example of a naive or primitive ignoramus but rather of a realist whose head was as hard as anybody's so far as the regularity of nature is concerned. He saw the exception in Mary's case only because he had a pristine conviction about the rule. Believing in miracles does not at all mean any hazy notion about the regular operation of the laws of nature but rather the opposite.

Next Lewis tackles what he regards as the modern fallacy that the articles of the Christian creed are unacceptable because they are primitive in their imagery, for instance, the statement that God "came down from Heaven" rather than, as we prefer today, "entered the universe" and the notion that since hell "fire" is a metaphor it means nothing more serious than remorse. He insists that such metaphorical conceptions reveal just as supernatural a cosmos as modern abstractions and, what is more significant to his purpose, that both the so-called primitive and the modern and supposedly unmetaphorical imagery are equally figurative. To call God a "spiritual force" or "the indwelling principle of beauty, truth, and goodness" is to make one or both of two mistakes—to suppose one has escaped metaphor into some more realistic imagery, or actually to hide from reality in a verbal smoke screen.

Lewis declares that because most accounts of miracles are probably false, a standard of probability is needed. How can we determine a real from a spurious claim of miracle? One way is by the "fitness of things," a method actually deep in the best of science, a conviction as real as the color of one's hair. It was this conviction that earlier led to the very possibility of science. People expected law in nature because they believed in a Legislator. A modern agnostic science will yet discover how the omission of God inevitably leads to improbabilities in the uniformity of nature. It is a dangerous thing to make nature absolute, because claiming too much you are likely to end up with too little. "Theology offers you a working arrangement, which leaves the scientist free to continue his experiments and the Christian free to continue his prayers."

This fitness of things tells us that the miracle of the Resurrection is on a different level from someone using her patron saint to find her second best thimble. The Resurrection is a part of an immutable and eternal plan, not a last-minute "expedient to save the Hero from a situation which had got out of the Author's control." The whole story is actually about Death and Resurrection. The grand miracle is that of the Incarnation, a part of an eternal plan. Christ is indeed the corn king of mythology but not for the reason ascribed by the anthropologists. The death and rebirth pattern is in nature because it was first in this eternal plan, a plan going back before both nature and nature religions. There is rebirth in nature myths, but the Resurrection of Christ is described in the Bible as a completely unique event. The whole of creation shadowed, "mythologized," in a thousand ways the event that was to change all of history.

Miracles, which Lewis subtitles *A Preliminary Study*, is directed not at the subtleties of theological parlance but at people who really want to ask the question of whether miracles are possible. It is addressed to people of naturalistic and pantheistic minds, groups Lewis believes to include the great mass of people today. He holds that "an immoral, naive and sentimental pantheism" is the chief obstacle against Christian conversion in our time. Most people in effect regard God as incapable not only of miracle but of anything else. They have some place heard the usual anthropological accounts and hazily suppose that because these are modern they are more enlightened than the Christian revelation. Pantheism, says Lewis, is not new but very ancient and in fact the natural tendency of the human mind. Only the Greeks were able to rise above it and then only in their greatest men. Today it is manifest in theosophy, the elevation of a life force, and the race worship of the Germans under Hitler. The tragedy is that people suppose "each new relapse into this immemorial 'religion'" to be the last word in truth and fact.

God is not diffused in all things, as pantheism teaches, and neither are we contained in him as "parts," but God is the great Concrete who feeds a torrent of "opaque actualities" into the world. God is not a principle, a generality, an "ideal," or a "value" but "an utterly concrete fact." On the contrary, today our minds are congenial to "Everythingism," that is, that the whole show is merely self-existent and inclusive. The pantheist thinks that "everything is in the long run 'merely' a precursor or a development or a relic or an instance or a disguise, of everything else." Lewis is completely opposed to such a philosophy. He contrasts the pantheistic conception of God as someone who animates the universe much as you animate your body with the Christian idea of God as the inventor and maker of the universe, the artist who can stand away from his own picture and examine it.

LETTERS TO MALCOLM: CHIEFLY ON PRAYER

The rich conception of God as creative artist continues in the posthumous volume *Letters to Malcolm: Chiefly on Prayer.* In this book Lewis describes creation as a "delegation through and through" and argues that "there are no words not derived from the Word." Life is, or ought to be, a continuous theophany. Every bush is a Burning Bush, and the world is "crowded with God." Because sin defies not merely God's law but his whole creative purpose, it is more than disobedience—it is sacrilege. No physiological or psychological explanation of humanity goes deep enough. Neither the "I" nor the object is ultimate reality, and we are deceived when we take them as such. One great value of prayer is that it forces us to leave the continually impinging secularism of life and awaken to "the smell of Deity" that hangs over it. In prayer, as in the Lord's Supper, we take and eat. Understanding, desirable as it may be, is for the time replaced by a contact with ultimacy.

Our pleasures are "shafts of the glory as it strikes our sensibility." What we call bad pleasures are actually those obtained by unlawful acts. "It is the stealing of the apple that is bad, not its sweetness. The sweetness is still a beam from the glory." Lewis says that ever since he learned this long ago he has tried to make each pleasure of his life into a channel not simply of gratitude to God but of adoration. He thinks the difference is significant. "Gratitude exclaims, very properly, 'How good of God to give me this.' Adoration says, 'What must be the quality of that Being whose far-off and momentary coruscations are like this!' One's mind runs back up the sunbeam to the sun."

Lewis calls this book more nearly autobiography than theology and says that he has often simply "festooned" theological ideas with his reflections. Some years ago he wrote me that he had done a book on prayer but was not satisfied with it. That he still felt the tentative nature of some of his conclusions may be evident in the fact that he has put the book in the form of offhand letters to an old college friend.

Had we not known before, this volume would leave little doubt that *A Grief Observed*, the book that appeared under the name N. W. Clerk, is by Lewis, for here we find numerous poignant allusions to the "great blow," i.e., the death of his wife, and the deep love he had for her. It also gives us the best glimpse anywhere into the practical aspect of Lewis's prayer life. He had a lengthy list of people, some of whom he had prayed over for a long span of years and some of whom he knew simply as "that old man at Crewe" or "the waitress" or even "that man."

In this book Lewis repeats the idea discussed in an appendix to *Miracles* that our prayers are granted, or not, before the beginning of time. In the initial act of creation God dovetailed all "future" spiritual and physical occurrences. Our difficulty in understanding this is that we experience in time the things that to God are outside time. The acts of men, whether prayer or sin, are not "predetermined," for there is no "pre" with God. Because we cannot, like God, experience life in an "endless present," it does not at all mean that we are not, living or dead, eternal in God's eyes. Of a good act we may say with equal validity, "God did it" and "I did it."

Lewis's remark that he believes in Purgatory can best be understood in terms of his conviction that God continues his beatitudes in the soul after death, that there is a "farther in and a higher up" and that all eternity perhaps involves a growth. Like Dr. Johnson, Lewis thinks that the closer one comes to the purity of heaven the more he will wish for some preparation, some hallowing of the soul, before it takes up its new citizenship. Purgatory is for him a place not of retributive punishment but rather of purification in which the saved soul "at the very foot of the throne, begs to be taken away and cleansed."

Then there is in this book the same profound sense of the reality of heaven that has permeated all of Lewis's mature thinking. As usual, and with particular meaning in this his last book before his death, Lewis closes with a discussion of the Resurrection and the joy of heaven. He repeats that he came to believe in God before he believed in heaven and adds that even if the "impossible supposition" that there is no Resurrection were true, he would still take his stand on the side of Christianity. After his speculations concerning the nature of the resurrected body, he concludes that if he is incorrect something even better than he has imagined will be the Christian's happy discovery at death.

MERE CHRISTIANITY

Lewis begins this book with two facts that he calls "the foundation of all clear thinking." One is that people everywhere have the curious idea they ought to behave in a certain way, the other that they do not in fact so behave. The notion of right and wrong is not local and cultural but lodged deeply in the moral wisdom of mankind. We can call this "constant" in the world the law of human nature, or the moral law, or the rule of decent behavior. This law is not the "herd instinct" but rather directs the instincts. It is not a social convention inculcated by education but rather a real morality which measures conventions and systems. There is a big difference between the law of nature and the law of human nature. The former includes such laws as that of gravity and tells you, for instance, what a stone actually does if you drop it. But the law of human nature tells you what people ought to do and fail in doing.

The materialist view of the universe is that it simply happened and that our earth and its people are what they are by strange or lucky accidents. The other view is the religious one that the universe came into being as the result of a conscious Person. If the second view is true, we must assume that such a Person is the creator of the facts as we observe them, not something to be discovered inside the facts. There is a third in-between view called creative evolution or emergent evolution or the life-force view, which produces a kind of tame God. Lewis wonders if this view is not the world's greatest illustration of the folly of wishful thinking. The moral law, on the contrary, is as hard as nails and suggests that the universe is governed by an absolute goodness.

Now among people who think there is a God, one class sees him as more or less animating the universe and such that if the universe expired he would expire with it. Another sees him as very separate from the universe and opposed to the bad things in it. But this second view leads to the important question of how a benevolent God should create a world in which badness could enter. People who get to thinking about the justice of God often conclude that the world is simply senseless. But strangely, their conclusion proves that one part of the world is not senseless, namely, their own idea of justice.

Although Satan tries to destroy all good in the world, God woos people back to him through conscience, good dreams or myths, the scriptural depiction of his dealings with the Jews, and, by far the greatest, his own Son and Redeemer. This Son was either all he claimed to be or else a lunatic or worse, and he claimed to put us right with God not through following his teaching but through baptism, belief, and Holy Communion. The mystery of Christianity has unfathomable depths but its reality is genuine. The Christian has Christ actually operating in him.

From the next section of *Mere Christianity*, which deals with Christian behavior, I shall mention only a few of Lewis's exceptions to common viewpoints. He says that Moses, Aristotle, and the great Christian teachers of the Middle Ages all agreed against the lending of money at interest, one of the main things on which our present economy is based. As to Christian giving, the only safe rule is to give more than we can spare. Like Christianity, psychoanalysis claims to put the human machine right. The philosophy of Freud is in direct contradiction to Christianity, but psychoanalysis itself is not when it tries to remove abnormal feelings connected with moral choices. Christianity is concerned primarily with the choices. A person's choices through a period of many years slowly turn him or her into a heavenly or hellish creature. This is why one who is getting worse understands badness less and less.

Marriage, despite modern views to the contrary, is for life. Novels and movies have misled us to believe that "being in love" should be a normal lifetime expectation, whereas it is properly no more than the explosion that starts the engine of a quieter and different sort of love. Forgiveness is much unpracticed as a Christian virtue. To love one's neighbor does not at all mean making out that he is a nice fellow when he is not; we are only asked to love our neighbors as we love ourselves, and what is very lovable in any of us? The great vice loathed by all when observed in another person yet common to all of us is pride, "the complete anti-God state of mind." It can subtly reside like a spiritual cancer at the very center of even a religious person. In the Christian sense, love is not a condition of the feelings but of the will. You are not to be always weighing whether or not you "love" your neighbor but proceed as if you did and then you will come to a genuine love. The hope of heaven is not escapism. The failure of Christians to think effectively of another world is a cause of their ineffectiveness in this world. In the attempt to satisfy a deep longing that haunts us, we may try ocean voyages, a succession of women, hobbies, and other things. Yet the longing is from God and only God can satisfy it. "If I find in myself a desire which no experience in this world can satisfy, the most probable explanation is that I was made for another world." Dependence on one's moods will allow one to be neither a good atheist nor a good Christian. Faith consists in holding on to things your reason has accepted despite moods that may overtake you and the recognition that one's own efforts are to be swallowed up in Christ's indwelling power.

Both *Miracles* and *Mere Christianity* are intended as simple presentations of orthodox views. One section of the latter volume Lewis submitted in manuscript to an Anglican, a Methodist, a Presbyterian, and a Roman Catholic for their criticism and discovered only minor differences from his own view. The difference between these books and most others, particularly theological, on the same subjects is resident in Lewis's ability to select the basic issues from the corpus of their vast theological history and to present them in apt analogies, homely illustrations, clear insight, and classically simple diction. His method is proof that a sanctified imagination is a legitimate tool for any Christian apologist.

One theologian who objected to *Miracles* did so partly on the ground that Lewis was, as he said, crude in visualizing the Trinity as like a cube of six squares while remaining one cube. But was not this the very method employed by our Lord who seemed invariably to turn to things close at hand as illustrations of holy things—vines, and fig trees, and lamps, and bushel baskets, and even vultures. It was likewise St. Paul's method when he spoke of sounding brass and tinkling cymbals or the resurrection of Christ as the firstfruits. Indeed it was St. Augustine's method in *De Trinitate* and has been the method of great writers ever. Lewis points out that Plato, one of the great creators of metaphor, is "therefore among the masters of meaning." He holds that the attempt to speak unfiguratively about high abstractions is likely to result in "mere syntax masquerading as meaning" and indeed that metaphor, while not primarily the organ of truth, is the great organ for the depiction of essential meaning either in this world or others.

Chapter 4

EVERYMAN'S THEOLOGIAN

Kilby examines a few key concepts in Lewis's writing: pain, redemption, sanctification, and that mysterious, unbidden nostalgia that gently pulls us toward heaven. This article first appeared in Christianity Today *in January 1964.*

The death of Clive Staples Lewis on November 22, 1963, removed from the world one of the most lucid, winsome, and powerful writers on Christianity. We have reason to thank God that such a man was raised up in our time to become, as Chad Walsh has put it, the apostle to the skeptics. "His books exposed the shallowness of our atheist prejudices; his vision illumined the Mystery which lay behind the appearances of daily life," said one man who turned to Christ from Communism, alcoholism, and attempted suicide. "Without his works, I wonder if I and many others might not still be infants 'crying in the night,'" said another intellectual who had turned from atheism and Communism to Christianity.

Sixty-four when he died, Lewis had been converted at the age of thirty after a long span of atheism. He thereafter produced more than a score of books, both expository and fictional, to set forth his conception of the meaning of Christianity. Millions of copies have been read and widely acclaimed by both theologians and laymen all over the Western world. Nearly all of his books are now available in paperback, a good sign of their wide acceptance.

His best-known book is *The Screwtape Letters*, a brilliant story in which an undersecretary to the High Command of Hell writes letters of instruction and warning to his nephew Wormwood, a junior tempter in charge of a young man in England at the time of World War II. Wormwood is in trouble from the beginning because he has failed to prevent his "patient" from becoming a Christian. Screwtape suggests many devices for reclaiming the patient's soul. He must prepare for the time when the first emotional excitement of conversion begins to fade. He must turn the thoughts while in prayer, from God to his own moods and feelings. When the patient prays for charity, Wormwood must cause him to start trying to manufacture charitable feelings in himself. He must also stir up irritations between the patient and his mother. He must persuade the young man to think of devils as comic creatures in red tights and tails. He must cause the patient to believe that his "dry" periods are signs that God is unreal. The young man must be introduced to smart, superficially intellectual, and skeptical people who will teach him to despise "Puritanism" and love religious flippancy, and he must be persuaded to shoulder the future with all its cloud of indefinite fears rather than live in a simple, immediate dependence on God. He must be made spiritually resentful and proud. If possible, he must be brought to love theological newness for its own sake and to think of the "historical Jesus" rather than the Jesus of the Gospels. The patient's prayer life must be rationalized so that if the thing he prays for does not come to pass, he will see it as proof that petitionary prayers simply do not work, or if it does come to pass, as nothing more than the operation of natural causes.

In this book both human and divine conduct are seen from the viewpoint of hell. One of the best things is the devil's-eye conception of God, who is observed as having none of the high dignity and austerity of hell but rather as "irredeemably vulgar" and bourgeois-minded, a hedonist who invented pleasure and filled the world full of happy things like eating, sleeping, bathing, playing, and working. Hell hates God's undignified stooping to communication and fellowship with a man on his knees. Hell's intelligence department, though it has worked hard to do so, has never been able to discover one great fact about God—that is, his disinterested love for verminous man and his wish to make every man more individual, more himself in the right sense, rather than, as is the custom in hell, simply to absorb him. Whereas in hell there is nothing but competition and terrorism, the swallowing up of all who by shrewdness and power one is able to overcome. God loves distinctiveness. Hell's unity is dominated by a constant lust to devour; but God aims at the paradox of infinite differences among all creatures, a world of selves, like that of a loving family. God loves "otherness"; hell hates it. Hell hates God's complex and dangerous world pervaded with choices, a world that God has inseminated with all sorts of realities that carry their hidden winsome reminders of himself, such as beauty, silence, reverence, and music. Concerning the last, hell hopes to one day make the universe one unending noise.

Lewis's book called *Mere Christianity* is a direct treatment of many of the ideas that have been deliberately turned upside down in *The Screwtape Letters*. He begins this book with two facts that he calls "the foundation of all clear thinking." One is that people everywhere have the curious idea that they ought to behave in a certain way: the other is that they do not in fact so behave. The notion of right and wrong, he says, is not local and cultural but is lodged deeply in the moral wisdom of mankind. There is a big difference between the law of nature and the law of human nature. The former includes such laws as that of gravity and tells you, for instance, what a stone actually does if you drop it. But the law of human nature tells you what people ought to do and fail in doing.

Atheism, says Lewis, is too simple. Christianity is complicated and "odd," yet with the density of reality itself, not something you would easily have guessed. Take the matter of free will. Why did God give men free will if he knew they would misuse it? Because free will makes evil possible, it is also the only thing that makes joy and love and goodness possible. Without free will men are toys on a string. With free will they have vast possibilities for good as well as evil. If men choose evil, God's law will withhold from them the happiness they thirst for. This, he says, is the key to all history.

Later on in *Mere Christianity* Lewis declares that Christ was the first "real man" and that he made it possible for us to be real if we only will. To gain this reality, the Christian must each day shove back his own wishes and hopes and let God's "larger, stronger, quieter life come flowing in." It is not God's purpose, says Lewis, to bring people barely within the gates of heaven; he intends their absolute perfection, and late and hereafter will direct toward that end. "When He said, 'Be perfect,' He meant it. He meant that we must go in for the full treatment. . . . It may be hard for an egg to turn into a bird: it would be a jolly sight harder for it to learn to fly while remaining an egg. We are like eggs at present. And you cannot go on indefinitely being just an ordinary, decent egg. We must be hatched or go bad."

Lewis has written books on miracles, on pain, on love, and on the dangers of an unlimited trust in science. In *Miracles* Lewis discusses, among many other things, his belief that most people today are afflicted with "chronological snobbery," that is, the idea that people in an older time could accept miracles because of their ignorance of the laws of nature. Joseph, Lewis points out, was fully as wise as any modern gynecologist on the main point of Mary's situation—that a virgin birth is contrary to nature. In finally accepting the situation as miracle, Joseph was affirming not only the miracle but, equally, the law of nature itself as it applies to childbirth. Joseph is by no means an example of a naive or primitive ignoramus; rather, he was a realist whose head was as hard as anybody's as far as the regularity of nature is concerned. He saw the exception in Mary's case only because he had a pristine conviction about the rule.

In the *Problem of Pain* Lewis begins with his once sufficient reasons for being an atheist—a vast and mostly lifeless cosmos with a nature "red in tooth and claw," and the like. But one significant question, he adds, never arose in his mind: "If the universe is so bad, or even half so bad, how on earth could human beings ever come to attribute to it the activity of a wise and good Creator?" If we had never supposed God to be good, there would of course never have arisen any problem of pain. The problem is conditional. "If God were good, He would wish to make his creatures perfectly happy, and if God were almighty, He would be able to do what He wished. But the creatures are not happy. Therefore God lacks either goodness, or power, or both." Thus Lewis puts the case before beginning to answer it.

Among Lewis's most popular books are the space trilogy *Out of the Silent Planet*, *Perelandra*, and *That Hideous Strength*. The first involves a visit to the unfallen world of Malacandra (Mars). In the second a demon-possessed man from earth does his best to bring about the fall of Perelandra (Venus). In the third a group of scientific-minded but evil men almost bring England to a satanic reign. Also popular with both children and adults are Lewis's seven Narnia stories, which recount the adventures of youngsters who escape into another and wonderful world and are protected by Aslan the great Lion (Christ). One critic has said that these books marked "the greatest addition to the imperishable deposit of children's literature since the *Jungle Books*."

Doctrinally, Lewis accepted the Nicene, Athanasian, and Apostles' Creeds. He was never-failing in his opposition to theological "modernism." Some of his most biting satire is employed against it in both his fictional and his expository works. It is as ridiculous, he declared, to believe that the earth is flat as to believe in the watered-down popular theology of modern England. In *The Screwtape Letters* a major employment of hell itself is to encourage theologians to create a new historical Jesus in each generation. He repeatedly insists that, contrary to many modern theologians, it was less St. Paul than Christ who taught the terrors of hell and other "fierce" doctrines rather than sweetness and vapid love. Lewis hated the depiction of Christ in feminine modes. In the Narnian stories Aslan is always pictured as more than a tame lion. Lewis believed that God is not to be bargained with but to be obeyed. Christ is Deity himself, the Creator, coexistent with the Father, yet also his only-begotten Son, the penalty of the law, Prince of the universe, the "Eternal Fact, Father of all facthood," the Everlasting and Supreme Reality, perfect God and perfect man, the best of all moral teachers but not merely that.

Though Lewis denies the doctrine of total depravity (one wonders whether he understood its full theological implications) on the grounds that man has the idea of good and that if he were totally depraved he should not know it, this denial does not preclude Lewis from representing man everywhere as a horror to God and a miserable offender. Some people, he says, suppose that the Incarnation implies a special merit in humanity: actually it implies "just the reverse: a particular demerit and depravity" because "no creature that deserved Redemption would need to be redeemed. . . . Christ died for men precisely because men are *not* worth dying for."

The most vivid picture of what it means to be saved—and Lewis does not hesitate to use this word—is the transformation of Eustace from a dragon back into a person in *The Voyage of the Dawn Treader*. Eustace tells how he remembered that a dragon might he able to cast its skin like a snake and began to work on himself. At first the scales alone came off; but as he went deeper, his whole skin started to peel off and finally was able to step right out of it altogether. Eustace then started to wash himself, but when he put his foot into the nearby pool of water he saw that it was as hard and rough and scaly as it had been before. So he began again to scratch and finally peeled off another entire dragon skin. But once again he found under it another. At this point Aslan appeared and said, "You will have to let me undress you." Though Eustace was deathly afraid of Aslan's claws, he lay down before him. His fears were justified, for the very first tear made by Aslan was so deep he felt it had gone clear down to his heart. When the skin was at last off, Eustice discovered it was "ever so much thicker, and darker, and more knobbly-looking than the others had been." Afterward Aslan bathed and dressed him in new clothes, the symbolism of which is clear enough.

Lewis assures his readers that he believes the Bible to carry the authority of God, and he insists that we must "go back to our Bibles," even to the very words. The biblical account, says he, often turns out to be more accurate than our lengthy theological interpretations of it. It is all right to leave the words of the Bible for a moment to make some point clear, but you must always return. "Naturally God knows how to describe Himself much better than we know how to describe Him." Lewis believed that some great catastrophe was ahead for man and that the Second Coming may be the next great event in history.

Certain themes run all through Lewis's books, whether expository or fictional. One is that every living being is destined for everlasting life and that every moment of life is a preparation for that condition. Like Albert Camus, Lewis believed death to be the most significant fact in the interpretation of life: yet, unlike Camus, he was convinced that man is primarily made for eternity.

With Socrates, he held that true wisdom is the "practice of death." Another theme in Lewis is that God is the creator, transformer, and ultimate possessor of common things; that God is the inventor of matter, of sex, of eating and drinking, and of pleasures. Lewis also teaches all through his books that the only way Christians can attain full happiness is to obey God implicitly. "It is only our daily bread that we are encouraged to ask for. The present is the only time in which any duty can be done or any grace received."

But perhaps the most persistent theme in Lewis is that of man's longing for Joy. He calls this longing "the inconsolable secret" that inhabits the soul of every man, a desire that no natural happiness can ever satisfy. It is a lifelong pointer toward heaven, a nostalgia to cross empty spaces and be joined to the true reality from which we now feel cut off. The culmination of this longing in the rhapsodic joy of heaven is, for me at least, the strongest single element in Lewis. In one way or another, it hovers over nearly every one of his books and suggests that Lewis's apocalyptic vision is perhaps more real than that of anyone since St. John on Patmos.

Until a short time before his death Lewis was the distinguished occupant of the chair of medieval and Renaissance English at Cambridge University. He was one of the best literary critics of our time and an expert in philology. Notable among his scholarly writings is *The Allegory of Love*, which has been called "the best book of literary history written by an Englishman in this century." At the same time he was a Christian of no uncertain stamp. He managed the difficult feat of successfully integrating his scholarship with his religion. If we add to these things the gifts of a lively imagination, a vigorous and witty mind, and a brilliance of language, we can discover why his books have sold widely and why his readers are steadily on the increase.

Chapter 5

HIS FATE AMONG THEOLOGICAL CRITICS

In 1958 Norman Pittenger, a liberal Anglican theologian, published a severe criticism of C. S. Lewis both as a theologian and as a "Defender of the Faith," in "A Critique of C. S. Lewis" (Christian Century *75 [1958]). Dr. Kilby wrote this spirited defense, which was published later that year in* Christianity Today *in December 1958.*

Though I am no theologian I venture to disagree with most of W. Norman Pittenger's recent criticisms of the writings of C. S. Lewis. Dr. Pittenger concedes that Lewis writes charmingly and provocatively in some of his books, particularly those of a fictional character, but he does not believe that Lewis's writings have much theological value. My own judgment is that Lewis has done more to clear the theological atmosphere of our time and to create a deep interest in Christian things than many theologians together. Lewis's avoidance of theological jargon (I use the word in no derogatory sense) is a studied avoidance and should not be taken as ignorance. It seems to me that such an assumption of ignorance is the basis of Dr. Pittenger's wrong critique of Lewis. But to some of the particulars.

THE SENSE OF DECENCY

Dr. Pittenger says that Lewis is crude, even vulgar. As examples, he violates our sense of decency by attempting to explain the Trinity by the figure of a cube which is "six squares while remaining one cube," and by saying that Christ was either what he claimed to be—the Son of God—or else a madman. I believe that one of Lewis's greatest contributions to orthodox Christianity is his demonstration that a sanctified imagination is a legitimate tool for any Christian apologist. If Dr. Pittenger thinks a cube may not be used to illustrate the Trinity, what can he say of Jesus's own invariable use of things close at hand to illustrate holy things—vines, and fig trees, lamps, and bushel baskets, and even vultures? Or what can he say of Paul's allusions to sounding brass and tinkling cymbals or the resurrection of Christ as the firstfruits? Or of St. Augustine's historic analogies in *De Trinitate*, confessedly inadequate but nonetheless helpful for pedagogical purposes? In his *Weight of Glory* Lewis says, "Perfect humility dispenses with modesty." Can it be that we have a false modesty on spiritual things, a modesty in which the "classical view" (a favorite idea in Dr. Pittenger's criticism of Lewis) is substituted for a downright eagerness to set forth the reality of Christ?

THE BOOK AND THE TIMES

Again, Dr. Pittenger says that Lewis's Christianity is often not orthodox. At the same time Lewis is said to hold to an "uncritical traditionalism" and to be dogmatic in his proclamation of it. Dr. Pittenger says that Lewis proceeds in his books by a "smart superficiality" and does not present a "credible theology." Dr. Pittenger makes fairly clear as he goes along what he believes to be credible theology. He declares that never in the Synoptic Gospels is there either statement or implication that Christ claimed to be the

Son of God. He is upset with Lewis for using the Fourth Gospel so uncritically. The validity of our Lord's unique place, says Dr. Pittenger, does not rest on such "mechanical grounds" as Lewis advances but on "the total consentient witness of all Christians from the apostles' time." Lewis is declared to be "too cavalier about the actual historical Jesus," who is described by Dr. Pittenger as "a Prophet who announced the coming of God's kingdom and who may even have thought that he himself was to be the Anointed One, or Messiah, who would inaugurate it." In other words, Dr. Pittenger diminishes the impact of the Fourth Gospel, holds to a "credible theology" based to a considerable extent, apparently on general belief through the ages which he interprets as denying that Christ was the unique Son of God, and at the same time accuses Lewis of unorthodoxy and "uncritical traditionalism." Lewis's faith, says Dr. Pittenger, is not a reasoned one. Instead, Dr. Pittenger prefers a faith "open and reasoned . . . built on history, confirmed in experience, checked by reason, and demonstrated in Christian life." (Note the double emphasis on reason.) He is unhappy with Lewis for his preferring "the Pauline ethic based on man's sinfulness and helplessness" (Dr. Pittenger's language) to the Sermon on the Mount. Isn't Dr. Pittenger himself behind the times here? Does current theology divide Paul's ethic from Jesus's?

Furthermore, says Dr. Pittenger, the sophisticate Lewis "pretends to be very simple indeed" by taking what the church has said in the Scriptures "as the last word." What does Dr. Pittenger put beside this for his own authority? He repeatedly accuses Lewis of failing to take cognizance of recent theological research. Lewis, for instance, confounds "the Fall" (quotations Dr. Pittenger's) "with an event in history," and confuses "biblical myth" concerning Adam with "a literal description."

GOD AND HIS WORD

But Dr. Pittenger's article is taken up in large measure with a somewhat detailed criticism of Lewis's *Miracles*. Again it seems to me that Dr. Pittenger is far-fetched in his denunciation. He describes Lewis's book as "one of the worst books ever written on the subject." In the first place, Dr. Pittenger appears to forget that Lewis, as Chad Walsh has well said, is the "apostle to the skeptic." No one who has read the Bible with any care could possibly be unaware that it teaches the omnipresence of God. God dwells in the heart, but he also dwells in the heavens. It is therefore altogether proper for Lewis to speak of God as being outside his creation. In the second place, throughout the whole of *Miracles* Lewis makes clear that all his discussion is, of necessity, metaphoric. His effort is to deny the deterministic and deistic conception that God is *confined* to his creation. Hence his metaphor of "intervention" to the idea of which Dr. Pittenger objects.

In appendix B to *Miracles* and elsewhere Lewis makes his metaphoric usage very clear. "If God directs the course of events at all then he directs the movement of every atom at every moment; 'not one sparrow falls to the ground' without that direction." Does this sound as if God is an absentee landlord? Dr. Pittenger's own list of quotations from St. Augustine and others show that they also spoke metaphorically of miracles. In fact, his quotation from St. Augustine contains the same word—"above"—to which Dr. Pittenger seems to be objecting in Lewis.

Lewis is also accused of being fifty years behind the times for not knowing that a self-explanatory universe is out of date. No "respectable philosophical writer and no first-rate scientist" during the last half century has held to a deterministic universe, says Dr. Pittenger. Only ignorant people are "naturalists" in Lewis's sense, and there he has proceeded in his "smart superficiality" to knock down a straw man. To answer Dr. Pittenger on this point it is perhaps sufficient to let the reader think a moment for himself. It is true that at some point in their studies many scientists have acknowledged that they were confronted by a mystery or have even spoken of the whole universe as mysterious, but that is no indication whatever that they have come over to the side of the angels. Admittedly, deistic-type mechanism is passé, but is this all there is to materialism? A great many philosophers and theologians are wrong unless our zeitgeist may properly be described as "naturalistic" in Lewis's precise meaning. Whatever they may imply or print or state on occasions, men live as if no miracle is possible, and it was this condition to which Lewis was addressing himself—not to a "classical" theory of miracles.

It might be well to stop for a moment and cite from a couple of reputable science-philosophers who hold to a nonsupernatural view of life. In his William Vaughan Moody lecture at the University of Chicago in 1931, Anton Julius Carlson said, "As I see it, the supernatural has no support in science, it is incompatible with science, it is frequently an active foe of science." Here, then, is one reputable scholar who can hardly be described as anything other than a "naturalist." In Bertrand Russell's *Why I Am Not a Christian*, published last year, he says: "There are some who maintain that physiology can never be reduced to physics, but their arguments are not very convincing and it seems prudent to suppose that they are mistaken." Also, a little later, "God and immortality, the central dogmas of the Christian religion, find no support in science." Can this reputable scholar be described as anything other than a "naturalist"?

Lewis is also accused of writing a book on miracles without looking at the words translated "miracle" in the Old and New Testaments. Isn't this a little too much? I do not know what sort of Hebrew scholar Lewis is, but I do know that he reads Greek with as much facility as most of us read English. Dr. Pittenger tells us that had Lewis read his Greek New Testament he would have been more fully aware of the *Sitz im Leben* of the miracles described there, i.e., he would have noted that though they are symbolically accurate they are not necessarily factually so. I suppose it would do little good to quote the New Testament itself against Dr. Pittenger, since he can assume the same symbolistic finality for all situations, but one does not need to be a theological student to notice that thousands swarmed around Christ in his days on earth simply because of what they at least supposed to be miracles—just plain miracles without "classical" or scholarly qualifications.

NATURALISM IN OUR BONES

Could it be that Dr. Pittenger's objection to *Miracles* arises in part from an unstated criticism? In the last chapter of *Miracles* Lewis gives an unmistakable warning to his readers: "If . . . you turn to study the historical evidence for yourself, begin with the New Testament and not with books about it. . . . And when you turn from the New Testament to modern scholars, remember that you go among them as sheep among wolves. Naturalistic assumptions, beggings of the question such as that I noted on the first page of this book, will meet you on every side—even from the pens of clergymen. . . . We all have Naturalism in our bones."

In all my reading of Lewis I think one of his very best qualities is his avoidance of technically theological language. It is the very thing that has made him spiritually thrilling to thousands of people around the world. This directness, this "orthodoxy," is the element Dr. Pittenger appears to dislike most. There is of course a place for theologians and all the fine points of theological discourse. As to C. S. Lewis, I am sure that he would be the first to acknowledge that his works are not flawless. But let not the theologians smother this man who brings into the soul the fresh air of spiritual reality.

Chapter 6

ON IMAGINATION AND REASON

Kilby responded to many requests to write on Lewis; some of these articles are brief or redundant, and they are not included here. On several occasions though he had the opportunity to expand in some detail on a particular aspect of Lewis and his thought, and we have included those more substantial pieces. He was asked to contribute something on Lewis's effectiveness as a communicator to Carolyn O'Keefe's collection, C. S. Lewis, Speaker and Teacher. *Kilby begins with essentially the same account of his 1953 meeting as in the earlier* Kodon *article, adding only the small detail that "all during our conversation he kept working with his pipe, but, if I recall correctly, he never got it really going," and goes on to add impressions from other sources of Lewis as a speaker, focusing above all on Lewis's unique blend of clear reasoning with powerful imagination.*

A recent, ground-breaking book by another former Oxford English professor, Iain McGilchrist (The Master and His Emissary: The Divided Brain and the Making of the Western World) *casts a great deal of light on Lewis's effectiveness as a communicator.*[12] *McGilchrist, disillusioned with how a sheerly analytical approach to literature kept one from meeting a work as a living thing, left literature for science and became a psychiatrist. In that capacity, without leaving behind his literary sensibility, he has done important work on the implications of the fact that*

12 Iain McGilchrist, *The Master and His Emissary: The Divided Brain and the Making of the Western World* (New Haven: Yale University Press, 2009).

our brains are profoundly divided. The left hemisphere simplifies things for the purpose of manipulation and use; the right hemisphere meets things in all their complexity, newness, and mystery. Both are necessary, but our culture keeps elevating the manipulative part of our brain ("the emissary") over the true "Master," which understands mystery, and meets it with metaphor. In Lewis, McGilchrist might say, the hemispheres were in particularly good balance. Intriguingly, McGilchrist says a great deal also about the right hemisphere's openness to longing, Sehnsucht, *which Lewis calls "sweet desire." Unlike so much reductive neuropsychological literature, McGilchrist is not so much explaining away as he is helping us understand the mystery of our consciousness in a world that is a gift and a miracle. Both Lewis and Kilby would have admired this. McGilchrist's analysis casts a great deal of light also on Kilby's analysis of the appeal of Tolkien to modern/postmodern culture. (See below, chapter 17: "The Lost Myth and Literary Imagination.")*

My own brief personal experience with Lewis was that of every other American I have heard of who visited him. That is, I found him a man of great courtesy, candor, outgoingness, deep friendliness, quietness of spirit, and manifesting a genuine interest in affairs other than his own. Billy Graham told me of his lengthy visit and of the manner in which Lewis promptly made him feel completely at home.

In later years I once talked with Professor Nevill Coghill at Merton College, Oxford, the longtime friend of Lewis, and he mentioned some similarities between Lewis and the famous Dr. Samuel Johnson. When I incorporated this into a preface I was writing and one of the publishers involved objected to using it, I wrote Professor Coghill of the incident, to which he answered:

> I cannot understand how anyone could possibly object to it. There he was, like the Reynolds portraits (bar the wig) thick-set, full-fleshed, deep-voiced, learned, rough, golden-hearted, flattening in dispute, a notable wit, kindly affectioned, with a great circle of friends, some of them men of genius like Tolkien, untidy, virtuous, devoted to a wife untimely lost, liable to give his house over to be occupied, or partly occupied, by people less well-endowed than himself, dispenser of secret charities, a Tory and a High Churchman. Could anyone since Dr. Johnson be so described except Jack Lewis? And every word true in its fullest sense. When I say "learned," when I say "virtuous," I do not mean them in the tomb-stoned sense, where the marble fossilizes flattery, but in their most rigorous meanings.[13]

Among other pictures of Lewis, one of the most interesting to me is that of a visit he made to London in 1944 to talk to the Christian Fellowship of the Electric and Musical Institute in Middlesex. Mr. John S. A. Ensor, who arranged the occasion, not only allowed me to have his correspondence with Lewis but also wrote me of his own impressions of him. The question arose of the best manner of presentation, and Mr. Ensor suggested simply allowing the men present to ask Lewis questions, to which Lewis replied: "Now that you mention questions at the meeting it suddenly occurs to me that the best meetings I've ever had have been *all* questions, i.e., I've announced myself as a one-man Brain's Trust on moral and religious questions."[14]

Someone had wondered whether Lewis's Oxford accent would be understood in London circles, to which Lewis wrote Mr. Ensor:

---

13 Letter from Nevill Coghill, July 7, 1967 (in the files of the author).

14 Letter from C. S. Lewis, March 13, 1944 (in the Lewis Collection, Wheaton College).

To anyone who is interested in this vexed question, I wish you'd circulate the real answer, which is as follows:

1. The first time I heard my own voice on a record I didn't recognise it and was shocked. Moral:
   A. No man knows what his own accent is like.
   B. No man's accent is there because he has chosen it.
   C. It may not be the accent he likes. If all my critics would hear their own voices they'd be very surprised.
2. The whole matter is misunderstood as long as people insist on looking at accents as subjects of approval or disapproval. They are simply accidental phenomena, to be studied as one studies different varieties of beetles. Taken in *that* way they are very interesting and often reveal much history.
3. My own accent is so far from voluntary that I have actually tried to retain my original North of Ireland—and apparently failed.
4. What do they want me to do? I could try mimicking some other accent but there'd be great danger, at my age, of producing only a horrible mixture.[15]

As plans for the meeting matured, the matter of an honorarium came up, to which Lewis wrote Mr. Ensor: "I take money for lecturing on subjects on which I'm a professional (e.g., English Literature), but not for lecturing on subjects on which I'm an amateur (e.g., Theology)."[16]

When the time of the visit arrived, Lewis was to be met at Paddington Station. To help in identification, he wrote Mr.

15 Ibid.

16 Letter from C. S. Lewis, April 28, 1944 (in the Lewis Collection, Wheaton College).

Ensor: "I am tall, fat, clean shaven, don't wear glasses, and shall be in corduroy trousers, probably with a walking stick."[17] In later years Mr. Ensor wrote me:

> He did not seem "fat." He was dressed in well-worn tweed jacket and corduroy trousers with fawn raincoat, and would seem undistinguishable in appearance from scores of other ordinary folk. Looked rather older than expected, although in fact two years younger than I. Had a solitary and detached air, which was deceptive because we almost instantly established an easy and friendly conversation. . . . When we arrived at the E. M. I. Head Office at Hayes, he was taken to a small tea party for refreshment prior to the meeting. Here he met the then President of the Company and several senior executives who had accepted invitations. Although all these men were stylishly dressed and distinguished in their own fields, it was an eye opening experience for me to see the deference with which he was treated in this company.

There were some two hundred present. The director read the questions. Mr. Ensor reported how "all the answers were given spontaneously and most eloquently for about one hour non-stop."[18]

When Lewis made this trip to Middlesex he was forty-five years old and widely known both as an Oxford scholar and professor and a powerful explicator of the Christian faith. In both branches of this rather unusual combination he had published books which won high acclaim.

Now the great and I think all but unique essential ingredient in Lewis's makeup was a remarkable combination of two qualities

17 Letter from C. S. Lewis, March 31, 1944 (in the Lewis Collection, Wheaton College).

18 Letter from John S. A. Ensor, December 9, 1965 (in the Lewis Collection, Wheaton College).

normally supposed to be opposites. I mean, on the one hand, a deep and vivid imagination and, on the other, a profoundly analytical mind. Even more remarkable, it was not that these qualities lay in him side by side and disconnected but that by some good alchemy they were organically joined. An easy instance of what I mean is Lewis's *Screwtape Letters*, where by the power of imagination the reader is allowed to see his own motives and actions as they are viewed by devils in hell, yet the wide distribution of this book indicates that Lewis put his finger on the pulse of spiritual problems as substantially as any professional theologian could wish. A writer in *The Saturday Review* said that Lewis was "a powerful, discriminating and, in the proper sense of the word, poetic mind, great learning, startling wit, and overwhelming imagination." Actually reason and imagination are joined in Lewis's communication—both written and oral—because they were first joined in his thought and life.

The imaginative strain was particularly apparent, as might be expected, in Lewis's childhood. The family's move when he was six to a big new house in Belfast gave him and his older brother Warren a new world of their own. "I was the product of long corridors," he wrote, of "empty sunlit rooms, upstairs indoor silences, attics explored in solitude, distant noises of gurgling cisterns and pipes, and the noise of wind under the tiles."[19] He lived long stretches of unalloyed happiness in his imagination. One cannot forget the nostalgia with which he tells, long after the event, of a time when his brother carried into their nursery a little toy forest that he had made of moss and twigs and flowers on the top of a biscuit lid and of the consequent bliss when, standing one summer's day beside a flowering currant, the memory of that event returned to him "as if from a depth not of years but of

19 C. S. Lewis, *Surprised by Joy: the Shape of My Early Life* (New York: Harcourt, Brace & World, Inc., 1955), 10.

centuries,"[20] the two experiences joining to create in him a lifelong love both for the forms and freshness of nature and for the significance of nostalgia, of longing.

In Lewis imagination led early to creativity, and even before he could write, he used to compose stories, which he would dictate to his father on Saturday evenings. A little later he was putting other stories down in his own boyish hand. His Animal-Land was patterned on a geography that included India and the Himalayas, and he warned his readers that his stories need not necessarily be taken as history—that they might be "only legends." At fifteen he was deeply involved in a project that is almost unbelievable. Preparing for admission to Oxford, he had gone for tutorial study under W. T. Kirkpatrick in Great Bookham, Surrey, and there fallen in love with the countryside and also the glories of Greek literature, which he was romping through in the original under Kirkpatrick's tutelage. Earlier he had come to love the whole world of Norse mythology, so now he undertook to write a full-length drama about the Norse gods but built upon a model that was strictly Greek classical. He wrote his boyhood friend Arthur Greeves explaining in detail the contents of *Prologos*, *Parodos*, episode 1, episode 2, episode 3, and *Exodos*, and he urged Arthur, who was talented as a musician, to begin writing the necessary music.[21] Lewis had already begun to write poetry and at twenty published a volume of lyrics called *Spirits in Bondage*.

This imaginative and creative side of Lewis remained as a major strain and ran like a clear stream in all his oral and written communication throughout his life.

But now I wish to devote a good deal of attention to another and equally significant side of Lewis and one that, as I said, was seemingly opposite. This side, unlike the other, apparently came

20 Ibid., 16.
21 Letter from C. S. Lewis, undated but probably Autumn, 1914 (in the Lewis Collection, Wheaton College).

rather suddenly into existence when Lewis, at fifteen, went to study under Kirkpatrick. That side was cold-blooded reason. Lewis's own account of how his training began is vivid. The tall, lean, muscular, and bearded tutor met him at the railway station, and they started for his home. Looking about, the boy began to make conversation, saying that the scenery of Surrey was much wilder than he had expected.

> "Stop!" shouted Kirk with a suddenness that made me jump. "What do you mean by wildness and what grounds had you for not expecting it?"
>
> I replied I don't know what. . . . As answer after answer was torn to shreds it at last dawned upon me that he hadn't really wanted to know.[22]

Thus in less than five minutes after they met, Lewis began to feel the sting and forcefulness of a method that he was himself to acquire and exercise for the rest of his life.

The most noteworthy application of the method was that the young atheist Lewis, studying under the atheist logician Kirkpatrick, eventually discovered that true rationality led to the road away from atheism and toward holiness, toward God. Though the road was long—some fifteen years—it became clearer and clearer to the young man who entered Oxford, went away to war, was wounded, reentered Oxford, was graduated with honors, and settled down as instructor that "a young Atheist cannot guard his faith too carefully."[23] God simply closed in on him. The taut rationality and devastating dialectic he had learned from his tutor was largely the means to his salvation. He discovered that a man cannot be intellectually honest with God and fend him off for long.

22 Lewis, *Surprised by Joy*, 134.
23 Ibid., 226.

The emphasis on reason is everywhere apparent in Lewis's works, fictional as well as expository. In *The Pilgrim's Regress* it is Reason who rescues John from the psychoanalytical prison, slays the Spirit of the Age, offers the prisoners freedom, and leads John back toward the main highway and directs him to Mother Kirk and salvation. Later in the story Reason appears as John's enemy, as he supposes, and forces him with a brandished sword into the right path, the very event that had transpired in Lewis's own experience. In *Screwtape* one of the devil's purposes was to keep the Christian out of arguments about religion. From the hellish point of view what was wanted was a quiet drift into worldly-wise common sense. Argument would inevitably lead from personal to universal issues, and universals tended to circumvent the insidious schemes of hell.

The most pronounced depiction of the powers and also the shortcomings of rationality appears in *Till We Have Faces.* There the Fox, the Greek tutor of a pagan king's daughters, taught them to reason everything out much as Kirkpatrick had taught Lewis. The Fox explained all the elements of life, physical and metaphysical, as the outworking of natural and reasonable causes with nothing whatever left over. But later in the novel, the Fox, now in limbo, abjectly confesses that his rationalism had been as clear but also as thin as water. Orual, the leading character in the novel, who had learned her own analytical methods from the Fox, was also dismayed when in limbo she discovered her supposedly airtight case against the supernatural to be little more than a lifelong repetition of a few rather shoddy complaints.

Never does Lewis make fun of reason as an effective instrument, even in the hands of the enemies of Christianity. In *Perelandra*, for instance, Ransom has to confess that at least a portion of the Unman's case is shockingly logical even when in this novel that case threatens to be the cause of a second Fall. It is of course this utter willingness of Lewis to present both sides that has made him a great influence on his generation. In *That Hideous Strength*, Ransom says of his friend MacPhee at St. Anne's, "He is our skeptic; an important office."[24] In the same book, Frost, director of Belbury, explains that much of what one takes for thought is simply a by-product of the blood and nervous tissues, and that friendship, fear, resentment, and all social relationships are purely chemical in origin. In what it considered the latest scientific spirit, Belbury set out to treat men as machines that "have to be worked" and intended ultimately to supplant birth, breeding, and even death with its own particular brand of Rationality.

Against the sterile and decimating technology of Belbury, Lewis in this novel presents two antitheses. One is the enthronement of the real "goddess Reason, the divine clearness" represented by the ancient and worthy, though almost wholly destroyed, strain of true Christianity in Britain. The other is represented by the utter beingness of Mr. Bultitude, the bear who did not know that his friends were people and that he was a bear. What he did know supremely was that "goodness occurred and he tasted it."[25] Mr. Bultitude was always in that glorious state of pre-Adamic consciousness that men can only experience in some occasional moment of nostalgia and longing, an experience of "a potent adjective floating in a noun-less void" of pure quality. Like Chesterton, Lewis was a man unutterably appreciative of being itself, such as that in a bear or a blade of grass.

Lewis's conception of reason can, I think, be reduced to two propositions. The first is that of necessity any predication assumes a standard, a norm of some sort, a yardstick. Anything that can be designated thought must be to a greater or less degree involved with the marshaling of ideas into coherent schemes and coercive arguments. An imbecile is what he is because nothing can be error

---

24 C. S. Lewis, *That Hideous Strength* (New York: The Macmillan Company, 1946), p. 211.

25 Ibid., p. 362.

to him. A man can aim a gun at falsehood only when the gun is set against the shoulder of what he, rightly or wrongly, regards as truth. The second is that an adequate standard or norm must rise above the noetic and discursive, that is, reason must give way to a greater thing called Right Reason or, as I have mentioned, the "divine clearness."

Both of these propositions are illustrated throughout Lewis's works but are perhaps best illustrated in the three Riddell Memorial Lectures delivered at the University of Durham and later published in his small volume called *The Abolition of Man*. There he begins by citing from a British schoolbook the declaration that when a person calls a waterfall sublime he is making a remark not about the waterfall at all but only about his own feelings. What the authors of this schoolbook are doing, says Lewis, is implanting in the minds of children the idea that all value judgments are subjective and dependent on the accidental factors such as mood or occasion and that there is no more accurate procedure than this. There is really no such thing as a yardstick by which to measure a waterfall or anything else. Such response as one gives is simply relative to the person and the occasion.

Quite contrary to the textbook makers, Lewis holds to what he calls the doctrine of objective value, i.e., "the belief that certain attitudes are really true, and others really false, to the kind of thing the universe is and the kind of things we are."[26] He gives this example: it is a fact that children are delightful even though he himself does not enjoy the society of small children. When Lewis measures his attitude by the objective value rather than by a psychological response varying according to the mood and the occasion, he is able to recognize it as a defect and to acknowledge that life still demands of him a certain response whether he happens to make it or not. Attitudes, he told his

---

26 C. S. Lewis, *The Abolition of Man* (New York: The Macmillan Company, 1950), 12.

university audience, can be judged reasonable or unreasonable as they conform or fail to conform to Reason.

Even those who go about debunking values practice better than they preach by assuming, often unconsciously, a value of their own. While teaching children that values are subjective and perhaps trivial, the textbook authors are themselves demonstrating that one value is not so, namely, the value assumed by them in the very act of writing such a book. This is apparently a value independent of mood and occasion and is presumably important, else they would not go to the trouble of doing the textbook in the first place. And what is that value actually? That there really are no significant values. Reason thus is used to deny reason, and proof is used to prove that proof is chimerical. All arguments denying the validity of thought, says Lewis, "make a tacit, and illegitimate, exception in favour of the bit of thought you are doing at that moment. It has to be left outside the discussion and simply believed in, in the simple old-fashioned way."[27] On the contrary, Lewis believes the validity of thought is central and "all other things have to be fitted in round it as best they can."

The other idea in *The Abolition of Man* is similar but more subtle. It is the effort, in our time moving forward with dispatch via scientific progress, to reduce all things to "merely." For instance, the sun is merely matter, energy, heat, mass, an assumption very far from the belief of the early Greeks that the sun was a god and godlike in its glory. Likewise man is reduced to material—such an object as Susanne Langer describes to illustrate her own complete atheism: man, she says, is "an organism, his substance is chemical, and what he does, suffers, or knows, is just what this sort of chemical structure may do, suffer, or know. When the structure goes to pieces, it never does, suffers, or knows anything again."[28] On the contrary, the world for Lewis is not merely factual, nor "merely"

27 C. S. Lewis, *Miracles* (New York: The Macmillan Company, 1947), 30.
28 Susanne Langer, *Philosophy in a New Key* (Cambridge, Massachusetts: Harvard University Press, 1951), 40.

anything, and "to 'see through' all things is the same as not to see." That is, reason is unworthy of itself until it rises above "merely." Abstraction is unavoidable, he feels, but the abstractor must be pertinently aware of the procedure.

In his autobiography, Lewis tells of one of the great intellectual milestones of his education. It arose from reading Samuel Alexander's *Space, Time, and Deity*, where he learned that an experience and the later thought about that experience are two entirely different things that must never be regarded as one. He discovered:

> You cannot hope and also think about hoping at the same moment; for in hope we look to hope's object and we interrupt this by (so to speak) turning round to look at the hope itself. Of course the two activities can and do alternate with great rapidity; but they are distinct and incompatible. . . . In introspection we try to look "inside ourselves" and see what is going on. But nearly everything that was going on a moment before is stopped by the very act of our turning to look at it. Unfortunately this does not mean that introspection finds nothing. On the contrary, it finds precisely what is left behind by the suspension of all our normal activities; and what is left behind is mainly mental images and physical sensations. The great error is to mistake this mere sediment or track or by-product for the activities themselves.[29]

In another place he put the matter very succinctly:

> The more lucidly we think, the more we are cut off: the more deeply we enter into reality, the less we can think.

29 Lewis, *Surprised by Joy*, 218–19.

> You cannot study Pleasure in the moment of the nuptial embrace, nor repentance while repenting. . . . But when else can you really know these things? "If only my toothache would stop, I could write another chapter about Pain." But once it stops, what do I know about pain?[30]

In *Surprised by Joy* Lewis tells of his pre-Christian excursions, some of them very serious, into philosophies such as those of Bergson, Schopenhauer, Bertrand Russell, Berkeley, Hegel, occultism, stoical monism, anthroposophism, realism, and absolute idealism. The last was in Lewis's student days the dominant philosophy at Oxford. He came eventually to the conviction that idealism, taken seriously, was actually "disguised Theism."[31] He found that he could incorporate science into his theistic system but that he could never fit Christianity into a scientific cosmology. He wrote:

> Granted that Reason is prior to matter and that the light of that primal Reason illuminates finite minds, I can understand how men should come, by observation and inference, to know a lot about the universe they live in. If, on the other hand, I swallow the scientific cosmology as a whole, then not only can I not fit in Christianity, I cannot even fit in science. If minds are wholly dependent on brains, and brains on bio-chemistry, and chemistry (in the long run) on the meaningless flux of the atoms, I cannot understand how the thought of those minds should have any more significance than the sound of wind in the trees. . . . I believe in Christianity as I believe that the Sun has risen not only because I see it because by it I see everything else.[32]

---

30 Lewis, "Myth Became Fact," *World Dominion* (September-October, 1944), 269.
31 Lewis, *They Asked for a Paper: Papers and Addresses* (London: Geoffrey Bles Ltd., 1962), 164.
32 Ibid., 164–65.

Lewis felt that most of the other popular explanations of things suffer the same inconsistency. Psychoanalysis, for instance, tends to find man "merely" a bundle of complexes, but we should hardly have psychoanalysis in the first place if the promulgator of that philosophy were himself considered to be simply a bundle of complexes. Again, the Marxist "proves that all thoughts result from class conditioning except the thought he is thinking while he says this." Thus too of behaviorism, logical positivism, or any other philosophy intending explanation by simplicism, reductionism, or naturalistic methods. They are, as G. K. Chesterton said, "in the clear and well-lit prison of one idea."

Lewis reminds us of the old problem of scientific explanation itself. If you start out to explain a rose you can ascribe the color to light waves impinging on optic nerves and scent reaching the nostrils, and the like, until no actual rose is left. Such explanations remove us farther from the object we wish to understand. An object does not consist of the elements into which it can be resolved. Like many others, Lewis felt that since the sixteenth century the system of "truncated thought" at the heart of science has increasingly tended to supplant not only metaphysical and theological thought but true reality itself. He was convinced that reality is more than physical objects, on the one hand, and abstract concepts, on the other; it involves the "concrete but immaterial" and the possibility of a naked contact with the Almighty himself.

Now up to this point I have considered mainly the negative side of Lewis's view of reason. If the systems we have mentioned are in error, what is correct?

First, Lewis believed that reason can never properly exist on its own. The plant called reason must have its roots in a deeper soil and its leaves spread out to a more ambient air. Since the human mind is "wholly incapable of inventing a new value," it must look outward toward a changeless standard. Such a standard is in fact a necessity. "Our ideas of good," he says, "may change, but they cannot change either for the better or worse if there is no absolute and immutable good to which they can approximate or from which they can recede."[33] One must either accept God as that absolute or inevitably be forced to some lesser, more passing substitute that will become in effect an absolute of man's own making.

When God was, as he says, "closing in" on him, Lewis was overwhelmed with the idea that God was Reason itself, the very Logic (*Logos*) of the universe. At the same time he was convinced of God as far more than reason, or of reason becoming personal and requiring surrender. He looked back on his long debate with God and discovered that "when you are arguing against God you are arguing against the very power that makes you able to argue at all."[34] Up to that time Lewis's nonimaginative universe had been bounded by reason but with some troublesome preternatural elements omitted or else stuffed into a corner. Now he concluded that reason in the normal sense would be forever insufficient and that something resembling Milton's Right Reason was necessary. He saw with Alfred North Whitehead that, "apart from a complete metaphysical understanding of the universe, it is very difficult to understand any proposition clearly and distinctly."[35] And he also saw with William James that, "when we see all things in God and refer all things to Him, we read in common matters superior expressions of meaning."[36] Reason he discovered is the "spearhead of the Supernatural," but that that reason is conditioned both

33 C. S. Lewis, "The Poison of Subjectivism," *Religion in Life* (Summer, 1943), 356–65.

34 C. S. Lewis, *Mere Christianity: A Revised and Enlarged Edition, with a New Introduction, of the Three Books "The Case for Christianity," "Christian Behaviour," and "Beyond Personality"* (New York: The Macmillan Company, 1952), 38.

35 Alfred North Whitehead, *The Function of Reason* (Princeton: Princeton University Press, 1959), 68.

36 William James, "Find the Balance," *Time*, August 26, 1957, 34.

by Satan's darkening of man's intellect and also by the human condition itself. "A man's Rational thinking," he concluded, "is just so much of his share in eternal Reason as the state of his brain allows to become operative: it represents, so to speak, the bargain struck or the frontier fixed between Reason and Nature at that particular point."[37]

God is not only the source of all facthood but of all order as well, and the source of the moral order. God being absolute and the Creator of all things, "the real laws of the universe are not broken ever."[38] Perhaps this is what St. Paul had in mind when he told the Corinthians that "after all, we can make no progress against the truth; we can only work for the truth."[39]

After Lewis's conversion he found that Right Reason could easily include in the sum of things not only a Logos or logic but also a personal God of both justice and love. It could accept at once both reason and faith. Faith, he found out, does not consist of tenaciously holding on to a belief without evidence or in the teeth of evidence. A scientist will weigh evidence in a certain way in his laboratory, but he will not use the same process to "believe" in his wife, children, and friends. A Christian believes in God not because he finds him by laboratory methods but by actual contact with him. The Christian is something like the electric eel, which knows more about electricity than all electrical engineers put together.

In his communion with God, the Christian moves "from the logic of speculative thought into what might perhaps be called the logic of personal relations. . . . *Credere Deum esse* turns into *Credere in Deum*. And *Deum* here is this God, the increasingly knowable Lord."[40] The strict logician versus the believer is illustrated in

37 Lewis, *Miracles*, 49–50.
38 Lewis, *That Hideous Strength*, 440.
39 2 Corinthians 13:8 (J. B. Phillips translation).
40 Lewis, *They Asked for a Paper*, 196.

That Hideous Strength. Knowing the menace hanging over them, the rationalistic MacPhee wants to act on the known evidence and finds it impossible to understand Ransom's quiet waiting for orders from a metaphysical world. In a similar way Psyche in *Till We Have Faces* lived inside the glorious reality of her palace and her lover while her sister, the rationalizing Orual, found it utterly impossible to make any sense of the situation.

And now I can return to what I have said of the imaginative and creative side of C. S. Lewis and endeavor to describe the organic joining of that and the rational side.

No longer confined to a God made largely in his own image, Lewis as a Christian discovered a universe increasing simultaneously in wonder and in mystery, a universe more to be celebrated than to be cerebrated. He was like his character Ransom who on the voyage to Mars discovered what he had abstractly called "space" was now, when he was in the midst of it, a warm and thrilling reality "tingling with fullness of life for which infinity itself was not one cubic inch too large." Lewis could now take a new and enlarged look at everything and see cosmic connections everywhere by the use not of reason alone but of Right Reason. He could reexamine mythology and anthropology and conclude, in opposition to Frazer, not that man created God but rather that mythology is the result of "gleams of celestial strength and beauty" moving upon the minds even of pagan and sinful men. He saw that the world, including its evil, is neither a duality nor an absurdity, but rather the particular sort of world described by St. Paul and Jesus Christ.

Possessor of a God large enough to be inevitably mysterious, Lewis could nose around in all corners and gaze at the magnificent "oddities" he ran into. There was, for instance, *Sehnsucht*, that longing in every man, that ineluctable cry at the very roots of man's being that keeps man forever restless until he rests in

God. Lewis could welcome the numinous or built-in awe from man's deep intuition of more than the eye sees and the ear hears. He could try out his friend Charles Williams's "co-inherence" and substitution and discover that he could actually relieve the intolerable cancer pains in his wife's thigh by taking them into his own.[41] Like Chesterton, he now could readily accept the ineffable richness of the universe and the sensuous world as generous gifts of its Creator. In his poem "On Being Human" he declares man to be better off than even angels in his ability to feel, smell, taste, hear, and see.[42] Lewis could also fling his imagination forth to depict an unfallen planet and the delightful children's world of the Narnia stories.

Lewis's hierarchy now included God, Right Reason, the numinous, myth, reality, and joy. He saw the opposite hierarchy as one beginning with agnosticism or atheism and having for its chief members reason, naturalism, scientism, sexuality, such modern jangles as advertising and idiotic sophistication, and what Daniel J. Boorstin calls pseudo-events. He saw clearly the subtleties by which the ego falls into the hands of hell.

Lewis's position on reason and Right Reason may perhaps best be summed up by an essay of his called "Meditation in a Toolshed."[43] He tells of standing in a darkened toolshed in his yard and seeing through a crack at the top of the door a beam of light from the sun outside. "From where I stood that beam of light, with the specks of dust floating in it, was the most striking thing in the place. Everything else was almost pitch black. I was seeing the beam, not seeing things by it." When he moved so that the beam fell on his eyes the whole picture was changed. "I saw no toolshed, and (above all) no beam. Instead I saw, framed in

---

41 Jocelyn Gibb, ed., *Light on C. S. Lewis* (London: Geoffrey Bles, 1965).

42 C. S. Lewis, *Poems,* ed. Walter Hooper (London: Geoffrey Bles, Ltd., 1964), 34–35.

43 C. S. Lewis, "Meditation in a Toolshed," *Coventry Evening Telegraph*, July 17, 1945, 4.

the irregular cranny at the top of the door, green leaves moving in the branches of a tree outside and beyond that, 90-odd million miles away, the sun." He concluded that these two views represent two radically different ways of seeing things. Take, for instance, a young man in love with a girl. "The whole world looks different when he sees her. Her voice reminds him of something he has been trying to remember all his life, and ten minutes casual chat with her is more precious than all the favours that all other women in the world could grant." But let a scientist come and describe the situation. "For him it is all an affair of the young man's genes and recognized biological stimulus." One is looking along the beam, the other simply at it.

Lewis believed that our century has misunderstood Christianity by the illogicality of having not looked along the beam. "It has been assumed . . . that if you want the true account of religion you must go not to religious people, but to anthropologists, that if you want the true account of sexual love you must go not to lovers, but to psychologists; that if you want to understand some 'ideology' . . . you go not to those who live inside it, but to sociologists." The physiologist may come along and assure us that the mathematician's thoughts are simply minute physical movements of the grey matter in the brain. "But then what about the cerebral physiologist's own thought at that very moment? A second physiologist, looking at it, could pronounce it also to be only tiny physical movements in the first physiologist's skull." And so on.

Over against such beliefs, Lewis upholds the power of Right Reason. To be genuinely rational he thinks that "we must pray for the gift of Faith, for the power to go on believing, not in the teeth of reason, but in the teeth of lust, and terror, and jealousy, and boredom, and indifference, that which reason, authority, or experience, or all three, have once delivered to us for truth."[44] Only Right Reason is sufficient for these things.

Of course he had no objections to analogical reasoning and in fact, like Plato and others before him, used it freely. A certain theologian thought Lewis's speaking of the Trinity as like a cube of six squares was a vulgarism, but apparently the theologian forgot the vast array of Christ's own metaphors of vines, fig trees, lamps, and bushel baskets to illustrate spiritual truths.[45] Neither had Lewis an objection to anthropomorphic views of God, believing that man has no choice but to make, i.e., to understand, all things in his own image. He often pointed out the fact that seeing God as an old man with a white beard was no whit less anthropomorphic and far more comprehensible than seeing him as a great Force or Power.

I recall in my youth hearing of Plato and supposing that if I ever tried to read him I should be overwhelmed with the intricacies of philosophical propositions. Then I remember my happy surprise in actually finding in Plato groups of friends sitting around casually with cups in their hands and talking of packasses and smiths and cobblers and carpenters and beds and tables and magical rings and caves and dogs and birds, and all in a spirit of wit, banter, personal innuendo, and general delight. Always the situation and the conversation were utterly human. Reason is at the bottom of everything, light-footed and joyous, filled with anecdote and story. It is as broad as the heavens and at the same time as homespun as a country village.

Such is quite precisely the kind of situation in which I think C. S. Lewis would have found himself at home. In fact, he loved few things better than a group of close friends sitting about a fireplace

---

44 C. S. Lewis, "Religion: Reality or Substitute?" *World Dominion* (September-October, 1941), 277–81.

45 C. S. Kilby, "C. S. Lewis and His Critics," *Christianity Today, III* (December 8, 1958), 13.

or out on a vigorous cross-country walk with body at ease and mind receptive to the warm flow of ideas and when everybody was prepared, as his friend Nevill Coghill says, for "thunderous disagreements and agreements."[46] Lewis loved the truth but never, if it could be helped, in abstraction. He always preferred the poetic over the prosaic even when he was writing prose. His stories, he said, always began with a picture, not, as one would suppose from remembering his Christian interests, with ideas or "truths."

I have mentioned Lewis's appearance before the Christian Fellowship of the Electric and Musical Institute in Middlesex. One of the questions asked him there had to do with the Christian answer to the problem of pain and bereavement. He answered that the best way of response to such experiences is regarding them as proper punishments. "Imagine," said he in a figure that would not be unworthy of himself, "a set of people all living in the same building. Half of them think it is a hotel, the other half think it is a prison. Those who think it is a hotel might regard it as quite intolerable, and those who thought it was a prison might decide that it was really surprisingly comfortable."[47] Or how could the unique calling of Christ be better depicted than when a little girl in one of his stories wants a drink of water but finds the lion Aslan (Christ) between her and the water.

> "Are you not thirsty?" said the Lion.
>
> "I'm *dying* of thirst," said Jill.
>
> "Then drink," said the Lion.
>
> "May I—could I—would you mind going away while I do?" said Jill.
>
> The Lion answered this only by a look and a very low growl. . . .

46 Gibb, *Light on C. S. Lewis*, 55.

47 *Answers to Questions on Christianity* (Hayes, Middlesex: Electric and Musical Industries Christian Fellowship, 1944), 9.

> "I daren't come and drink," said Jill.
>
> "Then you will die of thirst," said the Lion.
>
> "O dear!" said Jill, coming another step nearer. "I suppose I must go and look for another stream then."
>
> "There is no other stream," said the Lion.[48]

In such illustrations I believe we find the essential Lewis.

First there is the man of reason and common sense placing before us the simple fact of a thirsty child, a nearby stream, and an obstacle. But then the situation is not localized to mere adventure but includes the man-to-God and God-to-man framework of Right Reason. And finally the experience is presented not as "statement" but as symbol, and the symbol is organic to an imaginative encounter between a little girl and a lion.

I have had letters from children or teachers of children, from college students, from businessmen, and from scientists, philosophers, and theologians who have spoken with enthusiasm of C. S. Lewis. The chapters that follow suggest the variety of his talents as lecturer, preacher, teacher, conversationalist, radio broadcaster, and writer. Long ago Lord Bacon said: "Discretion of speech is more than eloquence; and to speak agreeably to him with whom we deal is more than to speak in good words or in good order." Lewis knew the art of putting good words in good order and, better still, how to draw close to his audience by cutting a straight path through the mental and spiritual underbrush in which most people are lost most of the time.

---

48 C. S. Lewis, *The Silver Chair* (New York: The Macmillan Company, 1953), 16–17.

Chapter 7

ON MUSIC, WORSHIP, AND THE SPIRITUAL LIFE

In this very substantial article Dr. Kilby, along with Linda Evans, explores exhaustively the important—and often overlooked—role of music in Lewis's thought and work. In addition to the light it casts on Lewis, the article is useful for the articulation it gives to certain recurring themes in the debates over forms of worship music in the church. Lewis had strong feelings about worship music (many of them negative), and it is interesting to imagine what he would make of the current discussion. But the greatest strength of this article is the way it points to the absolute centrality in Lewis's work of music as a metaphor of holiness, and of heaven itself.

For ease of reference, the following abbreviations are used in this chapter:

AG	*Letters to Arthur Greeves, 1914–1963*
AL	*The Allegory of Love: A Study in Medieval Tradition*
AT	*Arthurian Torso*
CR	*Christian Reflections*
EIC	*An Experiment in Criticism*
FL	*The Four Loves*
GD	*The Great Divorce*
GID	*God in the Dock*
LETS	*Letters of C. S. Lewis*
LM	*Letters to Malcolm: Chiefly on Prayer*
MBW	*Major British Writers*
MC	*Mere Christianity*
MN	*The Magician's Nephew*
NP	*Narrative Poems*
OSP	*Out of the Silent Planet*
PC	*Prince Caspian*
PEREL	*Perelandra*
POEMS	*Poems*
PPL	*A Preface to Paradise Lost*
PR	*The Pilgrim's Regress*
ROP	*Reflections on the Psalms*
SBJ	*Surprised by Joy: The Shape of My Early Life*
SC	*The Silver Chair*
SIB	*Spirits in Bondage*
SL	*The Screwtape Letters*
SLE	*Selected Literary Essays*
SMRL	*Studies in Medieval and Renaissance Literature*
SP	Letter to Sister Penelope, nos. 50–51
TAFAP	*They Asked for a Paper*

TDI	*The Discarded Image*	WG	*The Weight of Glory*
THS	*That Hideous Strength*	WHL	Letter of W. H. Lewis, 24 July 1968
VDT	*The Voyage of the Dawn Treader*		

C. S. Lewis's frequent mention of his dislike for church hymns has led some readers to conclude that he had little taste for music. However, an examination of his writings reveals that music remained for Lewis a glory, a joy, and a fundamental motif thought his works.

Scores of allusions to music from Lewis's letters (mostly unpublished) make it clear that at fifteen and sixteen, Lewis felt music to be an utterly essential part of his life. He knew the catalogs of gramophone records thoroughly and which records would last the longest. The piano compositions of the romantic composers, Chopin, Beethoven, Grieg, and Schubert, were among his favorite.[49] But as all readers of Lewis's autobiography know, his greatest love at this period was the story and music of Richard Wagner's operas. Through the literature of Longfellow at the age of nine, Lewis discovered the legends and myths of northern Europe and returned to them as the largest element in his life at about thirteen.[50] Even before he heard a note of Wagner's music, he was so deeply struck with a mere synopsis of *Das Rheingold* that he promptly sat down and began the writing of a heroic poem on the same subject. A few months later he was transfixed with joy when he actually heard a recording of "The Ride of the Valkyries."[51]

This early enthusiasm built itself into the rhythm of Lewis's life. The longing to know all about Valhalla and the Valkyries led him forward into the scholarly investigations of myth and

49 Once he wrote to his boyhood friend that he had just met "the prettiest girl I ever have seen in my life . . . she is just like that grave movement in the 'The Hungarian Rhapsody' (or is it the 'dance') that I love so much" (AG, 43).

50 LETS, 110–11.

51 GID, 278; SBJ, 76.

medievalism. At fifteen, as part of his preparation for entrance to Oxford, he was reading Homer and Greek drama in the original. Loving what he read and being beset with a constant desire to write, he wrote an opera about the Norse gods in the dramatic pattern of the Greeks. He tried persuading his friend Arthur Greeves, who had musical talent, to compose music and design scenery for it, but the project, "after an extremely short and happy life, died a painless death."[52]

His overwhelming desire for many years was to write the most musical of all literature—poetry. His two earliest books are poetry, and almost half of the poems in his first publication make reference to song, music, or singing.[53] His later poems show a great variety of lyrical forms. Even his titles often give away the design: "Evolutionary Hymn," "Science-Fiction Cradle Song," "Coronation March," etc. His childhood fancies of

> Subterranean rivers beside glimmering wharfs,
> Hammers upon anvils, pattering and yammering,
> Torches and tunnels, the cities of the dwarfs[54]

kept up their beat in such later poems as his "Narnian Suite," which has the subtitle, "March for Strings, Kettledrums, and Sixty-Three Dwarfs," and "March for Drum, Trumpet, and Twenty-One Giants."[55] Many of these poems show a predominance of the strong beat and exhilarating tones of bagpipes, flutes, tabors, drums, and the dance.

---

52 SBJ, 151. Years later Lewis commented, "My whole Norse complex–Old Icelandic, Wagner's *Ring* and (again) Morris. The Wagner is important; you will see if you look, how *operatic* the whole building up of the climax is in *Perelandra*" (LETS, 205). Oxford musicians composed an opera based on the same book but had not produced it before Lewis died; Lewis was said to have been so moved by the musical score that he wept when it was introduced to him at a gathering in a home of some friends.

53 SIB, passim.

54 POEMS, 9.

55 POEMS, 6–7.

In his narrative poem *The Nameless Isle*, an enchanted flute is the instrument of temperamental magic.

> The dwarf deftly drew the flute out,
> Gold and glittering. Grinned while he spoke . . .
> He laid his lip to the little flute.
> Long and liquid,—light was waning—
> The first note flowed. Then faster came,
> Reedily, ripple-like, running as a watercourse,
> Meddling of melodies, moulded in air,
> pure and proportional . . .

The "dwarf fluted off his flesh away" and became "the fairest thing." The same music causes the marble statues to come alive, and they all continue in a procession as the Bride and King sing praises to one another.[56]

Even in literary criticism Lewis makes constant allusions to composers and musical works, showing evidence of the manner in which music and literature accentuate each other in his thinking.[57] He speaks of the "lightness and liquidity" of Shelley's *Witch of Atlas* and feels that we must go to music, particularly to Mozart, to find a parallel to this quality of Shelley's poetry.[58] Charles Williams's "world is one of pomp and ritual, of strong, roaring, and resonant music,"[59] and his "word music equaled by only two or three in this century and surpassed by none."[60] Virgil's hexameters are "more like the slow movement of the Seventh

---

56 NP, 112–14, 120–22.

57 Lewis makes special mention of Plato's widely ignored philosophy of music in *The Discarded Image*, 56.

58 SLE, 200.

59 AT, 199.

60 AT, 194–95. Citing how Taliessin's song (in Charles Williams's "Star of Percivil") brings a barbarian girl running to him, Lewis points out that such power, often manifest in music, suggests the danger of "a poet, a musician, an actor . . . as seducer" if they wish to adopt such a practice (AT, 136). Cf. Plato on music and morality.

Symphony and less like the *Walkürenritt*."[61] In his criticism of Spenser, Lewis writes, "Those who have attempted to write poetry will know how much easier it is to express sorrow than joy. That is what makes the *Epithalamion* matchless. Music has often reached that jocundity; poetry, seldom."[62]

In *A Preface to Paradise Lost*, Lewis restates the conventional comparison of Milton's style to organ music but thinks it more "helpful to regard the reader as the organ and Milton as the organist."[63] He writes, "We are his organ: when he appears to be describing Paradise he is in fact drawing out the description of the manipulation of Milton, "as if readers were so many Hammond Electric Organs."[64] May we briefly mention that the chief irony of this raillery lies in the fact that Lewis's least favorite instrument was the organ.[65]

In Lewis's popular children's stories, music is often inevitable to the story. At one point in *Prince Caspian* dozens of fauns, the boy Caspian, and dwarfs dance to the faint beat and clear music of reedy pipes.[66] Also in *Prince Caspian*, dryads and naiads make lovely music with stringed instruments on the occasion of Aslan's arrival.[67] In another book, *The Silver Chair*, Jill escapes from the underworld up through a hole in the ground and peers out in amazement at the "great Snow Dance." Fauns, dryads, and dwarfs stamp the complicated dance steps with the music of "four fiddles, three flutes, and a drum." It was "wild music, intensely sweet and yet just the least bit eerie too, and full of good magic" as

61 SLE, 284. Comparing English poetry to Old French: "Ours is 'all instruments,' theirs is the 'lonely flute'" (AL, 135). "The Italian stanza is all clear bell-like music" (SMRL, 118).

62 MBW, 95–96. Also speaking of Spenser, "He can be as prosaic as Wordsworth: he can be clumsy, unmusical, and flat" (AL, 318).

63 PPL, 40.

64 Robert Martin Adams, *Ikon: John Milton and the Modern Critics* (Ithaca, NY: Cornell University Press, 1955), 38.

65 SBJ, 234.

66 PC, 67–68.

67 PC, 117.

opposed to the concealed bad magic of the Witch's thrumming of her stringed instrument—her mesmerizing voice "cooing softly like the voice of a wood-pigeon from the high elms in an old garden at three o'clock in the middle of the afternoon."[68]

But music plays a deeper role too. One of the greatest scenes in all of Lewis is the great lion Aslan pacing to and fro with stately grace singing the enchanting land of Narnia into existence. Aslan began his song in the utter dark with tones so deep that it seemed the voice of earth itself. The song was wordless and at first hardly a tune at all, yet so beautiful as to be almost beyond bearing. Then Aslan was joined by many other voices higher than his own, "cold, tingling, silvery voices," as points of light appeared above and turned out to be stars ("morning stars sang together"). That this is celestial music is indicated by the fact that both Andrew and the Witch, who are evil, hate it. Eventually Aslan sang into existence the rising sun, trees, green grass, flowers, and as the music swelled, the rest of nature broke forth. The power of the music to make things grow was so strong that a bar from a telephone that which had been accidentally carried into Narnia grew up into a lamppost.[69] When it is time for "The Beginning of the End of the World," in a later book of the same series, an old man and his daughter sing a "high, almost shrill, but very beautiful" "cold kind of song, an early morning kind of song" joined with "far wilder tones and in a language which no one knew"—the source of these additional voices being thousands of great white birds flying from the center of the rising sun.[70]

In Lewis's other books music often accentuates a poignant experience. In the novel *Till We Have Faces*, along with music being part of the worship of Ungit, the Fox sang compelling and tender Greek poetry to Orual. After Psyche's palace had been destroyed,

68 SC, 185–8.
69 MN, 90–96.
70 VDT, 171–73.

the face and voice of the One who pronounced judgment on her was free from anger. The voice "was unmoved and sweet, like a bird singing on the branch above a hanged man."[71] In the first book of Lewis's space trilogy, Ransom longingly recalled the sound of singing in his Malacandrian valley—"great hollow hound-like music from enormous throats, deeper than Chaliapin, a 'warm, dark noise.'"[72] When in the paradisal land of Perelandra, Ransom woke up to "Eve" "singing to herself in a low voice," and later when she tells Ransom who she is, he had "the feeling that it was not she, or not only she, who had spoken. No other sound came to his ears, for the sea and the air were still, but a phantom sense of vast choral music was all about him."[73] Ransom observed strange animals, one that had "the mouth wide open as it sang of joy in thick-coming thrills, and the music almost visibly rippled in its glossy throat."[74] After Ransom had succeeded, almost at the cost of his own life, in destroying the Unman, he had a long recuperation in which a glorious song

> now high in the air above him, now welling up as if from glens and valleys far below . . . floated through his sleep and was the first sound at every waking. It was formless as the song of a bird, yet it was not a bird's voice. As a bird's voice is to a flute, so this was to a cello: low and ripe and tender, full-bellied, rich and golden-brown: passionate too, but not with the passions of men.[75]

In *The Screwtape Letters*, the diabolical Screwtape speaks of "that detestable art which the humans call Music . . . a direct insult to

71 *Till We Have Faces*, 173.
72 OSP, 168.
73 PEREL, 56, 64.
74 PEREL, 304–5.
75 PEREL, 197–98.

the realism, dignity, and austerity of Hell."[76] A beautiful house and garden on earth impresses Screwtape as "one vast obscenity" bearing a "sickening resemblance to the description one writer made of Heaven; 'the regions where there is only life and therefore all that is not music is silence.'"[77] The aim of hell is to keep people ignorant of "the incalculable winds of fantasy of music and poetry" because such things "are always blowing our whole structure away."[78]

Lewis has the tendency of reserving the images of song, play, and dance for the highest things. The loveliest and most awesome music is begotten by the most glorious occasions and characters. For example, the discord in Lewis's poem *Dymer* is resolved as new sounds are heard.

> And from the distant corner of day's birth
> He heard clear trumpets blowing and bells ring,
> A noise of great good coming into the earth
> And such music as the dumb would sing.[79]

This is in contrast to the wild music of King Lust.

> They beat the devilish tom-tom rub-a-dub;
> Lunging, leaping, in unwieldy romp,
> Sing Cotytto and Beelzebub.[80]

The evil is heard again, in the single, nauseating, and growing pitch sounded in the Witch's Hall in *The Magician's Nephew*.[81]

---

76 SL, 57–58. Milton's Satan, fallen from heaven, realizes his cue "to grow numb voluntarily to decline on a lower plane of being . . . to avoid great literature and noble music" (PPL, 103).

77 SL, 113.

78 SL, 144.

79 NP, 91.

80 NP, 72. Likewise in Milton's *Comus,* "song" is reserved for only Sabrina and the Lady. Comus and his rout make "noise."

81 The digression of Milton's Satan and his angels advances with each book until they are only capable of sounding a universal hiss and appearing as a mass of

However, in *That Hideous Strength*, Jane, after meeting the goodness of Ransom, "reflected with surprise how long it was since music had played any part in her life, and resolved to listen to many chorales by Bach on the gramophone that evening," for she was "in the sphere of Jove, amid light and music and festal pomp."[82]

Later, Jane and the other rejoicers of St. Anne's celebrate life in clear opposition to the deathly gibberish of Belbury's banquet a few miles away.

> For never in her life had she heard such talk—such eloquence, such melody (song could have added nothing to it), such sky rockets of metaphor and allusion.[83]

> Arthur—the only musician among them—was bidden to get out his fiddle. The chairs were pushed back, the floor cleared. They danced. What they danced no one could remember.[84]

At the same time, the Glund-Oyarsa, King of Kings, has entered the Blue Room upstairs.

> Kingship and power and festal pomp and courtesy shot from him as sparks fly from an anvil. The pealing of bells, the blowing of trumpets, the spreading of banners, are means used on earth to make a faint symbol of this quality. It was like a long sunlit wave, creamy-crested and arched with emerald that comes on nine feet tall, with roaring and with terror and unquenchable laughter. It was like the first beginning of music in the halls of some King so

swarming serpents (*Paradise Lost*, X, 529–43).

82 THS, 151–52.

83 THS, 321.

84 THS, 326.

> high and at some festival so solemn that a tremor akin to fear runs through young hearts when they hear it.[85]

In view of the unparalleled joy at St. Anne's later in the book, it would seem appropriate for Lewis to have some vast symphonic music coming into the story, but he does not. The elephants who escaped from Belbury come to St. Anne's and in the bright moonlight, "almost brighter than day," dance in the garden. "High, high they lift their feet. And they go round and round. And oh, look!—how they lift their trunks. And how ceremonial they are. It is like a minuet of giants."[86] He uses "the liquid light and supernatural warmth of the garden," the song of birds, the two bears, the ceremony of sex, and the quiet joy as contrasted to the jolting jars from afar. But there really is no music except in their souls, inaudible to our ears.

In *Pilgrim's Regress*, the style of song issued from the mouths of the characters reveals what they are essentially. Savage can only bellow two songs lauding violence and the old heroic values;[87] Superbia and the Dragon can only "croak" about themselves.[88] John, the hero of the allegory, decidedly dislikes the modern music of the twenties when he hears Victoriana sing some neo-Romantic ditty with a little toy harp, the bearded Phally croon a swampy song with a tom-tom, and skinny Glugly sing with an infant's "goo-gooing."[89]

Those acquainted with Lewis's writing will not be surprised to learn of his antagonism to much modern music. One objection he had to modern music is much the same as his objection to newspapers—both are in a state of constant change.[90] He felt that "nearly all those treacly tunes and saccharine poems" expressing

85 THS, 326–27.
86 THS, 454.
87 *Pilgrim's Regress*, 106–7.
88 Ibid., 183–92.
89 Ibid., 50–54.
90 EIC, 4.

affection are false and odious. "They represent as a ready-made recipe for bliss (and even goodness) what is in fact only an opportunity. There is no hint that we shall have to do anything: only let Affection pour over us like a warm shower-bath and all, it is implied, will be well."[91] Any person, he declared, whose mind is filled with sentimental songs and his body full of alcohol is bound to have a low estimate of love.[92]

He felt that much modern music is no exception to the common tendency toward "progressive specialization and impoverishment." An opera by Mozart, for instance, "is the ancestor of the modern serious opera and of the revue.[93] The separation of the low-brow from the high-brow in its present sharpness is a comparatively recent thing: and with the loss of the old unified function all curb on the eccentricity of real artists and the vulgarity of mere entertainers has vanished."[94]

In view of Lewis's deep interest in both music and Christianity, it is deserving to note his lifelong antagonism to hymns of the last century and a half and, to a smaller degree, to church music in general. He has a whole collection of objections to these hymns. One is that the airs themselves are often like the airs of certain popular songs, "intrinsically vile and ugly," inviting "vulgar swagger or lacrimose self-pity": and hence he "cannot hear them as neutral patterns of which good use might possibly be made."[95] The lyrics are mostly bad, often sentimental and "lugubrious," causing

---

91 FL, 62.

92 MC, 86.

93 Speaking of Mozart's operas, "It is not sufficient to say that a work designed for the popular market may sometimes by a happy freak, outshoot its mark. The thing has happened too often to be called a freak" (SLE, 272–73).

94 "Perhaps this change is seen most clearly in the history of opera. A modern composer underlines his evil characters or places with discords. An old composer was content with making a courtesan's song soft and melting or a tyrant's song loud and declamatory; within that very general limit he then made each simply good of its kind. Thus Wagner gives Alberich ugly music to sing: but Mozart gives to the Queen of Night music as beautiful as he gives to Sarastro" (SMRL, 116).

95 EIC, 25.

thought in hymns to become confused or erroneous.[96] Lewis's rejection of hymns went back far and deeply. His long reluctance to turn to God was in part owing to his fixed antagonism to the "sentimentality and cheapness" of so many Christian hymns.[97] Many hymns and sermons on the subject of the crucifixion were disagreeable to him because they endlessly harped "on blood as if that was all that mattered."[98]

Lewis asks whether hymns constitute a truly spiritual or only an aesthetic aspect of worship. Instead of genuine worship, there is the danger of an "aesthetic religion of 'flowers and music,'" which for Lewis is far from the calling of God to active obedience.[99] Lewis more than once voices his strong objection to the weak-looking Christ and effeminate angels in nineteenth-century painting, noting that by contrast in the Bible, angels comforted people in the terror and awe of their appearance, by saying, "Be not afraid." Readers of the Narnia series know how often Lewis says, "Aslan is not a tame lion."

Though A. L. Rowse believed as Lewis did about many things, there was one point on which they were in total disagreement, and it was Rowse's frank confession of his religion as being solely aesthetic. The Bible was for him tedious, but singing, in which he excelled, was a thing for its own sake even though mostly experienced inside the church. Lewis felt that many devout Christians, if they faced the truth, might find their real interest in hymns no more devout than Rowse's: that any tune and almost any words, as long as they mentioned Christ, might for large numbers of people

96 CR, 2. "On the lowest intellectual level, people who find any one subject entirely engrossing are apt to think that any reference to it, of whatever quality, must have some value. Pious people on that level appear to think that the quotation of any scriptural text, or any line from a hymn, or even any noise made by a harmonium, is an edifying sermon or a cogent apologetic" (TDI, 205).

97 CR, 13.

98 LM, 85–86.

99 GID, 328–29.

sitting in a church be little more than an exercise in rhythm, tune, and the joining of voices.

But Lewis had a deeper objection to hymns. It involved his conviction toward worship itself. It may seem crotchety for him to say he has no enthusiasm for "the fussy, time-wasting botheration" of church services, "the bells, the organizing."[100] He claimed to have a sort of spiritual gaucherie that made him unapt to participate in any rite.[101] He preferred a church "free from stunts" where the eyes are inevitably drawn to the altar and where everything is quietly centered on Christ.[102] The Eucharist in particular involves worship, and nothing but worship—an act in which every moment and every movement of priest and people is wholly worship. If some in the congregation cannot sing hymns, the necessary unity and responsiveness of the worship may be broken. It is the sort of objection that Lewis and many other devout Anglicans have to impromptu prayers: one's mind must not be diverted, for instance, from worship itself to a concomitant inquiry whether the priest is using orthodox terms or not. Many devoted Christians in denominational churches, if they think intently on this subject, may notice how worship itself may be entirely absent from a service. It is one of the places where Lewis, who has sometimes been held up by evangelicals as less than orthodox, may prove a good deal more orthodox than themselves. For Lewis, one goes to church to worship and for no other purpose.

Lewis assumes "from the outset that nothing should be done or sung or said in church which does not aim directly or indirectly either at glorifying God or edifying the people or both"; church music may glorify God like clouds and such by being "excellent in

---

100 SBJ, 220-21.

101 While defending the ritual style of Milton, Lewis states, "When our participation in a rite becomes perfect we think no more of ritual, but are engrossed by that about which the rite is performed; but afterwards we recognize that ritual was the sole method by which this concentration could be achieved" (PPL, 60).

102 LM, 9, 100.

its own kind," not by claim of its own quality.[103] People singing or shouting their hymns is a pleasant, wholesome thing, like a "pint of beer" or a "dip in the sea."[104] Lewis doubts whether congregational singing or the trained choir is any more edifying than other popular pleasures.[105] If the congregation objects to "high-brow church music," it is perhaps best to have fewer, better, and shorter hymns and a fine organist to play somewhat "down" to a congregation, who in turn seeks to understand something higher musically than it is used to. In this way, "discrepancies of taste and capacity will, indeed, provide matter for mutual charity and humility."[106]

Lewis warned of the naive idea that "our music can 'please' God as it would please a cultivated human hearer."[107]

> That is like thinking under the old Law, that He really needed the blood of bulls and goats. To which an answer came, "Mine are the cattle upon a thousand hills," and "if I am hungry, I will not tell *thee*." If God (in that sense) wanted music, He would not tell us. For all our offerings, whether of music or martyrdom, are like the intrinsically worthless present of a child which a father values indeed, but values only for intention.[108]

Although Lewis's lifelong attitude toward church music was essentially negative, he admitted the possibility of positive qualities. One is that even though "heaven is not really full of jewelry any more so than it is really the beauty of Nature, or a fine piece of music,"[109] there is a blessed faith—"a child's or a savage's faith which finds no difficulty" in accepting "the harps and golden

103 CR, 94.
104 Ibid., 95.
105 Ibid., 96.
106 Ibid., 96–97.
107 ROP, 50; CR, 98–99.
108 CR, 98–99.
109 TAFAP, 202.

streets and the family-reunions pictured by hymn-writers. Such faith is deceived, yet, in the deepest sense, not deceived; for while it errs in mistaking the symbol for fact, yet it apprehends Heaven as joy, plentitude, and love."[110]

Lewis thought that any natural thing that was not sinful in itself could become a servant of the spiritual life, but not automatically—that when it wasn't a servant it became either "just trivial (as music is to millions of people) or a dangerous idol."[111] He felt that the emotional effect of music could be a distraction and certain emotions could be mistaken for religious emotions when actually

> They may be wholly natural. That means that even genuinely religious emotion is only a servant. . . . The love we are commanded to have for God and our neighbour is a state of the *will*, not of the affections (though if they ever also play their part so much the better). So that the test of music or religion or even visions if one has them—is always the same—do they make one more obedient, more God-centered and neighbour-centered and less *self-centered*? "Though I speak with the tongues of Bach and Palestrina and have not charity, etc.!"[112]

Humbleness is another important quality that one may learn even from a very poor hymn when he sees it being sung "with devotion and benefit by an old saint in elastic-side boots" in the next pew and realizes he is probably a far better Christian than oneself.[113] In this connection he reports his expectation on first becoming a Christian, to "do it on my own, by retiring to my rooms and reading

110 TAFAP, 176.
111 LETS, 268.
112 LETS, 268–69.
113 GID, 61–62.

theology" rather than going to church at all, but later, he found that a Christian must "fly his flag" by assembling with other Christians and taking an active part in the public worship of God.[114] He came to see that there was an emotional as well as an intellectual approach to God. He discovered that "the simple, emotional appeal ('Come to Jesus') is still often successful."[115]

Then Lewis's opinion on any subject needs to be examined in the light of his far-reaching Cambridge inaugural address, for thereafter examining other possibilities, he declared that the greatest change in the history of the Western world occurred about the turn of the nineteenth century, and he was convinced that it was, contrary to popular opinion, a change for the worse, music being no exception. The best church music, especially the great Masses, was written before this change.[116]

In his review of Lord Cecil's *The Oxford Book of Christian Verse* (*Review of English Studies*, Jan. 1941), Lewis defends hymns against Cecil's charge that "the average hymn is a by-word for forced feeble expression." Lewis says: "Now it is true that all hymnbooks are full of very bad poems." He thinks that Cecil is mixing literary criticism and private judgment in his statement. "Many bad English hymns are translations of very good Latin hymns," and these hymns belong often in the class of "occasional" poetry, which is often very bad. This is a modern phenomenon. Poets worked to order but were great within that commission. "But in the last few centuries we have unquestionably lost the power of fitting art into the process of life." The hymn of the Middle Ages had no difficulty.

114 Ibid.; WG, 30. "The idea of allowing myself to be put off by mere inadequacy—an ugly church, a gawky server, a badly turned-out celebrant—is horrible. On the contrary, it constantly surprises me how little these things matter, as if 'never anything can be amiss when simpleness and duty tender it.' One of the golden Communions of my life was in a Nisson hut. Sometimes the cockney accent of a choir has a singularly touching quality" (LM, 101).

115 GID, 244.

116 GID, 279–80.

Perhaps the best summary of Lewis's opinion of hymns is evident from an article called "Correspondence with an Anglican who Dislikes Hymns" in *The Presbyter*. On July 13, 1946, Eric Routley wrote Lewis for the Hymn Society of Great Britain and Ireland asking him to become a member of a panel to whom new hymns might be sent for an assessment of their merits. Lewis wrote Mr. Routley that he was "not in sufficient sympathy" with the plan to take part. "I know," he said, "that many of the congregation like singing hymns; but am not yet convinced that their enjoyment is of a spiritual kind. It may be; I don't know. To the minority, of whom I am one, the hymns are mostly the dead wood of a service." To which Mr. Routley wrote Lewis at length, pointing out many potential faults in church music and noting that there is a difference between the Eucharist in the morning and the evening or a preaching service where hymns may be more appropriate to the declared Word of God. But Lewis continued to decline participation in the panel, confessing, however, "I was wrong if I said or implied [in his previous letter] that (*a*) variables, (*b*) active participation by the people, or (*c*) hymns were bad in principle. I would agree that anything the congregation *can do* may properly and profitably be offered to God in public worship." He went on to state his objections:

> In modern England . . . we can't sing—as the Welsh and Germans can. Also (a great pity, but a fact) the art of poetry has developed for two centuries in a private and subjective direction. That is why I find hymns "dead wood." But I spoke only for myself and a few others. If an improved hymnody—or even the present hymnody—does edify other people, of course it is an elementary duty of charity and humility for me to submit. I have never spoken in public *against* the use of hymns: on the contrary I have

> often told "high-brow" converts that a humble acquiescence in anything that may edify their uneducated brethren (however frightful it seems to the educated "natural man") is the first lesson they must learn.[117]

Several times Lewis wrote to his friend Arthur Greeves expressing a fear of losing his taste for music. Many conjectures can be drawn as to why Lewis thought he was losing his musical faculty. One is that the concentration of his literature studies left no time for enjoyment of music. However, if this were true then it would be more likely that the rarity of music would make each encounter with music more meaningful. Perhaps Lewis attended inferior musical functions and the artists performed badly, and it *was*, as Lewis described, "all just meaningless sound."[118] However, Lewis gives additional reason. It involved his constant endeavor to recapture the fading Northerness, looking for the "Joy" that might turn up in any context. He searched "while reading every poem, hearing every piece of music, going for every walk" but constantly destroyed it by introspection and only tasted Joy when startled into self-forgetfulness.[119] "And we once thought we could be happy with books and music," said Lewis.[120] It was only after Lewis's conversion to Christ[121] that he was able to say, "I am getting back more of my old pleasure in music all the time."[122] After sorting out and playing his recordings, which dated back to the beginning years of his friendship with Arthur Greeves, Lewis wrote,

117 GID, 330–31.
118 AG, 50.
119 SBJ, 168–69.
120 AG, 284.
121 SBJ, 237.
122 AG, 544–45.

> Lying on the study sofa and hearing these familiars I had sensations which you can imagine. And at once (here is the advantage of growing older) I knew that the enemy would take advantage of the vague longings and tenderness to try and make one believe later on that *he* had the fulfillment which I really wanted: so I baulked him by letting the longings go even deeper and turning my mind on the One, the real object of all desires, which (you know my view) is what we are *really* wanting in all wants.[123]

A parallel account of this realization appears in *The Pilgrim's Regress*. John, the autobiographical and chief character of Lewis's allegory, also longs, but it is a longing for the Island and for its accompanying music.[124] When the sight of the Island is withheld from him, John becomes angry, searches for it, and accepts substitutes. Mr. Halfway's singing reminds John of the Island and begins to bring the sweetness of longing with it; however, "the rapture does not last but dwindles into technical appreciation and sentiment."[125] Toward the end of his journey, John sings a prayer to his Landlord.[126] His song is like the glorifying songs that Venture and the Guide sing later.[127] After John finally meets the Desire of his desires, he is able to dance and delight in the music

123 AG, 406–7.
124 "A music that resembled / Some earlier music / That men are born remembering" (POEMS, 76).
125 PR, 23, 32, 44.
126 "Our prayers, and other free acts, are known to us only as we come to the moment of doing them. But they are eternally in the score of the great symphony" (LM, 110).
127 These songs are of victory and prayer, praising the spontaneous mode of David's Psalms, Deborah's song of triumph, and the Magnificat. Lewis had very high regard for all three of these (CR, 115–20). "Praise almost seems to be inner health made audible. Nor does it cease to be so when, through lack of skill, the forms of its expression are very uncouth or even ridiculous. Heaven knows, many poems of praise addressed to an earthly beloved are as bad as our bad hymns, and an anthology of love poems for public and perpetual use would probably be as sore a trial to literary taste as *Hymns Ancient and Modern*" (ROP, 94).

of an old fiddler and not destroy his pleasure by hunting for the Island in every note.

> The books or the music in which we thought the beauty was located will betray us if we trust in them; it was not *in* them, it only came *through* them, and what came through them was longing. These things—beauty, the memory of our past—are good images of what we really desire; but if they are mistaken for the thing itself they turn into dumb idols, breaking the hearts of their worshippers. For they are not the thing itself; they are only the scent of a flower we have not found, the echo of a tune we have not heard, news from a country we have never yet visited.[128]

Lewis suspected that most of his enjoyment was emotion produced out of his "own imagination at rather slight hints (it may be even accidental hints) from music."[129] He therefore did not think it "any very real commendation" to say that he "was greatly moved by" listening to a recording of *The Planets* by Holst.[130] While the extra-musical wandering into one's imagination, away from what is being heard, is normally poor, he thought it conceivable that those meanderings might produce a greater work of art than the composition heard in the ear at the time.[131] Lewis thought that this was what could possibly have happened "when Keats looked at a Grecian urn."[132] Similarly, we can speculate whether the extra-musical experience Lewis had with *The Planets* may have

---

128 TAFAP, 200.

129 AG, 639. "It is no use offering me a drug which will give me over again the feelings I had on first hearing the overture to *The Magic Flute*. The feelings, by themselves—the flutter in the diaphragm—are of very mediocre interest to me. What gave them their value was the thing they were about" (CR, 139). See also TAFAP, 169–70.

130 AG, 630.

131 EIC, 23.

132 EIC, 18.

played a singular part in the origination of *That Hideous Strength* when the five gods descend upon St. Anne's in the majestic power and distinction of each planet with the "sweet, immeasurable sound" of the spheres: with the "*Gloria* which those five excellent Natures perpetually sing."[133] However, this speculation seems unlikely when we learn that *That Hideous Strength* was written *before* the above-mentioned encounter that Lewis had with *The Planets*. The resemblance between these two works evidently caught the attention of Lewis's friend Sister Penelope, for he wrote her back shortly after *That Hideous Strength* was published, replying:

> About Holst's *Planets*. I heard Mars and Jupiter long ago and greatly admired them but have heard the complete work only within the last six weeks . . . his characters are rather different from mine I think. Wasn't his Mars brutal and ferocious?—in mine I tried to get the *good* element in the martial spirit, the discipline and the freedom from anxiety. On Jupiter I am closer to him; but I think his is more "jovial" in the *modern* sense of the word. The folk tune on which he bases it is not regal enough for my conception. But of course there is a general similarity because we're both following the medieval astrologers. This is, anyway, a rich and marvelous work.[134]

We leave open to the reader the course of any further speculation.[135]

In his later teens Lewis shared his love of Northerness and music with his friend Arthur Greeves. He was a pianist who, in Lewis's opinion, not only rendered the passages correctly but also played

133 SMRL, 52; THS, 327.
134 SP, 50–51; LETS, 209.
135 The early chapters of Lewis's *An Experiment in Criticism* should be examined by anyone particularly interested in pure and program music.

with "fire and abandonment."[136] Another musical influence at this time was Mrs. Kirkpatrick, his tutor's wife, who introduced a variety of piano compositions to him. (He was especially taken with Chopin's Preludes.) The symphonies of Beethoven and Sibelius, as well as piano music, attracted Lewis. Renewed appreciation for Beethoven occurred when he went to Oxford and fifteen years later, when he was "completely converted" from a previous dislike of the choral part of Beethoven's *Ninth Symphony* during the attendance of a "magnificent philharmonic performance," where he "seldom enjoyed anything more."[137] Sibelius was described by Lewis as the only composer who "exercised the same enchantment" over him as Wagner did in his youth. His "glorious" symphonies were "not *noble* like Beethoven" but "inarticulate, intimate, enthralling, and close to one like Nature itself."[138]

One of Lewis's earliest musical discoveries was the opera. He not only loved to listen to available gramophone recordings of this compacted art form but also yearned to attend them.[139] Of the operas that he did attend, he knew exactly what he liked and did not like about them. Novelties in the way of staging were

136 AG, 35.

137 SBJ, 188; AG, 586. "Did I (also) tell you that Warnie has complete sets of all the Beethoven symphonies, and that we have a whole symphony each Sunday evening? This is one of the best hours of the week" (AG, 574). Of another concert Lewis wrote, "I thought I knew the symphony [*Fifth Symphony*] from Warnie's records, but Beecham [the conductor] brought things out of it that I never dreamed of" (AG, 579). "How *tonic* Beethoven is, and how festal—one has the feeling of having taken part in the revelry of giants" (AG, 586).

138 AG, 590. Mozart was likewise a favorite, and Lewis often praised the Overture to *The Magic Flute* (TAFAP, 169–70). In his journal covering his undergraduate life he tells of a chance conversation with two friends: "Miss Wardale, apart from a few sensible remarks on Wagner, was content to sit back in a sort of maternal attitude. . . . Coghill did most of the talking, except when contradicted by me. He said that Mozart had remained a boy of six all his life. I said nothing could be more delightful; he replied (and quite right) that he could imagine many things more delightful" (LETS, 85).

139 In early letters, Lewis often complains that he does not have money to buy the records he longs for, such as a solo by Chaliapin in Myerbeer's *Robert Le Diable*. He particularly enjoyed the orchestration of Puccini, the "Church Scene" of Gounod's *Faust*, and the Prelude to *Aida* (AG, 220, 34 49, 89). He wrote that if he had to choose (from a certain scheduled program) he would prefer attending the operas *Aida* and *The Magic Flute* to *Carmen* or *The Lily* (AG, 76).

"always rather interesting," but Lewis preferred "quiet, tasteful, plain decorations to tawdry splendid things."[140] He desired the continuity of orchestration and disliked the gaps that occurred between arias and recitatives when they were treated as "numbers" in a concert.[141] Of a particular production of *Faust* he could have done without the "crowded stage, the conventionality, the noisy comic opera scenes of drinking," which "were really too much after the 'Valkyrie.'"[142] Even after reveling in a performance of *Tosca*, he thought the opera was not "with the solemnity[143] of the 'Valkyrie,'" which was beyond anything he had seen or "hoped to see so gloriously unoperatic in the silly sense."[144] This second opera of Wagner's *Der Ring des Nibelungen* made such an impression on Lewis that he concluded "all Italian opera is merely a pastime compared with the great music-drama of Wagner."[145] Thus a lifetime partiality to the *Ring* continued to develop without faltering.[146] Even when Lewis was disappointed with other productions of the cycle, repeatedly his old dream returned as he once described it:

---

140 AG, 32.

141 AG, 212, 220. Ransom had "always disliked the people who encored a favorite air in the opera–'that just spoils it' had been his comment" (PEREL, 45).

142 AG, 219.

143 Insisting that solemnity need not to be gloomy or oppressive, Lewis writes, "A great mass by Mozart or Beethoven is as much solemnity in its hilarious gloria as in its poignant *crucifixus est*" (PPL, 16).

144 AG, 220.

145 AG, 213. Lewis did not remain faithful to all the favorite compositions of his youth. "How on earth can we ever have liked" Delibes's *Cortage de Bacchus* from the *Aprez-midi D'une Faune*? "It seemed to me the merest music hall patriotic song rhetoric on the brass pretending to be something better" (AG, 407).

146 "I did not enjoy the *Rheingold* this year nearly as much as I enjoyed *Siegfried* last year–neither at the time nor in memory. Oddly enough the hammer passage which you mention I actually disliked. I had enjoyed it on your gramaphone [sic], but at Covent Garden it seemed to me so much cruder and before it ended (and I thought it would never end) nearly ridiculous. You must think my loyalty to the *Ring* is wavering. The main causes of my disliking the *Rheingold* were (a) Our having very bad seats (b) My not liking the man who sang Alberich" (AG, 553).

> I hope you can see the whole scene—the light slanting through the fir trees, the long elder branches swaying and then swooping down with a rustle of leaves, the click-click of the shears, and the heavy odors of crushed vegetation. In that fir wood I suddenly got a terrific return the other day of my earliest Wagner mood—the purely Nibelung; Mime, mood before the Valkyries rose on my horizon. You know—very earthy, and smith-y, and Terrtaric. How *inexhaustible* these things are. You think you have done with a thing—whoop!—it's all back again, strong as ever.[147]

Lewis felt he could "boast no musical education," nor did he play a musical instrument, yet his knowledge and perception of musical philosophy and history were applied in accordance with the medieval belief that the arts were not to be separated.[148] He held frank delight toward certain music—a delight aided by the melody and the imagination of his heart.[149] True, his classical scholarship was far superior to his musicianship. Even Lewis claimed, "but then literature is my province, and in music I can only afford to enjoy the music that really suits me."[150] However, Lewis's mind did not fragment the arts; music sang with literature and held hands with dance, and the logician's wholeness flowed throughout his works.

---

147 AG, 506, 484. "I will by no means join in the modern depreciation of Wagner. He may, for all I know, have been a bad man. He may (though I shall never believe it) have been a bad musician. But as a mytho-poieic poet he is incomparable" (CR, 84).

148 CR, 94.

149 Lewis "never had any musical education but was, so to speak, born with a taste for good music" (WHL).

150 AG, 219.

Chapter 8

INTO THE LAND OF THE IMAGINATION

In an evangelical Christianity that was preoccupied with rational arguments, Kilby was a fervent apologist for the Christian imagination. (More of his observations on creativity and imagination are available in the companion book on aesthetics.) He was certainly no enemy of careful thinking; he simply realized that without image and story our life, and the gospel, is one-dimensional. The festschrift presented to Dr. Kilby in 1971 was very appropriately titled Imagination and the Spirit, *and in all his teaching Kilby was concerned to open the doors that let us "into the land of the imagination." And of course, even more than Lewis's keen logic, it was his ability to think in terms of image and story that attracted Kilby to him so strongly. In the following essay, from* Christian History, *Kilby first argues for the centrality of the imagination to our humanity and in Scripture, then proceeds to illustrate the way it functions in Lewis's work.*

Every normal person is blessed with imagination. Imagination operates ceaselessly and is capable of tying together even grotesque elements of matter and spirit. The apple that is said to have fallen on Isaac Newton's head launched him into a set of meanings that culminated in his laws of gravitation and motion. In his theory of relativity Einstein combined complicated mathematical equations with images of trains rushing into distant space. The best scientists know that great discoveries are not made simply by experiment and reason but sometimes in mental gyrations as great, even as delightfully humorous, as Alice's adventures down the rabbit hole.

There is hardly one of Lewis's expository works in which he fails to allude to the imagination. Lewis defined reason as the natural organ of truth, and imagination as the organ of meaning.

The whole enterprise of art—music, sculpture, literature, even architecture—is particularly dependent upon consistent imagination. And is not life itself also, at least in the portions of it that seem really to live? Owing to the Great Mistake of Eden, life tends habitually to settle into the prosaic and ordinary. Indeed, is it not symbolic of fallen man that a steady smell of roses leaves them odorless? Imagination is necessary to the worthwhile life.

IMAGINATION IN THE BIBLE

Some devout Christians fear imagination is inevitably evil, yet the Bible is almost embarrassingly imaginative. Lewis insists that the reader of the Bible, without losing sight of its primary value, must always remember that it is literature. "Most emphatically," he says, "the Psalms must be read as poetry." We remember such highly imaginative passages as "Let the floods clap their hands, let the hills be joyful together," and Christ as the great storyteller describing a man who built his house upon sand and a sower who went forth to sow. He compared the kingdom of heaven to a grain of mustard seed and described himself as "the true vine." God, the greatest of imaginers, gives all men power to imagine, just as he gives them free will. Either can lead to steady and joyful devotion to him or else to everlasting misery.

Lewis believed that the modern imagination has fostered more than the usual quota of villainy, having too often searched out the devious and febrile in all the litter corners where sin lurks. In the final chapter of *The Screwtape Letters,* Lewis describes hell's view of our times. At the Tempters' Training College for Young Devils, Screwtape speaks his gratitude for the abundance of souls now entering hell but bemoans their quality, souls "hardly worth damning," and harks back to periods of more substantial sinners such as Henry VIII, Farinata, or even Hitler. Lewis also believes that people in our time have, for whatever cause, tended to avoid the great positive potentials of love and holiness. "How little people know who think that holiness is dull. When one meets the real thing . . . it is irresistible."

THE CHRISTIAN NOVELIST

In the one meeting I had with C. S. Lewis, we discussed the Christian novelist. When I mentioned the term, Lewis instantly responded with a comparison to the Christian carpenter. Each is simply a Christian doing his particular work, doing it well or badly. "If a man who cannot draw horses is illustrating a book, the pictures that involve horses will be the bad pictures, let his spiritual condition be what it may," he said. Of course the Christian writer should avoid "mendacity, cruelty, blasphemy, pornography," and "aim at edification insofar as edification is proper to the kind of work in hand." If the story is about Jack and the beanstalk he dare not allow Jack to stop on the way up and recommend high-growing bean seeds. A story must be true to the known rules for successful composition: content from one sentence to another requires not trickery but honesty and wisdom.

Take an instance from the beginning of the Narnian adventure *The Silver Chair.* Jill Pole has played the egotist and got her friend Eustace Scrubb into trouble. Shortly afterward she comes upon a Lion (the capital is Lewis's), which turns and moves slowly back into the forest. Jill then hears running water and finds herself very thirsty, whereupon she plucks up her courage and steals carefully from tree to tree in its direction. She comes upon an open glade from which the sight of the enticing water ahead mightily increases her thirst. Ready to rush forward, she suddenly checks herself because there, between her and the stream, is the Lion lying quietly with its head raised and its paws out in front. It is looking straight at Jill. The two face each other for a long time.

Jill's thirst is now so persistent that she must have water even if the Lion catches her. In a "heavy, golden voice" the Lion finally asks, "Are you thirsty?"

"I'm *dying* of thirst," Jill promptly responds.

"Then drink," says the Lion.

Hesitantly Jill suggests that the Lion go away while she drinks, to which a low growl is the only response. Then she says, "I daren't come and drink."

"Then you will die of thirst."

Taking a step nearer, Jill says, "I suppose I must go and look for another stream then."

"There is no other stream."

Now frantic with thirst, Jill proceeds to the sparkling stream and drinks "the coldest, most refreshing water she has ever tasted."

Apart from "no other stream," this whole episode is simply good narrative. Yet we can imagine the many Scriptures that ran through Lewis's mind as he wrote: "If any man thirst, let him come unto me, and drink . . . none other name under heaven whereby we must be saved . . . whosoever drinketh of the water that I shall give him shall never thirst . . . though he slay me, yet will I trust in him . . . the wages of sin is death," and more.

We must not of course suppose that the manner in which Lewis presents this episode is the only possible way. What it does imply beyond question is that *The Silver Chair* is a story and therefore must above all keep literary faith. At the same time the record is abundantly clear that Lewis's Narnian stories have conveyed the Christian way to millions of children and adults. One of my friends wrote me at some length of how, over a period of some ten years, he had slowly lost total contact with God, and how one day while reading *The Lion, the Witch and the Wardrobe* to his children he was suddenly overcome with remorse and tearfully recommitted himself to the Savior.

MEANING AND MYTH

Even one consummate value may redeem an otherwise poor writer. Lewis joyfully spoke of George MacDonald as his literary "master" despite a whole array of faults he found in him. One such fault was the quite common one of unnecessary sermonizing. What Lewis found valuable in MacDonald was "fantasy—fantasy that hovers between the allegorical and the mythopoeic." Lewis believed that ultimate meanings tend to fall into metaphor, allegory, and myth, types in which a Christian writer should feel he is on home ground. Lewis calls myth at its best "a real though unfocused gleam of divine truth falling on human imagination." He had such an ideal in view in all his creative works, particularly in what he considered his best story, *Till We Have Faces*. Myth, he says, "deals with the permanent and inevitable."

The scope of Lewis's imagination, if not as profound, is as wide as that of Dante and Milton. He tells how happy he was, after dwelling imaginatively on the infernal motives and intrigues of hell in *The Screwtape Letters*, to return to normalcy. Not only does he present for us these supernatural characters but also devilish-minded, even devil-possessed ones, right here on earth. In *That Hideous Strength* Belbury's destructive might is set against the quiet Christianity of St. Anne's, one feverish with bustle and trickery and the other calmly, even in the threat of world insurrection, awaiting the will of God. In *The Great Divorce* people are allowed to go up from the murkiness of hell and stand warmly welcomed into the permeating glory of heaven, and yet, with only one exception, they refuse heaven and return to hell. The thing they will never let go is their "proper pride." They continue, even after the pains of hell, to choose self over God. The painter urged to come inside rejects heaven when he learns it is without coteries and the worship of Big Names. Even the bishop, who has grown to love questions better than answers, rejects heaven in the interest of his little theological society in hell where he is admired for his papers on the speculative aspects of religion.

THE IMAGINATIVE PROCESS

Though many have tried, no one has ever been able to explain the imaginative process, no doubt because successful creativity is as large as life itself. Lewis gives a fragmentary sketch of how *The Lion, the Witch and the Wardrobe*, one of his Narnian stories, came to be. It began, as his stories generally did, with a mental image, this time of "a Faun carrying an umbrella and parcels in a snowy wood." This initial bit first lodged in Lewis's imagination when he was about sixteen, long before he became a Christian. Years later, he says, he sat down to see if he could make a story out of it. Had he not in the meantime given himself completely to God, it would probably have become a good story as such, but now "Aslan came bounding into it." Not only that, Aslan "pulled the whole story together." Would the story become a Christian tract? Amazingly, Lewis in this book tied narrative interest and profound theology together, and we experience not only a multitude of details related to the death and resurrection of Jesus Christ but also note that he died on a stone table representing the law of Moses.

Lewis accepted imagination as one of the great and varied gifts of God. As a Christian he saw it a worthy avenue of spiritual witness. He believed, however, that it should never become a "device" or frame on which to hang a sermon. For Lewis, the principle on which we must daily operate is a simple honesty which takes its life and its liberty from a living experience of the triune God.

Chapter 9

THE JOY-MINDED PROFESSOR

Dr. Kilby was intimately acquainted with joy, as those who knew him readily remember. In Lewis he found not only one whose writings could make joy palpable and present but also one who could trace the meaning of joy all the way back to its source in God. It is no surprise then that when he tries to make a case for the importance of joy to the Christian, he turns to Lewis for illustration.

Judging by a Bible concordance, the word *joy* appears to be more important for a Christian believer than the word *prayer*. At least the first occurs more often than the second. As we know, the Psalms are full of joyful praise for God's glory and strength and blessings. Paul tells the Thessalonians to "rejoice evermore" (1 Thess. 5:16). He urges the Ephesian Christians to sing and make melody to the Lord "in your heart" and not to get drunk on wine but (my own interpretation) get drunk on the Spirit (Eph. 5:18–19).

And yet in most Christian churches this "inebriety in the Spirit" is noteworthy by its absence.

Almost the last person we might expect to urge the practice of joy would be a university lecturer, professional scholar, and logician like the highly regarded and influential Clive Staples Lewis. The forty books of this British Christian are not only still in print but also tremendously popular twenty-two years after his death. Yet it seems that no modern writer has more often or more feelingly stressed the importance of practicing joy.

It is altogether fitting that C. S. Lewis should call his autobiography *Surprised by Joy*. "We are halfhearted creatures," he said, "fooling about with drink and sex and ambition when infinite joy is offered us."

Christians, he believed, are promised joys here and now and indescribable joys after death. We are eventually to "drink joy from the fountain of joy."

Like Christians generally, Lewis believed that joy existed in all its perfection in the Garden of Eden. He believed also that even fallen man experiences a distant echo of Edenic joy on occasion. Sudden stabs of joy are likely to arise out of quite natural circumstances, yet they should not be considered merely an accident but one of the ingredients with which God has made the world.

Every man every day of his life is being called by God. "When we see the face of God, we shall know that we have always known it," Lewis declared.

Joy is there for anyone who wants it enough. One who did want it sufficiently was John (in Lewis's *The Pilgrim's Regress*).

Once in youth he heard a distant music and had a vision of a calm sea and a wonderful island in the midst of it. Not knowing why, John sobbed with joy at the sweetness and the piercing beneficence of the vision. He knew instantly that this, and this alone, he must have.

He left off everything else and started out in search of it. He took a road that went straight as an arrow, but before long the first of a long series of enticements took him to the right or to the left.

The first was Mr. Enlightenment, who offered John a ride in his buggy and, after much talk, the assurance that God did not actually exist, something that John was at this stage glad to learn since he had tried fornication and feared heavenly punishment.

But shortly John learned, as he was to learn eventually from the other enticements to leave the main road, that Mr. Enlightenment's way did not lead to John's music and the glorious island he sought.

At long last John, weary and in rags, saw how foolish he had been ever to have left the main road. Shortly thereafter, he met those who offered him real fulfillment on condition that he totally "give himself up." To accomplish this, or rather to have it accomplished for him, he had to go down to the bottom of the Great Divide—that is, move from his unfulfilled worldliness and twisted motives to Jesus Christ.

Not long afterward John, traveling happily in this new land, came in sight of his island, where "the morning wind, blowing off-shore from it, brought the sweet smell of its orchards" and created in him a great purity and joy that he knew to be everlasting.

It is clear enough from this story that John represents you. And though you may misunderstand and maltreat the calling as John did, it continues to pierce you from time to time, calling you to Joy himself.

In the Garden of Eden, according to Lewis, "being, power and joy descended from God to man in the form of a gift and returned from man to God in the form of obedient love and ecstatic adoration."

That is the plan, the prescription, for real joy, as against mere entertainment or even the very proper ordinary pleasures of life. Men live too often on the dead level of not quite believing anything.

Evil takes over those who allow it to and leaves them like cows cropping the grass and unaware of the field. Because Lewis was so clearly conscious of hierarchy, he was able to write convincingly on the utter joys of heaven and the withering misery of hell.

How odd that often the stabs of joy in our lives are accompanied by pain.

After long exile, the Israelites were finally allowed to return to their beloved Jerusalem and begin the reconstruction of the temple. When its foundation was finally completed, there was a great convocation at which "the people could not discern the noise of the shout of joy from the noise of the weeping" (Ezra 3:13).

The depth of both joy and weeping involved not simply the occasion but recollections of their ancestors, especially David and Solomon, and of the sins of their forefathers and of the original temple.

Indeed, for them, as for us today, the visitation looks backward all the way to Eden, on the one hand to the ecstatic perfection of that garden and on the other, as the British poet John Milton said, to the forbidden tree that "brought death into the world, and all our woe." Joy derives from God yet bears the painful recognition of sin and death.

Pain is often the precursor of joy. An auto plunges off a cliff and the woman, though she survives, is trapped inside for four days without food or water in freezing weather. When finally rescued, she is asked, "Are you a religious person?" She responds, "I wasn't until four days ago; now I am."

Pain, says Lewis, is "God's megaphone to rouse a deaf world," and the traveler John learns that "security is mortals' enemy."

Most of us, when we are really honest with ourselves, know these things to be true. And most of us, when we act upon the set lesson, find joy the outcome.

For a long time during his early Christian life, Lewis wondered why we are commanded to repeatedly praise God. Don't we despise someone who requires continual assurance of his talents and virtues?

"Gratitude to God, reverence to Him, obedience to Him, I thought I could understand, not this perpetual eulogy."

But eventually he came to see that when we admire God, this "is simply to be awake, to have entered the real world; not to appreciate [God] is to have lost the greatest experience, and in the end to have lost all."

He discovered also that it is in the act of worshiping God that he communicates himself to us. Even the Cross gives us joy.

"Our life as Christians," he said, "begins by being baptised into death; our most joyful festivals begin with, and centre upon, the broken body and the shed blood. . . . Our joy has to be the sort of joy which can coexist with that."

It was not only Lewis's experience of Christian joy in his own life that led him to present Christ as the source of real joy in book after book but also his awareness of how little real joy there is in a world more and more fed on an upside-down sort of reality.

The great thing about Lewis's stories is that they do not simply recommend joy, or simply say that certain characters experience joy, but they carry winged joy directly into the reader's life.

Let's look at a young and sophisticated housewife (described in *That Hideous Strength*) who is very unhappy and likely headed for divorce from her equally sophisticated husband. Much against her will, she gravitates to the community called St. Anne's and there becomes acquainted with Christians who, in the midst of horrifying dangers, are calm and joyful. Living there, a whole new world begins to dawn on her. One day, walking alone down a mossy path in the garden, it happened.

> There was no form nor sound. The mould under the bushes, the moss on the path, the little brick border, were not visibly changed. But they were changed. A boundary had been crossed.
>
> She had come into a world, or into a Person. . . . There was nothing, and never had been anything, like this. And now there was nothing except this.

Jane becomes a Christian and a "right proper wife." God promises, Lewis said, to make each of us perfect, and he will get that process well under way in this life and complete it in the next.

In his classic *Mere Christianity* Lewis wrote: "When He said, 'Be perfect,' He meant it. He meant that we must go in for the full treatment. . . . It may be hard for an egg to turn into a bird; it would be a jolly sight harder for it to learn to fly while remaining an egg. We are like eggs at present. And you cannot go on indefinitely being just an ordinary decent egg. We must be hatched or go bad."

On the other hand, if we choose him, he will make "the feeblest and filthiest of us into a . . . dazzling, radiant, immortal creature, pulsating all through with such energy and joy and wisdom and love as we cannot now imagine, a bright stainless mirror which reflects back to God perfectly . . . His own boundless power and delight and goodness.

"If you want joy, power, peace, eternal life, you must get close to, or even into, the thing that has them. . . . Once a man is united to God, how could he not live forever?"

I have suggested that the emotions of joy and rejoicing are dominant in much of the Bible and also in the words of C. S. Lewis. He, once an atheist, came to a point at which he felt impelled to bow down and confess that God is God. Having earlier made out a written case against Christ, the time came when he had no intelligent choice but to confess Christ as the Son of God and as his own Savior.

Perhaps it was the great contrast between the negatives of atheism and the positives of Christianity that made it easy for Lewis to write of both heaven and hell and particularly to speak more meaningfully than any modern writer I know of about Christian joy.

He understood, as so many of us do not, what Paul meant when he wrote to the Corinthians, "Eye hath not seen, nor ear heard, neither have entered into the heart of man, the things which God hath prepared for them that love him" (1 Cor. 2:9).

Chapter 10

THE WITNESS OF HOLINESS

In whatever sphere C. S. Lewis is evaluated, whether as novelist, apologist, or professor, he is seldom considered for his single-minded pursuit of personal holiness. Yet Kilby observes that "a saint . . . confesses the blessed name and attempts to live blamelessly before God." Regarding that simple desire, concludes Kilby, Lewis was a genuinely holy man. Some recent biographies (particularly A. N. Wilson's) have added complexity to our understanding of Lewis's life (for example, in speculating on the nature of his early and long connection with Mrs. Moore, the mother of a friend from Lewis's military service, who lived in Lewis's house, under his care, for nearly thirty years). But they do not succeed in tarnishing the picture of personal goodness that Kilby sketches here.

When we think of the word *holy* we are likely to imagine the apostles or others from the Bible or else someone canonized by the Roman Catholic Church. Holiness, we suppose, belonged to some distant time when life was simpler and men really loved one another. But could there be a holy person just now in my block, in my town?

Could a shabby creature with receding hairline, nicotine teeth, and sloppy clothing—who lived in a house so desperately in need of repairs that one of its floors simply burst through—can such a man be a saint? A man who frequented a local pub and, in an anteroom where the smell of beer and smoke filled the air, talked and laughed so uproariously that other drinkers wondered if he and his friends were not drunk—can that sort of man be a saint? A big, hearty man capable of making a new suit look frowsy the second time worn and who enjoyed hiking twenty miles a day over hill and dale? A man who as scholar might ride roughshod over any opponent in intellectual debate?

If pressed, we should perhaps have difficulty in saying precisely what constitutes a holy person. Perhaps we would think of someone who possessed steadiness, quietness, contemplative habits, the regular reading of Scriptures and devotion to prayer. But less likely would we think of someone engaged in a busy, involved life.

Yet in C. S. Lewis both sets of characteristics met in a powerful witness to God's sanctifying grace.

Who is a saint? And what is holiness?

These questions, always considerations in the life of any Christian, struck me with unusual force on hearing a lecture on Lewis by his stepson Douglas Gresham, who, though he spoke warmly of Lewis as a Christian gentleman, insisted that he was "not a saint."

On the contrary, my own longtime reading of the works of Lewis has slowly but increasingly impressed upon me his real saintliness, his genuine holiness.

I think, for instance, that no one this side of our Lord himself was more insistent upon the need—the absolute need—of our forgiving the sins of others in the same proportion and completeness as our Lord forgives us when we ask. "Real forgiveness," Lewis said, "means looking steadily at the sin, the sin that is left over without any excuse, after all allowances have been made, and seeing it in all its horror, dirt, meanness and malice, and nevertheless being wholly reconciled to the man who has done it. That and only that, is forgiveness."

Of course Lewis wrote of forgiveness, but did he practice it?

At twenty-six Lewis was elected to a fellowship at Magdalen College, Oxford, one of the great universities of the world. He was expected to tutor pupils and deliver scholarly lectures. Oxford had been established by saintly men for the propagation of Christianity, but when Lewis went there it was far from its origin. Lewis found Magdalen "leftish, atheist, cynical, hard-boiled."

Yet in such an antagonistic atmosphere he became a Christian and in due course did not hesitate to write and publish books that would be sneered at by many of his colleagues. Not simply "religious" books—they might have been stomached—but works clearly intent on turning men to Jesus Christ.

One report went out that no one at Magdalen wanted to sit next to Lewis at table because he would immediately turn and ask, "Are you a Christian?" Both by nature and the dictates of good taste, Lewis was utterly opposed to putting anyone in a corner. Yet this was the sort of gossip that, along with his output of books on Christianity, finally prevented Lewis's being awarded a professorship—though he was regarded by many as the greatest scholar in the university.

For some twenty-five years Lewis knew what it was to be sneered at, to be called "saint" cynically, but still he was friendly with all his colleagues.

If Lewis had much to forgive at his college, he had more at home. At the time of World War I he had promised a buddy in the British army that, were the friend killed, he would attempt to care for his mother and her daughter. That led to long years of what Lewis's brother described as intolerable imposition, even domination, by a woman who possessed "an intense selfishness, an egotism, which excluded any pretence of interest in any subject but herself, and an arrogant and ignorant dogmatism on every topic however abstruse."

How quickly most of us would have conjured up plenty of excuses for escape from the promise made to a buddy leaving for the battlefront in France! But Lewis was steadfast to his promise during some thirty years of increasing vexation. When he spoke of the absolute necessity of forgiveness, he knew intimately what he was talking about.

Another deep conviction of Lewis's was that the greatest sin of all is pride, chiefly and finally choosing oneself over God. In book after book he endeavored to describe and illustrate the continuous and hellish exaltation of the self. In his *The Great Divorce* we have a bishop who after experiencing the literal tortures of hell is offered, but refuses, the heavenly country presented before him, choosing rather to return to the infernal regions and learnedly discuss with his ecclesiastical colleagues such subjects as how this fellow called Jesus had talents that might have carried him far in the world had he not unluckily come to an early death; or a mother who so "loves" her dead son that she neglects her living husband and children; or an artist who likewise refuses heaven when he finds he will not be recognized there as "somebody."

He emphasized that pride and the other "respectable" sins are the worst ones. Pride and spite he described as spiritual evils that men share with devils. "The essential vice, the utmost evil, is pride. Unchastity, anger, greed, drunkenness, and all that, are mere fleabites in comparison." Therefore the Christian must wage ceaseless war against it. A Christian needs every morning, before the duties of the day rush in, to renew his commitment to God, to become low before him and invoke his steady loving care. Let him remember that he is a creation of God and destined to live, not seventy years, but forever.

Lewis was a staunch believer in heaven and, by logical consequence, in hell. To most Christians both these concepts somehow manage to remain more or less hazy throughout life. Not so with

Lewis. As a very young man he had been sent to study under an atheist tutor whose practice it was to demand logical proof for any remark one might make. It was in such untoward circumstances that Lewis learned logic. But then that very logic started him doubting his doubts and swayed him away from his own then-professed atheism toward the way of holiness.

The practice of unfailing forgiveness and steady recognition of the hellishness of besetting pride are austere doctrines. But we can now turn to something deeply positive in Lewis's belief and practice.

God calls his children not only to right practices but also to the only genuine happiness, joy. If the face of the coin is obedience, its other side is the continuous recognition that God is, that he is my Creator and Savior, and that whatever my daily circumstances his joy is to remain in me forever.

No writer I know of outside the Bible actually conveys joy to his reader as does Lewis. He moves toward joyful scenes as instinctively as a hound on the trail. The reader finds himself not just told about joy but rather enveloped in unclouded beauty and deep inner satisfaction.

Lewis often spoke of "stabs of Joy," momentary glimpses that both satisfy and at the same time set one longing. We are all aware of the difference between simply being told that a character feels joy and, as we read, having a world of blessedness take possession of the deepest recesses of our being, in Lewis's words, "a sort of splendor as of eatable, thinkable, breathable gold."

In two of his books we are taken to the murky and treacherous confines of hell, but in others to the glories of heaven. In *Perelandra* we not only meet angelic powers but also find an unfallen Eve who, living in perfect fellowship with God, is unaware of the word "self." She is unaware of choice, yet is altogether free. The joy one feels in Lewis is not unlike that of Pentecost when the Holy Spirit came upon the apostles with "tongues like that of fire" and initiated such contagious enthusiasm that Christianity itself began to blaze its trail to the very ends of the earth.

Holding on the one hand to the fixed requirement of obedience to God and on the other to the joyful rewards of that obedience, it is not surprising that Lewis became an unusual defender of the faith. He was far less bothered about outright atheists or agnostics than about those who play around with biblical truth. Having been raised in a "modernistic" church, he was from the moment of his conversion the particular foe of church leaders who water down Christian doctrines.

In his youth Lewis had argued with his best boyhood friend that indeed a man named Yeshua had once existed but that "all the tomfoolery about virgin birth, magic healings, apparitions and so forth is on exactly the same footing as any other mythology." His complete about-face some fourteen years later left him with a sharp awareness of the two extremes in his opposition to deviations from scriptural truth. "We are told," he summarized, "that Christ was killed for us, that His death washed out our sins, and that by dying He disabled death itself. That is the formula. That is what has to be believed."

There is, finally, a great chasm between the joyful acceptance of Christ and rejection, whether outright or by neglect. "I would pay any price," he wrote, "to be able to say truthfully 'All will be saved.' But my reason retorts, 'Without their will, or with it?' If I say, 'Without their will' I at once perceive a contradiction; how can the supreme voluntary act of self-surrender be involuntary? If I say, 'With their will,' my reason replies, 'How if they will *not* give in?'"

Lewis loved utter privacy as much as any man ever did. Yet he willingly went into army camps during World War II and preached the gospel to soldiers. He also went on BBC radio and did the same sort of thing, activities that brought down upon him a vast sea of correspondence and interviews, all to be added to his extensive duties at Magdalen College. And of course his Christian books did the same. If it is argued that thus he also gained high reputation and a large income, it should be said that he gave away two-thirds of his income because of his deep-seated conviction that all one's possessions are a gift from God and must be used for his glory. As to giving of possessions, he held up the rule that the proper amount is simply "more than one can spare."

Was C. S. Lewis a saint, a holy man? The rather minimum evidence I have mentioned surely gives an affirmative answer, even such as to prod me into calling him a "real" saint and a person of particular and enticing holiness.

Who, according to Scripture, is saint, a holy person? Simply one who believes God and, in the words of the first Psalm, "delights in the law of the Lord." We remember Paul's account of his happiness that the Macedonians had taken up a contribution for "the poor saints which are at Jerusalem." At the end of Hebrews, the writer sends salutations to "all the saints." Paul also tells of how, before his conversion on the Damascus Road, he vigorously shut up in prison many of the "saints" of that city.

A saint, then—a holy person—confesses the blessed name and attempts to live blamelessly before God.

In his lecture on Lewis, Mr. Gresham declared that Lewis was "not a saint." Undoubtedly he did not wish to imply that Lewis was anything less than a devout Christian. Rather, perhaps he was thinking of the wide reading of Lewis's books (some forty million apparently now in print) as well as an outpouring of books and articles about him, and of the Lewis Societies and conferences and the danger of making him more than a man. Lewis himself would undoubtedly have responded to such things with warnings like Mr. Gresham's. Nevertheless Lewis was, by strictly biblical standards, a true saint, a genuinely holy man.

Chapter 11

BETWEEN HEAVEN AND HELL

Through his writing and speaking, C. S. Lewis indulged a delight in the prospect of heaven, but he was not ignorant of hell's terrors. A firm belief in the afterlife—and the importance of earthly decisions arrived upon before entering those realms—propelled him into the discipline of apologetics. He was eager that others share his hope.

Someone has said that men who can write readable books about religion are almost as rare as saints. Clive Staples Lewis, a tutor first at Oxford and then professor at Cambridge University until his death on the same day as President Kennedy's assassination, was such a man. Beginning in 1933 and ending with a posthumous volume recently published, C. S. Lewis produced more than a score of articulate books on religion, plus other volumes of scholarship in literature and philology and numerous periodical articles, prefaces, and poems.

Of *The Screwtape Letters*, the most popular of Lewis's works on religion, Leonard Bacon said it was a book "for which believer and unbeliever alike may give thanks . . . a spectacular and satisfactory nova in the bleak sky of satire." He felt there was justification for comparison of Lewis with Jonathan Swift. John H. Holmes, writing of Lewis's popular lectures on the British radio, said: "His clarity of thought and simplicity of expression have a magic about them which makes plain the most abstruse problem of theological speculation." Of Lewis's *Allegory of Love*, a study in medievalism,

Professor B. Evans wrote: "Out of the multitude of volumes on literary criticism there arises once or twice in a generation a truly great work. Such, I believe, is this study." Kenneth Tynan, one of Lewis's students at Oxford, said that he had at his fingertips more knowledge that he had ever known in another scholar, and Dom Bede Griffiths, a colleague of Lewis's, said that he had the most exact and penetrating mind he had ever encountered.

Lewis's books are often small, but they are seminal in their profound grasp of truth and their manner of silhouetting ideas. In religion he was a man who had discovered, with contagious conviction, that Christianity is the simple truth and that ordinariness is redolent with potentiality. Seven of Lewis's books on Christian subjects can be classified as fiction and seven as children's books. One of his books is his autobiography, and the others deal with the moral universe, Christian doctrines, and with what might be called the philosophy of Christianity. The fiction includes space travel to Mars and Venus, where the reader encounters Hrossa and Sorns and vegetation that is mountain high, barely visible beings called Eldils and evil men from Earth intent on taking over the entire universe. In the children's books one meets marsh-wiggles and Calormenes and Tarkaans and talking animals and dwarfs and giants and dryads and centaurs, a London cab horse that learns to fly and a delightful mouse called Reepicheep who is the epitome of bravery and honor; magic and glory, with delectable landscapes and with hairbreadth escapes, and finally what rarely happens in a children's book—the death of the characters. The most important figure in the Narnia series, as the children's books are called, is Aslan, the mighty lion who overcomes the White Witch and other enemies and turns ordinary people into stately kings and queens.

In his autobiography, *Surprised by Joy*, Lewis gave the clue to many of his themes. He called himself a "converted pagan living among apostate Puritans," who has taken as long to acquire inhibitions as others have needed to get rid of them. Early in life he moved into a satisfying atheism, but that state of mind eventually began to have its own brand of contradictions. "I maintained that God did not exist. I was also very angry with Him for not existing. I was equally angry with Him for creating a world." Once his reluctant mind became oriented toward the possibility of genuine Christianity, George MacDonald, G. K. Chesterton, George Herbert, Sir Thomas Browne, and, in their way, Hegel, Kant, and Bergson, together with contemporary colleagues at Oxford, carried him with increasing momentum toward the dreaded hour, as he said, in which he had to kneel and pray and "admit that God was God."

With such a background it was not surprising that Lewis became apostle to the skeptics. For many he was a great antidote to the intellectual and religious faddism of the twentieth century. He was decidedly opposed to what he called chronological snobbery—the notion that if a thing is not up to date it is probably untrue and that truth is like a machine that is bound to grow rusty and obsolescent. He scorned the idea that any generation is wiser than any preceding generation and that the old are necessarily wiser than the young.

Lewis was in fact out of sympathy with much in modern civilization. He regarded a great part of today's education, especially of the "new" variety, with little short of contempt. He had no use for the idea of the "adjusted" child, of "togetherness," and of slick mass education. He even opposed the "leveling" concept in democracy, with its resentment of superiority where that superiority is genuine. He advocated more individuality, more rebellion, and some place where the "utterly private" can exist. He thought that culture-mongers and the managerial or new ruling class are bringing into existence a dangerous society that he called Charientocracy.

Lewis gave what one critic described as a "strictly unorthodox presentation of strict orthodox." Perhaps the most striking instance of this orthodoxy is his view of hell and heaven. At a time when it is fashionable to lift the eyebrow at the notion of hell—and sometimes heaven—Lewis accepted both with complete seriousness. In fact, Lewis wrote with more cogency on the transcendent glories of heaven and the pejorative terrors of hell than any other man since the early centuries of Christianity.

The basic premise to the reality of both worlds lies in Lewis's remark, "There are only two kinds of people in the end: those who say to God, 'Thy will be done,' and those to whom God says, in the end, 'Thy will be done.'" Hence, heaven or hell for any individual is simply the result of a fundamental choice, and the free will is a fulcrum to an everlasting condition of being.

In *The Great Divorce*, people from hell take a bus ride to the purlieus of heaven, yet most of them refuse to go in. A painter urged to come inside rejects heaven when he learns it is without coteries and the worship of Big Names. A preacher who has grown to love questions better than answers rejects heaven in the interest of his little theological society in hell where he is admired for his polemical papers on speculative aspects of religion.

Lewis's images of hell suggest the terrible surrealism of Hieronymus Bosch, but his lively pictures of heaven are gloriously apocalyptic. Someone has said that heaven for Lewis is as real as a Sunday morning breakfast. The glory of this perfect world so completely permeated Lewis's mind that it shows up in almost any book he wrote.

In *Perelandra*, the unspoiled effulgence of that wonderful land infects the reader with a longing as intense as Lewis's own. In *Till We Have Faces*, Psyche goes down to Hades and brings up the casket of beauty that will transform the ugly Orual into Pscyhe's own beauty. Then these sisters await with overpowering sweetness, yet terror, the one whose coming purified and brightened the air, the one for whose sake the earth and stars and sun and all that was or would ever be existed. In that presence she discovers that her lifelong case against God was only words, words, words. Lewis conceives of heaven as a place where Christian virtues already practiced in this life come to their transcendent fulfillment.

Lewis believed that so-called realistic reading may be the worst possible preparation for real life.

A boy reading a school story may be deceived as no child is deceived by the fairy tale, for the school story may cause in him a desire for success and make him unhappy at being unable to attain it, while a boy reading the fairy tale "desires and is happy in the very fact of desiring." Likewise adults are not deceived by science fiction but frequently are deceived by stories in women's magazines suggesting, for instance, that the moment they are no longer in the state called "being in love" they are then justified in seeking a divorce.

"The real danger," Lewis wrote, "lurks in sober-faced novels where all appears to be very probable but all is in fact contrived to put across some social or ethical or religious or anti-religious 'comment on life.'"

There are people—especially those who set out to dislike him—who regard Lewis as nothing more than a popularizer of theological truths. But Lewis was not a mere popularizer. His naive, almost offhand touch and the utter simplicity of his style can easily be mistaken for popularization. But a closer look reveals a toughness and a consistency belonging to greatness; each reading increases one's respect for the profundity and meaning of their contents.

Chapter 12

TILL WE HAVE FACES

Kilby's early review of Till We Have Faces *recognizes its greatness, but reflects his sense that the book has many more secrets to reveal. As Lewis spent years writing it, Kilby spent years trying to understand it. This review is a very brief first attempt, and what follows is a longer, unpublished article in which Kilby probes the novel to much greater depth.*

THE STRAIGHT TALE OF BARBARISM

The central idea of this novel is that men's conception of God is commonly anemic, pale, and full of words. Even after one genuine glimpse of the shining palace across the river, Orual, the leading character, chooses to deny the vision rather than accept it. The soldier Bardia, kind and good at heart, is content religiously to give the gods their traditional worship and not worry too much about why he does so. The Greek slave Lysias, teacher of Orual and her sisters, denies the gods and holds firmly to nature and reason as ultimates. In the concluding section of the novel these people are forced to confess they were wrong. Orual's reading of her forty-year-old complaint against the gods becomes the answer to that complaint. She realizes it is only words, not truth. She comes to realize also that there has always been a deeper speech lying at the center of her soul, one that she was never willing to acknowledge. She comes to the shocking realization that God cannot speak to us openly or let us answer him because our words are simply "the babble that we think we mean." There is only one word we can speak to him and that is the mighty amen of contrition. Until then we really have no faces. God can have no essential dealings with us until rationalization and babble are hushed by the recognition of his being and sovereignty. Orual discovers that all her life she has simply wanted to be her own and consequently has left no room in the universe for God to exist. Even her supposed love for her sister turns out to have been only selfish. She finds that because she is totally empty inside she has had the lifelong tendency to usurp other people and things for her own ends.

This novel is an adaptation of the Greek myth of Cupid and Psyche. Lewis says he has worked on the general theme of the novel for most of his life. This is certainly the most difficult of his books (even beyond *Pilgrim's Regress*), but I believe it may be the most rewarding for those who are willing to spend time with it. Readers will long for a key to its meaning and will probably go to some interpretation if they can find one, but I should like to suggest that there is pleasure in ferreting out the symbols for oneself. As a beginning you can take Lewis's own brief words describing the story: "the straight tale of barbarism, the mind of an ugly woman, dark idolatry and pale enlightenment at war with each other and with vision, and the havoc which a vocation, or even faith, works on human life."

Lewis's little pictures—analogues with the Greek myth—in the latter part of the book are as beautiful as those in Bunyan's *Pilgrim's Progress*. In fact, the entire story qua story is told with the usual Lewis literary skill. It is only the symbols that will give one trouble. But then the symbols *are* the book.

The following paper is not only unpublished but undated; it was certainly written after Lewis's reply to Kilby's first attempts to understand it. That letter (W. H. Lewis, ed., Letters of C. S. Lewis *[New York: Harcourt Brace and World, 1966], 273) is illuminating for the novel, though it is prefaced by Lewis's disclaimer that "an author doesn't necessarily understand the meaning of his own story better than anyone else, so I give my account of* Till We Have Faces *simply for what it is worth." Kilby was clearly unsatisfied with the four "levels" of meaning Lewis proceeds to list, and keeps digging deeper in the book, as this careful essay illustrates.*

AN INTERPRETATION OF *TILL WE HAVE FACES*

This is, I think, unquestionably the most difficult of all of C. S. Lewis's books. Yet it may be the best of his books. I have read it at least a half dozen times, but the present reading suggests a wholly new story.

Perhaps the most noteworthy new view is that of the number of witnesses from the gods to Orual.

In the first place Orual is clearly aware that the blood of the gods is in her family. She begins with this "connection" with them, suggesting at once the Light "which lighteth every man that cometh into the world." The lengthy teaching of the Fox that the gods are lovely poetic inventions never quite wipes out a deep sense of their reality in Orual. When the Fox's death at the hands of her father seems imminent, she asks him, "Do you really in your heart believe nothing of what is said about the gods?" and she notices his trembling as his feelings overcome his Stoic philosophy (17–18). So even apart from Psyche, Orual experiences a general witness.

But it is chiefly through Psyche that the epiphanies take place. Orual loved (or thought she loved) Psyche, and Psyche's beauty and goodness were constant witnesses to her. Psyche was the first Christian in her tribe, and a glorious one at that, but Orual failed to look beyond her toward the god of the mountain, the brightest spot in Psyche's life (76). The at times overpowering, yet suppressed, supernatural force on Orual's existence keeps manifesting itself. When Psyche, in the palace prison and facing death, ironically repeats the Fox's fairtime philosophy about accepting misfortune, Orual says that it then "seemed to me so light, so far away from our sorrow. I felt we ought not to be talking that way, not now." Then she adds, "What I thought it would be better to talk of, I did not know" (69).

Then comes a series of overwhelming witnesses. The first is that the rain, the need for which was the cause of Psyche's sacrifice, actually followed that sacrifice. The fields were wet, the river refilled with water, the birds returned, and the people of Glome were happy in the belief that the gods had accepted their sacrifice and been placated.

Next comes Orual's finding of Psyche "alive" and looking healthier and happier than ever. Though Orual does not believe either in Psyche's palace or her loving husband, she sees before her an incontrovertible fact—her glorious sister full of life and warmth of welcome. And then, after their violent parting, Orual goes down at twilight to drink from the stream and momentarily, but truly, sees the palace. In her own words there it stood "solid and motionless, wall within wall, pillar and arch and architrave, acres of it, a labyrinthine beauty . . . like no house ever seen in our land or age. Pinnacles and buttresses leaped up . . . unbelievably tall and slender, pointed and prickly as if stone were shooting out into branch and flower" (132). Orual later stated her doubts about seeing the palace, but reading this account of its bulk and details one knows how she was fooling herself.

Another strong witness occurred on the second trip when Orual had won the victory over Psyche by commanding her to test her unseen husband and pledging her own suicide unless it was done. Yet promptly Orual was beset with the fear that she might have been wrong and that "a real god" is involved. She was terribly tempted to run back and stop what she had put into motion, but, she says, "I governed it" (169). What a difference had she succumbed.

For the Christian one of the great scenes of the book is what follows Psyche's forced testing of her husband. Lewis always wishes to say that "Aslan is not a tame lion," i.e., that there is another side to God than his love, and both aspects are clearly seen here. There is a great flash and thunder and lightnings and a vast flood. Then comes the voice that "even in its implacable sternness" was "golden." Her response, Orual says, is "the salute that mortal flesh gives to immortal things" (171). For a moment Orual experienced a theophany, the very face of God, and she said it was mainly the beauty, not the terror, that mastered her.

But now a new stage of both Psyche's and Orual's lives must begin, an oedipean wandering, particularly a wandering of the soul, day after day and year after year. The beginning of it is marked by "the passionless and measureless rejection" with which the face of God looked on her and a voice "unmoved and sweet, like a bird singing on the branch above a hanged man," said that Psyche was going out into exile and suffering, and then added, enigmatically, that "Orual shall be Psyche" (173–74).

Having undergone and successfully resisted the witness, Orual now begins to suffer the consequences. Yet one of those consequences is that God did not forsake her. The road back was a long, miserable road, and in many ways strikingly like the road taken by C. S. Lewis himself.

The story suggests two extreme sorts of response to God. One is that of Psyche herself. From earliest childhood her longing had been toward the mountain. Intuitively she believed she belonged there. She seemed natively to love and to possess religious virtues. She was born into a pagan home and a pagan city, yet she had a natural beauty of both body and soul. (All of us know of some pagan family today who produces a Psyche.) The other extreme type is represented by Orual, an instance of a person to whom God seemingly says, "I will have you, whether or no." St. Paul was such a man, and C. S. Lewis was another. At sixteen, Lewis wrote his boyhood friend Arthur Greeves of how God liked to get hold of some first-rate person and torture him with "cruelty after cruelty without any escape." He had nothing but contempt for "all the . . . tomfoolery about virgin birth, magic healings, apparitions, and so forth." After her experience beyond the mountain, Orual now realizes that the gods exist and, taking the anthropomorphic view, concludes that the gods hate her and intend to be revenged on her. She has heard that the gods sometimes turn men into beasts, so she puts her hand up to see if she can feel cat's fur or hog's tusks beginning to grow on her face (175). But her wounds are of another sort, the kind that most men are acquainted with.

For one thing, she says she went over the religious view of things "thousands of times" (72). Yet forgetting the pathos of the face and the voice she experienced in the storm, she retains her hatred of the gods. Sometimes she pities herself (209). Other times she becomes very hard. She wishes for the death of her father (202). She hardens herself. She decides to destroy the Orual of the past by plunging into her duties as the new queen, and for awhile she is successful. She kills a man in a duel. Meantime she concludes to hide her ugly face under a lifetime veil. Have we not seen people wearing this sort of veil, indeed have we not ourselves worn such a veil? Orual's experience proves it cannot hide her from God but only, in part, from the people around her.

She comes to wonder who "sends us this senseless repetition of days and nights and seasons and years" and feels it is "like hearing a stupid boy whistle the same tune over and over, till you wonder how he can bear it himself" (236). What a contrast this is with the Green Lady in *Perelandra*, who accepts at God's hand each day as a precious new gift, the best day of all. Orual does succeed in gaining a brief period of happiness, about the time she knows she is in love with Bardia and when she for a little appears to succeed in killing the old Orual (222).

Interestingly, once Orual falls down seriously before the gods and prays to them (150). There is no response. Yet she confesses that she came "without a sacrifice" and also requiring of the gods a sign. What a stroke of genius with which Lewis handles this experience of Orual's. There was a sign, not a new sign but a repetition of one of the clearest signs Orual had experienced of the gods. Had she not been warmly conscious that the dread drought ceased and the birds returned after Psyche's sacrifice on the mountain? She says that all the time she lay on the floor asking the gods for a sign there was rain on the roof. Rain, often a symbol in the Bible of God's presence and care, was for Orual also a sign. We can imagine what results might have ensued if her very abject confession before the gods had had no strings attached. Even with the strings the sign was there all the time and actually heard by her, yet without any spiritual recognition. She was not yet able to get her eyes opened to an unbargaining God.

What was the underlying problem of Orual? It was something that I think Lewis understood almost as well as any person in history—understood and desperately feared. It was the insidiousness with which the self crawls into every single crevice of a man's being. In this respect Orual was a replica of pagan and Christian alike.

Orual was in most respects an excellent and admirable person. She was reasonable, enthusiastic, brave, friendly, progressive, and a lover of justice. She was an excellent queen, efficient and just. She would have made a good neighbor. She vigorously took Psyche's part when she thought her sister unjustly sacrificed by the people of Glome. She hated her father's rages and was desperately ashamed of his cowardice when the lots were drawn for the sacrificial victim for the city of Glome.

Orual's great defect was selfishness and selfishness masquerading under the perfectly serious mantle of love. Orual is Maia. In Hindu religion Maia means "illusion." Maia is also "nature" or what Christians would call "the natural man." Almost from the moment of Psyche's birth, Orual loved her deeply, and as Psyche grew up she and Orual and the Fox spent deliriously happy days together. After Psyche's sacrifice on the mountain the world for Orual was like "a dead desert" (88). The trouble arose the moment it appeared that Psyche was to be lost to another (104). The Fox himself has to tell Psyche on one occasion that she hates, rather than loves, her sister. "There's one part love in your heart, and five parts anger, and seven parts pride," he tells her (148). Orual's agitated attitude that Psyche must not be sacrificed is in some respects like that of the disciples who told Christ that he must not go to the Cross.

Through the long years of Orual's successful queenship there was little cessation of the calling. She was constantly reminded, much as she tried to avoid them, of little memories of the happy days of childhood. The rain on the roof always spoke to her. But the beginning of her real enlightenment of the evil self-defensive attitude appeared when Orual visited the little temple in the woods and, full of astonishment, heard her own story retold as a myth. She was nonplussed about the priest's account of how the Orual of the myth really saw the palace, as she had carefully hidden that part of her experience from everybody. The only conclusion she could draw was that the gods themselves had somehow implanted that fact in the myth (243). But the thing that really incensed her was the claim of the myth that she hated Psyche (242). She had not taken the earlier hints of this seriously, and now she promptly concluded, in her insulted state of mind, to write down her case against the gods. She felt that if that terrible story that she hated her sister had gone abroad while Orual was yet alive, she must correct it by assuring the world of the truth, that is, of her great love for Psyche. It was the door that opened up for Orual all the "terrors, humiliations, struggles, and anguish" of her life, and she wanted the real facts to be known.

On this note the first book concludes.

The second opens with the remark, "I must unroll my book again." A whole new element had loomed up. The thing that caused the second account was the writing down of her case against the gods (253).

Orual now began to sort out the threads of the tangle in her mind—to review the whole of her life with a different viewpoint. Sometimes the sorting took place in her dreams, and once she found herself "separating motive from motive and both from pretext" (256). It was like a vast pile of different kinds of seeds needing to be separated but could not be. Then the first great blow to Orual's pride came in the form of a real event. Bardia died, and Orual went to comfort his widow and made the horrendous discovery that her love-hate of Bardia had destroyed him. Ansit told her, "Your queenship drank up his blood year by year and ate out his life." When Orual remonstrated and asked why Ansit never told her this, she answered that he was a soldier and she must not "make him so mine that he was no longer his." Note the double meaning here of (1) Orual's selfishness and (2) the way of God, who wants each man a free agent living the particular and peculiar life he has bestowed on him, rather than an automaton. (Psyche also loved Bardia but, like Ansit, she never thought of "devouring" him.) Orual now for the first time realizes that she is a destroyer of freedom in people's lives, that, like the legend of the Shadowbrute, the loving and devouring are all one.

"And now," says Orual, "those divine Surgeons [Lewis capitalizes the word] had me tied down and were at work." She had to confess to herself that in reality she hated Bardia. "A love like that," she said, "can grow to be nine-tenths hatred and still call itself love" (266). But to be able to see and say such a thing as that meant that now Orual was clearly on the right way. She was in position to get a new and correct view of the way things really are. Mainly she simply came to the end of herself. Thereafter she was "drenched with seeings." In his autobiography, Lewis tells how his "Adversary [God] began to make His final moves."[151] Later he adds, "Amiable agnostics will talk cheerfully about 'man's search for God.' To me, as I then was, they might as well have talked about the mouse's search for the cat."[152]

One thing Orual discovered is that people really are helped and made happy by the ancient and bloody Ungit, not the clean and pretty one set up by Arnom. Then she experiences the vision of her descent down through one Pillar Room after another until finally she comes all the way down to "living rock," where she must stand and see herself as she really is. She knows now that she has indeed been Ungit, "that all-devouring womblike, yet barren, thing." Under the burden of these things, she concludes to kill herself, but at the moment of flinging herself into the river, Shennit, a god, speaks to her. Even in her desperate intent to commit suicide, she is now on the way to God. The rebel in her is now gone, and she finds herself a "cold, small, helpless thing," a necessary condition to any real progress. "Die before you die. There is no chance after," says the god (279). Psyche had long

---

151 *Surprised by Joy*, 205.
152 Ibid., 214.

before told Orual, "If I am to go to the gods, of course it must be through death" (72), and I think it is not wholly out of place here to believe, looking back, that Psyche meant death to self.

But still Orual has a way to go. Her next step is self-reformation based on the Fox's philosophy. She fails. Fate, she believes, is against her. It is at this point that she has the vision of the rams of the gods whose "gladness" injures her. God will have no mere reformation. There is a way to successfully get the Golden Fleece—a way made apparent when Orual sees another woman able to procure it—to procure it from "the thorns" and thus win it without any effort.

Orual's last great stronghold is still to be destroyed. Of one great fact she has been sure: her love for Psyche. Now she has the vision of going into the Deadlands and finding there her father, the Fox, Batta, and others. In this judgment hall she is ordered by a veiled figure to read her lifelong complaint against the gods, but it does not work out at all as she expected. As she makes her complaint she discovers that she really preferred Psyche dead to Psyche made immortal (291). "She was mine. Mine!" the complaint said. The gods, she charged, are "a tree in whose shadow we can't thrive. We want to be our own. I was my own and Psyche was mine and no one else had any right to her. . . . You stole her to make her happy." She continues to read her complaint over and over (have you not known someone exactly like this?) until finally the judge stops her. He asks, "Are you answered?" and she says, "Yes."

Then we have that great page in the novel on which Orual confesses, "The complaint was the answer. . . . I saw well why the gods do not speak to us openly, nor let us answer. Till that word can be dug out of us, why should they hear the babble that we think we mean? How can they meet us face to face till we have faces?" (294).

But now, as in any good courtroom, the defendants must answer the plaintiff. The gods have been called into court. Orual fearfully asks the Fox what is likely to happen to her. In reply the Fox says that "whatever else you get, you will not get justice" (297). "Are the gods not just?" Orual asks. "Oh no, child," is the answer. "What would become of us if they were?" (297).

In the last beautiful and powerful portion of the story Orual finds not the justice but the love of the gods. By means of living pictures Orual learns of another attitude and another response toward the gods, mostly through seeing Psyche's means of sorting the seeds, acquiring the Golden Fleece, and filling the bowl with the water of death. When she asks how she could do such things and be happy, the answer is "Another bore nearly all the anguish." There seem to be at least two meanings here. One is that Love bore the anguish. Another is that in suffering Orual discovered the anguish of God over one lost to him, as Psyche seemed to be lost to Orual. God is jealous for what is truly his own (301). Orual learns that the cry of foolish men for heavenly justice is not at all a cry for justice but a mere muttering and whining.

Orual's "seeings" have now brought her almost full circle. Having discovered the nature of Love himself, she is prepared for the last great vision of Psyche going into the Deadlands to bring back the casket of beauty from "death herself." This trip illustrates the many-sidedness of myth as Lewis sees it. It has at least three important aspects. It is the token of Psyche's unswerving obedience to her husband. In Apuleius, Psyche, on the brink of success in her trip to and from Hades, failed because at the last moment her curiosity and the wish to have a little of the beauty in the casket for herself overcame her. Not so with Lewis's Psyche. Here she refuses to listen to the voices crying to her to take care and to return to safety and goes straightforward to the completion of her task. Orual herself was one who cried, "Come back. Come back." And now Orual discovers her own terrible mistake in the two visits she had paid to Psyche long before. But there is a third and significant overtone of another "descent into hell" in which by obedience to the point of bloody hands, feet, and side, an ineffable beauty was brought back to men. Like Orual, the reader at this point in the story is himself "drenched with seeings," and is as overjoyed as Orual herself at the glorious appearing of Love himself to replace her lifetime ugliness with a heavenly beauty.

Such, I think, is the main interpretation of this Christian myth. To state the entire implications of the story would mean, I think, to write a book larger than Lewis's.

The place of the Fox in the story is clearer than anything else, I think. For him nature and reason are "the whole," with allowances also for "custom" (85, 87). The gods are in nature. The Fox believes in the gods after the fashion of an "enlightened" man. They may be good for ignorant people, but after all he comes into Glome as an "expert" from abroad, as the man with the last word in philosophy and ethics. Finally he has to confess that his philosophy was as clear, but also as thin, as water. There is also the telling fact in his rationalism that it breaks down frequently when his heart is moved. The Fox seems to be Lewis's old tutor, the Great Knock, who was a logician and an atheist but who nevertheless on Sundays put on a nicer suit than usual in which to go out and do his gardening. One must not miss the significant postscript to the book, which says that the whole account was intended for the Greeks to read, that is, people today who are like the Fox.

I think the place of Ungit in the story is also very clear, at least in its main theme. Ungit's house is said to resemble "the egg from which the whole world was hatched" (94). This is obviously another allusion to Lewis's belief concerning the meaning of myth. Here it primarily means that pagan myths are often involved with blood sacrifices, and this Lewis explains is owing to an initial revelation to all nations of the essential nucleus of a theme that was made finally and fully clear in the incarnation and crucifixion of Jesus Christ. In the sweet-smelling little temple Orual found in the forest it was not blood that was sacrificed but flowers and fruit, if indeed there was any sacrifice at all. The difference between Ungit and the woodland temple was the difference between the sacrifices of Cain and Abel. Even in Glome, pagan as it was, the blood in some mysterious way "worked."

A troublesome element in the story is the "transformations" that keep appearing. The people of Glome say that as healer Psyche is Ungit and they worship her (32). Orual tells Psyche that she has always been her father and mother and kin—"and all the King too" that Psyche has ever had (158). "You also shall be Psyche," says the god to Orual (174). I think that one way at least in which Orual became Psyche was the long years in which Orual suffered the memory and the pain of her injury to Psyche. Without going into detail, we can perhaps best explain this element in the story by reference to the teachings of Charles Williams, Lewis's close friend, on co-inherence and substitution. Behind this conception is the idea that the world is inevitably a unity and therefore that men, made in the image of God, are capable of knowing and indeed undergoing the joys and sorrows of another. The most striking illustration of it in Lewis is the fact that for a period he took the pain from his wife's cancerous thigh and suffered while at the same time she was relieved of her pain.[153] The great co-inherence is suggested by a poem of Lewis's two lines of which run, "Nearly they stood who fall" and "Nearly they fell who stand."[154] How close Orual came to "standing" that time when she was all but overpowered with the idea of rushing back to Psyche and canceling the promise of Psyche to "test" her husband.

153 *Light on C. S. Lewis*, 63.
154 *Poems*, 102.

Bardia seems to be given us not only to show another instance of Orual's devouring but also to show the sort of man who might be found walking down most any street or even in churches. He is a Stoic, a man who "does his duty" (90) but, though a "god-fearing man" (99), really manages to leave the gods alone. He readily remembers the saying in Glome that "beyond the Tree, it's all gods' country" (100), but it is a saying, not a reality, to him. That belief is part of the mythology of Glome and illustrates Lewis's conception of how myth becomes encrusted with "filth," for Bardia and all the people of Glome had quite literally "brutalized" "the gods' country" by substituting a Shadowbrute for what Psyche and finally Orual knew to be the land of Love himself. (If we do not accept God, we tend to brutalize him.) Bardia is a prudent, courteous, hard-working, duty-fulfilling man (69) who gives the gods their due and otherwise steers clear of them.

Redival, by the way, is apparently the selfish, lustful worldling more concerned about "getting and spending" and a good time than anything else. Ungit means nothing to her. The interesting thing is that the resentful and hateful Orual, the rebel who vigorously makes her case against the gods, is the one who comes through, not Redival.

Finally we can say a word about the Apuleius myth that Lewis took as a source. There are clear agreements in Lewis and clear differences, and it makes an interesting study to examine them. In Apuleius we have a king with three daughters, the youngest worshiped as a goddess, a fact that makes Venus jealous and causes her to punish Psyche. An oracle in the old myth requires the exposing of Psyche to a kind of beast, and Psyche is then rescued by Westwind and carried, by prearrangement, to Cupid. Cupid requires Psyche not to see him as he visits her each night. The two other sisters come, see her beautiful palace, and become envious.

They persuade her to look on and be prepared to slay her lover. As punishment for this act, Psyche is forced to wander away, is captured by Venus, and put to impossible tasks such as sorting seeds, getting the Golden Fleece, and acquiring water from the lower world. The river Styx is common in Greek myth as the main river of Hades and to be crossed at death. Lewis changes the myth to suit his own Christian purpose. He makes much more of the sorting of the seeds, and particularly he has Orual on her visit get only that one fateful but sure glimpse of the palace of Psyche. In Apuleius Psyche gets herself in trouble by opening the casket of beauty, as I have mentioned already.

My present reading of the story has suggested to me all over again something of its almost unlimited mythic quality. There seems to be hardly a page—sometimes hardly a sentence—that has not its overtone about which one must ask, "Is there something else here?" For instance, the unseen lover of Psyche suggests more or less the whole relationship between the Christian and Christ. Though unseen, he is our great love and worthy of the test to "forsake all others." Even the sexual relation, as Bible students well know, is one of the important metaphors of the New Testament. Also this whole palace picture often suggests the glories of heaven as seen in the book of Revelation and the final goal of the Christian as the bride of the Lamb, as Psyche herself suggests the perfection of the church, "without spot or wrinkle."

One characteristic of a great book, said Mortimer J. Adler, is that it will not let you down if you try to read it well. By this standard I think that *Till We Have Faces* is surely a great book.

SECTION 2

J. R. R. TOLKIEN ON STORY AND THE POWER OF MYTH

Chapter 13

INITIAL ENCOUNTERS WITH J. R. R. TOLKIEN

Dr. Kilby acted as a tireless apologist for C. S. Lewis over many years. One of his main goals was to persuade evangelical Christians to read a pipe-smoking Anglican Oxford professor of whom they might be inclined to be suspicious—especially since (as Kilby was increasingly convinced) it was Lewis's imaginative works, even more than his theological and apologetic works, that were important. His relationship with the work of Tolkien was significantly different. To begin with it came much later. He does mention reading The Hobbit *at an early date, but the full* Lord of the Rings *wasn't published till 1957, and when I first heard Dr. Kilby refer to the works (in his Romantic poetry class in 1962), I had the distinct impression he didn't know them well yet, and they were a very minor part of the evening discussion group in the spring of 1964. The books were not well-known and were still hard to find.*

There was one set in the Wheaton Library, and I read The Fellowship of the Ring *in the spring of 1964. It ends with Frodo and Sam setting off alone toward Mordor, Pippin and Merry captured, and things looking very grim indeed. But the next two volumes were checked out, and there were no others to be found in stores or libraries. I went with the track team then on a spring trip to several southern colleges. When we got to a campus I would go immediately to the library to see if they had* The Lord of the Rings. *Alas, though most had Tolkien's early work* Beowulf: The Monster and the Critics, *none had the Rings story. Later that year I ordered eighteen hardback sets from Blackwell's in Oxford and sold them to interested students and faculty. Not till late in 1965 did the first paperback editions come out.*

But things changed quickly. I recall going along with Kilby to dinner at a graduate couple's apartment at the University of Chicago. They had discovered Tolkien and were eager to talk about him. The common interest here was not Christianity: it was Tolkien. As Kilby describes below, he met Tolkien in the summer of 1965, struck up a remarkable friendship, and spent the following summer (of 1966) with him in Oxford trying (unsuccessfully) to help bring The Silmarillion *to publication. The experience gave him a unique connection with Tolkien and his great story, and so he became much sought after as a speaker at fantasy conferences and the emerging Tolkien fan clubs. I remember going with Kilby and Glenn Sadler to a science fiction conference in Milwaukee where Kilby was a featured speaker. (Later we descended to the basement of the Marquette University library, where we looked at their seven-foot store of Tolkien manuscripts.) In such settings Kilby was no longer trying to persuade Christians that they ought to read fantasy; he was gently suggesting to a largely pagan and increasingly countercultural audience that the fantasy they loved had deep Christian roots.*

It was of course necessary to persuade Christians of this as well; for many, the widespread enthusiasm of pot-smoking flower children for The Lord of the Rings *was reason to be suspicious. That perhaps explains why the InterVarsity magazine* His *(to which Kilby was a frequent contributor) did not publish the following review until 1969.*

The interest in J. R. R. Tolkien's writings appears to be as strong as ever (my own arising when I read *The Hobbit*). Evidence is growing that Tolkien, C. S. Lewis, and Charles Williams will be grouped together as the "Oxford Christians." A 1966 dissertation by Mariann B. Russell at Columbia U. asserts the idea that these three men "shared a belief that the thrill of adventure stories could be related to Christian theology." She points out that though Tolkien's works are not specifically Christian oriented, there is undoubtedly an archetypal pattern of Christianity in them. This position is generally true of all the larger studies of Tolkien. Most emphatic of all is Dorothy E. K. Barber in her 1965 dissertation at U. of Michigan. She writes that the basis of *Lord of the Rings* is "the metaphor 'God is light.' . . . The story tells us how omniscient Good inevitably triumphs over deluded Evil." Darkness and light run their symbolic way throughout the story just as they do in the Scriptures and in men's lives.

Then also in *Lord of the Rings*, the nature of the quest seems to have Christian overtones. When the diminutive Frodo faces the hardships ahead, he insists that he's not the type for such things and asks, "Why was I chosen?" After he learns that it's not because of any special merit of his, he goes out to meet the perils, convinced that he's "called." If at all possible, he wants to destroy the evil that besets Middle-earth. He moves from one trial to another and discovers that if he's not to fail, he must command his will and dedicate himself. He never allows his longing for the easy ways or the peace of the Shire to change the intensity of his struggle. Yet he always seems aware, especially in times of unusual stress, that a more than natural help is available to him. He carries the One Ring with him, which is his source, if he chooses to use it, of almost unlimited power, and yet at the same time it's a token to him of his deliverance from evil.

Frodo may easily be seen as something of a Christ figure when he struggles up Mount Doom, where the One Ring will be destroyed forever. "There is no veil between me and the wheel of fire," he says. There where the price was a little less than death itself, he accomplished an earth-changing victory and afterward was rewarded by an apocalyptic happiness.

The war of Middle-earth grew out of the evil that originated during the First Age, when one of the angelic spirits revolted and brought destruction on the world. In the Second Age, another evil wish turned men into gods and they gained everlasting life unworthily and thus caused the destruction of Númenor from which only a few chosen people were saved.

A graduate student in a state university wrote that he had found *Lord of the Rings* the best reading of his entire life and wished he'd discovered the book in his teens so that he could have experienced what he described as its "therapeutic value." A mother wrote of first devouring the story while recuperating from the birth of a son and how she bewildered and alarmed her doctor and family by her strange references to black riders, elves, and orcs. For her the story illumined "the nature of reality, the glorious and tragic dimensions of the struggle between good and evil." "You," she wrote Tolkien, "have made courage and commitment and honor more meaningful." A young businessman in Oxford told me that he regarded this story as his "Bible" and that when he was confused and discouraged he went home and read from the book and was restored in mind and spirit.

My own experience in working with Professor Tolkien for a summer convinced me that though the story as he insists must not be read as allegory, nevertheless it has strong Christian overtones.

Thomas de Quincey pointed out that all true literature becomes "a Jacob's ladder from earth to mysterious altitudes above the earth" where only the dullest reader will not find meaning unlimited, and it is this sort of idea that gives credence to Guy Davenport's remark concerning *Lord of the Rings*: "For a generation that can't make head or tail of St. Paul, Mr. Tolkien has got Isaiah and St. Paul back before readers' eyes."

In a word, then, we're justified in feeling, as sensitive readers of this story always do, a deep religious, even Christian undertone. But it should be added that it is a story to be enjoyed, not a sermon to be preached.

Chapter 14

MYTHIC AND CHRISTIAN ELEMENTS IN *THE LORD OF THE RINGS*

The first point Kilby makes in this long and carefully thought article is not controversial, for the "mythic" character of Tolkien's story is beyond doubt. Nevertheless, Kilby's precise application of Mircea Eliade's discussion of myth—as a longing to live in "Great Time"—is illuminating. (What is ironic in the discussion is that now, half a century later, it is probably the case that Tolkien's story has done more than Eliade's analysis to focus our understanding of myth.)

But as Kilby makes plain in the first sentence, he was reluctant to disagree with his friend about the Christian elements in The Lord of the Rings. *But disagree he does, and Kilby's careful and detailed reflection makes a convincing case that, while never lapsing into allegory,* The Lord of the Rings *is still, on the mythic level, a profoundly Christian work.*

I am aware that my intention in this chapter is at once up against the stone wall of Professor Tolkien's denial that the story has any direct or allegorical implications. The story, says he, is "not 'about' anything but itself" and certainly "has *no* allegorical intentions, general, particular or topical, moral, religious or political." He declares in fact that he has a "cordial dislike" of allegory, and he says he began *The Lord of the Rings* just to amuse himself. To him it is "largely an essay in 'linguistic aesthetic,'" in which the story was made "to provide a world for the languages rather than the reverse."[1] Since hardly a page of this story can be read without clear and often momentous moral overtones, one seems to have little choice but to declare either that the author is really pulling one's leg or else to say with Edmund Wilson, a sworn foe of the story, that any pretensions to serious meaning in it is "all on the part of Dr. Tolkien's infatuated admirers."[2]

In view of this seeming impasse between my stated subject and Professor Tolkien's objections to such a subject, I should like for a moment simply to overleap his objections and later return to them.

For what I believe to be the most comprehensive account of myth I turn to Mircea Eliade's *Cosmos and History*. Eliade identifies as the leading characteristic of myth "a revolt against concrete, historical time" and a "nostalgia for a periodical return to the mythical time of the beginning of things, to the 'Great Time.'" Archaic or mythic man takes the long view and endeavors, by what Eliade calls "paradigmatic gestures," to live not in ordinary time but recapture the golden time. Man remembers somehow a period of such beauty, glory, elemental purity, utter freshness, and Edenic joy that "neither the objects of the external world nor human acts, properly speaking, have any autonomous intrinsic value. Objects or acts acquire a value, and in so doing become real, because they participate, after one fashion or another, in a reality that transcends them." Hence ordinary time—the sort identified with newspapers and the passing scene—have little interest. The true reality is that of a Golden Age that has long since disappeared, an age toward which the deepest yearning of the heart is turned, a true and trustworthy Reality that strongly

1 "Tolkien on Tolkien," *Diplomat*, October 1966, 39.
2 "Oo, Those Awful Orcs," *The Nation*, April 14, 1956, 312.

contrasts with the relative triviality of current events, the "getting and spending" of life. Mythic man is concerned with being rather than with mere living.

All the more stirring portions of *The Lord of the Rings* seem to be quite a perfect illustration of Eliade's characterization of myth. To make a simple hierarchal arrangement of peoples in Tolkien's story is itself to suggest the transcendent and mythic quality. On the bottom rung are the orcs and debased Gollum, creatures of the here-and-now who are filled with loathing for light and for anything originating in Lothlorien, such as Lembas, the Westernesse-made knives of Merry and Pippin, the very name Elbereth, and the like. At a much higher level are the hobbits, who recall their intricate genealogical connections and the quiet joys of the Shire. Again, the dwarves recall Durin, their first-age ancestor and the ancient glories of Moria where

> Beneath the mountains music woke:
> The harpers harped, the minstrels sang,
> And at the gates the trumpets rang.[3]

As with the dwarves, the vision of men is a long one. Sam and Frodo noted its far reach when at Henneth Annun in the woods of Ithilien, Faramir and his men before meals looked "towards Númenor that was, and beyond to Elvenhome that is, and to that which is beyond Elvenhome and will ever be."[4]

But it is the elves whose hearts are unceasingly aware of their ancient and transcendent past when "the secret fire was sent to burn at the heart of the world." King Theoden asked Gandalf about the "wizardry" by which the trees had destroyed Saruman's fortress. "It is not wizardry," said Gandalf, "but a power far older, a power that walked the earth, ere elf sang or hammer rang,"

3 *The Fellowship of the Ring*, Bk. II, Ch. 4.
4 *The Two Towers*, Bk. IV, Ch. 5.

Ere iron was found or tree was hewn,
When young was mountain under moon;
Ere ring was made, or wrought was woe,
It walked the forests long ago."[5]

Treebeard informs Merry and Pippin that the early Elves were the Adam-namers.[6]

These allusions are mainly to the glory of early Middle-earth, but there are even more Edenic allusions to Valinor and the Blessed Realm. We are told that "all lore was in these latter days fallen from its fullness of old."[7] Earendil's experience is an instance of reverence for the deep past. In the First Age, Earendil, desperate for aid for his people against Morgoth, built a glorious rune-protected ship and sailed "beyond the days of mortal lands." Lost in starless waters, he was visited by Elwing, who bound on him one of the three silmarils, which had long before been created by Feanor (whose name means "Spirit of Fire") to hold the light of the golden and silver trees. With this light he retraced his way and finally came to Elvenhome, "the green and fair," where he was clothed in elven-white and sent inland through the Calacirian entrance to

. . . timeless halls
Where shining fall the countless years,
and endless reigns the Elder King.[8]

There in the Blessed Realm he heard such sacred words and saw such visions that he could not again return to Middle-earth, whereupon the undefiled dwellers in Ilmarin built a majestic ship for him, and Elbereth Gilthoniel, Queen of the Valar and maker

5 *The Two Towers*, Bk. III, Ch. 8.
6 The Two Towers, Bk. III, Ch. 4.
7 *The Return of the King*, Bk. V, Ch. 8.
8 *The Fellowship of the Ring*, Bk. II, Ch. 1.

of the stars, set the silmaril on that ship as an everlasting light and set him as a star to travel through the skies. Whenever the elves see that star they are poignantly reminded of a glory hardly of this world.

In Middle-earth, Rivendell and particularly Lothlorien are symbols of Eliade's "Paradise." "Time doesn't seem to pass here,"[9] said Bilbo of Rivendell, and Professor Tolkien told me that he could not reread his own account of Lothlorien without emotion. The elves are always reminded by Lothlorien, their paradisal land, of the true paradise of the Blessed Realm, and in turn the succor Lothlorien gives to the members of the Fellowship, and even its natural enemy Gimli, creates a blessedness that is ever after to remain warm, elevating, and enticing in their memory. Thus the recollection of sacred time that echoes in Lothlorien becomes a reecho in Gimli and the others. Galadriel's phial of light, taken from Earendil's star and redolent of a light existing even before that, and so utterly comforting and protective to Frodo and Sam as they move toward the dark terrors of Mordor, is perhaps the best symbol in *The Lord of the Rings* of Eliade's Great Time, for around the phial clings the whole glory of the Age of Gold when "heaven" was emptied of some of its angelic beings who voluntarily descended to Middle-earth for the establishment of a kingdom commensurate with a heavenly vision that had been shown them. That phial contained light created before the sun itself, a light first resident in Telperion and Nimloth, the two trees, white and golden, that belonged to a period of some sixty thousand years before and more properly are outside time altogether. Here is a thing that can be held in the hand that is essentially paradisal.

Eliade's "paradigmatic gesture" is illustrated by the quality and quantity of allusions to such elements as this phial of light, but far more so by the songs. There is a tendency to sing both in times

---

9 *The Fellowship of the Ring,* Bk. II, Ch. 1.

of great joy and times of great stress. There is singing in Rivendell and Lothlorien and also in the horror of Moria and the farewell to Lothlorien and "the lady that dies not." In the hell of Mordor the songs, yet not altogether the memories, disappear for Frodo and Sam, yet after Orodruin and rescue the songs begin again. The truth is that Tolkien's world is arched with timelessness and thickset with a glory, a timelessness and glory felt by each member of the Fellowship but particularly poignant for the elves. Lovers of the story feel as if it is a thing not so much to be read as to be sung. It is a story of the movement from eternity to time and therefore of sadness. It is a book of infinite losses, of cosmic diminution, of paradise lost, and yet not without its *eucatastrophe* and *evangelium.*

Some of the most poignant turns of the story are those in which certain elves must decide between sacred and profane time, as in the case of Arwen Evenstar. The sad parting of the Fellowship at the end of the story is made far sadder by the farewell of Arwen Evenstar and her father after Arwen, for love of Aragorn, had chosen profane time. Arwen's general farewell was public, but her last meeting with her father Elrond, who belonged to sacred time, was private. "None saw her last meeting with Elrond her father, for they went up into the hills and there spoke long together, and bitter was their parting that should endure beyond the ends of the world."[10] Arwen's choice of profane time repeated the long previous love choice of another elf for a man, that is, of Melian the Maia, who filled the silence of Arda before the dawn with her voice. Thingol came upon her dancing in Nan Elmoth, loved her so much that they stood hand in hand for long years, and together they became the rulers of the Grey Elves.

I must now leave this meager illustration of *The Lord of the Rings* as myth in Eliade's sense and pass along to the main idea I wish to stress—that of the story as essentially a Christian narrative.

10 *The Return of the King,* Bk. VI, Ch. 6.

One of the most obvious Christian intimations, as others have pointed out, arises in the two worlds depicted—one all but angelic, the other hellish. There is a Fellowship of the good and upright and a parallel "fellowship" of the evil. To be sure, the evil is a company fettered together by its diabolical leader Sauron—whose name is strongly suggestive of saurian or reptilian—but its members have the effect of working as a body with relatively little internecine struggle or opposition. We are told that Mordor "draws all wicked things" to itself.

The most dominant symbol of these two worlds is the contrast of darkness and light. Sauron is called the Black Hand, Black Master, Black One, Black Shadow, Dark Lord, Darkness, Dark Power, the Enemy, the Lord of the Black Lands, etc. The Tower of Ecthelion standing high above the topmost walls of Minas Tirith "shone out against the sky, glimmering like a spike of pearl and silver, tall and fair and shapely, and its pinnacle glittered as if it were wrought of crystals; and white banners broke and fluttered from the battlements."[11] Sauron's tower, on the other hand, rises "black, blacker and darker than the vast shades amid which it stood."[12] The white tree is the symbol of the ancient Blessed Realm. White clothing is nearly always a symbol of goodness in the wearer, while the black robes of the Ringwraiths clearly identify their stealth and perpetual evil. At the Ford of Bruinen the black horses of the Ringwraiths contrast with the transcendent whiteness of Glorfindel's horse, which carries Frodo to safety. The same transcendency identifies Glorfindel himself, who is, we learn, one of the mighty of the Firstborn who had once dwelled in the Blessed Land.[13] Hardly is there a more dreadful picture in all of *The Lord of the Rings* than Shelob coming out of her black hole under a cliff with her great swollen body blotched with livid spots, her stinking

11 *The Return of the King*, Bk. V, Ch. 1.
12 *The Return of the King*, Bk. VI, Ch. 3.
13 *The Fellowship of the Ring*, Bk. II, Ch. 2.

belly, and her knobbly, hairy legs and claws.[14] What could save the diminutive hobbits from such an enemy? Not strength or ingenuity but the remembrance that they carry on their person the phial of light given them by Galadriel in heavenly Lothlorien. When they thrust this phial before the evil cluster of Shelob's eyes, it created a terror she had never experienced before, "the dreadful infection of light." Afterward the hobbits recollected that it was light from the Blessed Realm, a light to light them "in dark places, when all other lights go out."[15] The giver was Galadriel, "the Lady that dies not," and who bore about her a glory reminding one of the luminosity of Dante's Beatrice or of his image of the Virgin.

The light of sun, moon, and stars is hated by the orcs and other evil characters but loved by the good ones. Gollum looks up at the moon and blinks and says it is a "nassty, nassty, shivery light" that spies on him. The orcs travel at night because of their hatred of the sun, and Mordor is represented as a place where dark clouds often hover near the ground. The utter darkness of Moria and of the Barrows has a potency like that of Hades, which Job described as "a land of darkness, as darkness itself . . . where the light is as darkness."[16] The good people in *The Lord of the Rings* love light. Completely alone and feeling totally forsaken inside Mordor, Sam slips away from the sleeping Frodo to reconnoiter and, happening to look beyond the dark and treacherous mountain above him, saw a white star twinkling. "The beauty of it smote his heart . . . and hope returned to him. For like a shaft, clear and cold, the thought pierced him that in the end the Shadow was only a small and passing thing: there was light and high beauty for ever beyond its reach."[17] He returned to Frodo calm and hopeful and fell into an untroubled sleep. Earlier Sam, remembering the history of their

14 *The Two Towers,* Bk. IV, Ch. 9.
15 *The Fellowship of the Ring,* Bk. II, Ch. 8.
16 Job 10:22.
17 *The Return of the King,* Bk. VI, Ch. 2.

phial of light, said to Frodo, "We're in the same tale still," a suggestion of their solemn connection with ancient and sacred history. *The Lord of the Rings* is a story in which fixed and eternal things accommodate themselves to all the principal actions.

Again, the quest itself has the earmarks of a Christian dedication. When Frodo at the beginning of the story learns from Gandalf something of the dangers, he says: "I am not made for perilous quests. . . . Why was I chosen?"[18] It is the same question asked by Ransom when faced by the devil-possessed Unman in C. S. Lewis's *Perelandra.* And the same answer is given to Frodo and Ransom. To Frodo it was said, "You may be sure that it was not for any merit that others do not possess: not for power or wisdom, at any rate. But you have been chosen, and you must therefore use such strength and heart and wits as you have." Later at the Council of Elrond, Frodo, knowing now from his experience at Weathertop the malignancy of the Ringwraiths and learning the full magnitude of the task before him, quietly and "as if some other will was using his small voice," said, "I will take the Ring, though I do not know the way."[19]

That there is some superordinating power over Frodo and his friends is often suggested. There is a force "beyond any design" of Sauron, says Gandalf, as he explains the history of the Ring to Frodo. Bilbo, he says, "was *meant* to find the Ring," and therefore Frodo was also "*meant* to have it."[20] Elrond tells those present at the council that though they are seemingly there by chance, it is not actually so. "It is so ordered that we, who sit here, and none others, must now find counsel for the peril of the world."[21] A little later Aragorn tells Frodo pointedly that "it has been ordained" that he should hold the Ring.[22] Proud Boromir is a believer in strength

---

18 *The Fellowship of the Ring,* Bk. I, Ch. 2.
19 *The Fellowship of the Ring,* Bk. II, Ch. 2.
20 *The Fellowship of the Ring,* Bk. I, Ch. 2.
21 *The Fellowship of the Ring,* Bk. II, Ch. 2.
22 *The Fellowship of the Ring,* Bk. II, Ch. 2.

and power and finds it hard to understand Frodo's assurance that they must not trust "in the strength and truth of men."[23] Like MacPhee in C. S. Lewis's *That Hideous Strength*, Boromir thinks that in a time of great trouble it is foolish to wait for supernatural guidance and help. Though Tolkien feels that the Christian element in Lewis is too explicit, one finds frequent parallels in which the evil is hardly less transparent in Tolkien's story. In both a sovereign Good is constantly and consistently operative.

I have already mentioned the search for Christ images in modern literature. They are by no means infrequent in *The Lord of the Rings*. For instance, Gandalf's struggle with the fiery Balrog, a denizen of deepest and darkest underground, as both fall into a bottomless chasm, is strongly suggestive of Christ's descent into hell, and after Gandalf's resurrection—it is plainly called a resurrection—the Fellowship gazed on him with something of the same astonished joy that Mary Magdalene and others found at the tomb of Christ. Gandalf's hair, we are told, was "white as snow in the sunshine; and gleaming white was his robe; the eyes under his deep brows were bright, piercing as the rays of the sun; power was in his hand."[24] Gimli the dwarf sank to his knees and shaded his eyes from Gandalf's brightness. Later we learn that Gandalf is "filled with light," his head is "now sacred,"[25] he is a healer, does not require armor in battle, etc. We learn also that a whole year would not be sufficient for him to tell of his struggle with the Balrog underneath the earth.[26] It is sufficient that Gandalf says he has "no lasting abode"[27] in the earth, also that there has never been a day when he and other "wanderers" of the world have not guarded the Shire with watchful eyes.

I do not find it difficult to see as Christ symbols Frodo's

23 *The Fellowship of the Ring*, Bk. II, Ch. 10.
24 *The Two Towers*, Bk. III, Ch. 5.
25 *The Two Towers*, Bk. III, Ch. 5.
26 *The Two Towers*, Bk. III, Ch. 5.
27 *The Return of the King*, Bk. VI, Ch. 7.

commitment at Rivendell and most of his and Sam's journey after leaving their friends, and particularly the desperate journey through Mordor, the climax of that journey on Mount Doom, the sacrifice of life they expect to make, and the unexpected triumph and fruits of victory. Take as an instance Frodo's remark to Sam as they make the last struggle across the pits of Gorgoroth and up Orodruin and Frodo comes more and more under the burden of the Ring. He says to Sam, "No taste of food, no feel of water, no sound of wind, no memory of tree or grass or flower, no image of moon or star [note that now not even the stars can help] are left to me. I am naked in the dark, Sam, and there is no veil between me and the wheel of fire."[28] Does this not suggest something of the desperation that at least *we* feel as we go through the events of the last day or so of Christ's life on earth? Frodo resists the protection of the One Ring, throws off his orc disguise, and goes straightforward to his destiny. It seems to me that Frodo's last momentary determination not to destroy the Ring has at least a little in it of Christ's cry from the cross, "My God, why hast thou forsaken me?" A further hint of such a suggestion is the fact that in the darkness on top of Orodruin not even Galadriel's phial can throw much light.[29] At the last moment as Frodo and Gollum teeter on the edge of the precipice, Sam catches a visionary glimpse of them standing like personifications of Good and Evil, Gollum a creature "filled with a hideous lust and rage" and Frodo "a figure robed in white" holding at its breast a wheel of fire.[30] Good overcomes Evil, but the struggle ends in a cosmic climax.

Yet after the struggle comes the Triumph, and the reader is deeply stirred by the—to use Tolkien's own significant word—*eucatastrophe*. Sam and Frodo totter down to an ashen hill at the foot of Orodruin and there fall side by side to await death.

28 *The Return of the King*, Bk. VI, Ch. 3.
29 *The Return of the King*, Bk. VI, Ch. 3.
30 *The Return of the King*, Bk. VI, Ch. 3.

But then comes the "sent" eagles, and the faithful servants are picked up and carried away from the stench and the rivers of fire, and the next thing they know is a soft bed underneath beechen boughs glimmering green and gold through the lovely woods of Ithilien. Sam thought it was a dream but then discovered beside him Gandalf, "robed in white, his beard now gleaming like pure snow in the twinkling of the leafy sunlight." They learn that "the King" awaits them. Sam asks, "Is everything sad going to come untrue?" and is told yes.

> "A great Shadow has departed," said Gandalf, and then he laughed, and the sound was like music, or like water in a parched land; and as he listened the thought came to Sam that he had not heard laughter, the pure sound of merriment, for days upon days without count. It fell upon his ears like the echo of all the joys he had ever known. But he himself burst into tears.
>
> Then, as a sweet rain will pass down a wind of spring and the sun will shine out the clearer, his tears ceased, and his laughter welled up, and laughing he sprang from his bed.
>
> "How do I feel?" he cried. "Well, I don't know how to say it. I feel, I feel"—he waved his arms in the air—"I feel like spring after winter, and sun on the leaves; and like trumpets and harps and all the songs I have ever heard."[31]

The apocalyptic overtones of such a scene can hardly be avoided. But there is more.

The returning King they discover to have been their dear companion all the way, Aragorn the wandering ranger who has long guarded the world from dangers, who is believed to have strange powers of sight and hearing, who understands the languages of

31 *The Return of the King,* Bk. VI, Ch. 4.

beasts and birds and in other ways might symbolize the kingship and the omniscience, omnipotence and loving omnipresence of Christ. Aragorn has "taken back all his ancient realm. He will ride soon to his crowning."[32] When Frodo and Sam come into his presence, he at first gently recalls to them how they had originally disbelieved in him, but then he takes them by the hand, "Frodo upon his right and Sam upon his left," and leads them to his throne. There the two "nobodies" hear the "well-done" first of the King himself and then of all the people, and there is almost unspeakable joy.

> And all the host laughed and wept, and in the midst of their merriment and tears the clear voice of the minstrel rose like silver and gold, and all men were hushed. And he sang to them, now in Elven-tongue, now in the speech of the West, until their hearts, wounded with sweet words, overflowed, and their joy was like swords, and they passed in thought out to regions where pain and delight flow together and tears are the very wine of blessedness.[33]

The whole scene is evocative of the last pages of the Bible and also suggests St. Augustine's answer to a question that deeply perturbed him in his relationship to God:

> But what do I love, when I love Thee? not beauty of bodies, nor the fair harmony of time, nor the brightness of the light, so gladsome to our eyes, nor sweet melodies of varied songs, nor the fragrant smell of flowers, and ointments, and spices, not manna and honey, not limbs acceptable to the embracements of flesh. None of these I

---

32 *The Return of the King,* Bk. VI, Ch. 4.
33 *The Return of the King,* Bk. VI, Ch. 4.

> love, when I love my God; and yet I love a kind of light, and melody, and fragrance, and meat, embracement of my inner man: where there shineth unto my soul what space cannot contain, and there soundeth what time beareth not away, and there smelleth what breathing disperseth not, and there tasteth what eating diminisheth not, and there clingeth what satiety divorceth not. This is it which I love when I love my God.[34]

Since nothing less than the devilish enslavement of all Middle-earth to incarnate evil has been at stake, and since the meek and obedient have won the victory and inherited that earth, we feel that a poignant, epic, and indeed heavenly joy is appropriate.

But at the same time there hangs heavily over *The Lord of the Rings* the melancholy note of evil as an enduring fact. All three ages have seen devastating evil. When *The Silmarillion* is published it will be clear that Melkor, later called Morgoth, is nothing less than one of the angelic spirits who came into the world to make it after the pattern shown in "heaven" and who like Satan revolted and in due course enticed Sauron, another such angelic spirit, to become his servant in evil. In the Second Age the great revolt took place in Númenor and was engineered by Sauron, who had been brought to that lovely land as a prisoner. Both the cause and the result of the revolt are highly suggestive of biblical events. Sauron persuaded the Númenóreans that if they ignored the ban of the Valar and made their way over forbidden waters and once set foot on the shore of Aman the Blessed, they would be like the Valar and possess everlasting life.

The crime of the Númenóreans is very similar to that in Lewis's *That Hideous Strength*: it is nothing short of the intention of

34 Augustine, *Confessions*, translated by Edward B. Pusey (New York: Washington Square Press, Inc., 1962), 177.

turning men into gods. As a result of this revolt the island of Númenor was caused to sink into the sea. But, as with Noah, a few of the faithful are saved and make their way by ship from Númenor to Middle-earth and there establish themselves, finally, in such places as Rivendell and Lothlorien. Thus evil in *The Lord of the Rings* is cosmic and seemingly endless and will make forage of all good unless overcome by forces like those of the Fellowship and particularly by individuals committed as was Frodo. (The fact that the Fellowship consists of so varied a personnel as elves, dwarves, hobbits, and men is itself perhaps significant.)

Along with this continuing evil, however, comes always the possibility of redemption. The evil, in fact, clearly appears in people who were once good and therefore know the way back home. It is made completely clear that not even Morgoth and Sauron were evil in the beginning.[35] The tragedy of Saruman's great descent from membership in the White Council to a cackling lump of resentment and envy is sharp and strong in the story. But even in the moment of his lowest degradation when he makes an attempt upon Frodo's life, Frodo stops Sam from killing him. "He was great once," says Frodo, "of a noble kind that we should not dare to raise our hands against. He is fallen and his cure is beyond us; but I would still spare him, in the hope that he may find it."[36]

The Ringwraiths were once good men of Númenor who were enticed into Sauron's camp by a promise similar to that of Eden, i.e., the promise of knowledge.[37] In all these cases the compassion, I think, surpasses the norm of ordinary morality. It has the quality of mercy such as Portia calls "an attribute of God himself." When Frodo tells Gandalf that it was a pity Bilbo did not kill Gollum when he had the chance, Gandalf reprimands Frodo. "It was,"

35 *The Fellowship of the Ring*, Bk. II, Ch. 2..
36 *The Return of the King*, Bk. VI, Ch. 8.
37 *The Fellowship of the Ring*, Bk. I, Ch. 2.

says he, "Pity [note the capital] that stayed his hand. Pity, and Mercy: not to strike without need."[38] Frodo finally learns this Pity and practices it even after Gollum has spit in his face.

Again the conception of evil as having no essential being is remarkably suggested by the presentation of Sauron and his immediate henchmen as wraiths. We are told once that the horses the Ringwraiths ride are real but that the black robes worn by the Ringwraiths "give shape to their nothingness."[39] I have mentioned that Frodo took on ever so little the wraith-like quality by his use of the Ring at Weathertop. The skulking Gollum, we are told, is simply "the shadow of a living thing."[40]

In the same connection we can mention the inability of evil to create anything but only to mock. In the First Age it was believed that Morgoth captured some of the elves newly come into the world and slowly bred them into orcs in envy of the Eldar. This was regarded as one of his vilest deeds. He also made trolls in mockery of the Ents. Of the orcs, we are told, "The Shadow that bred them can only mock, it cannot make: not real new things of its own."[41] It did not give life to the orcs, "it only ruined them and twisted them." Philosophers and theologians have often noted the inessentiality of evil. C. S. Lewis says, "The Devil could *make* nothing but has *infected* everything."[42]

I think also that the element of will in the Tolkien story rises above that of simple Stoicism and takes on something at least of a Christian color. Frodo's heartfelt commitment to the cause does not save him and Sam from an increasing need to command their wills as they move deeper and deeper into enemy territory. Their whole way through Mordor is that of dedicated hearts careless of their own safety except as that safety pertains to the fulfilling of

38 *The Fellowship of the Ring*, Bk. I, Ch. 2.
39 *The Fellowship of the Ring*, Bk. II, Ch. 1.
40 *The Return of the King*, Bk. VI, Ch. 3.
41 *The Return of the King*, Bk. VI, Ch. 1.
42 *The Letters of C.S. Lewis* (London: Bles, 1966), 301.

their purpose. As they neared Mount Doom the weight of the Ring and the steadily increasing desire of Frodo to use it as a means of escape became a battleground in his inner parts and forced him over and over to will against the easy way. One of the powers of the Ring is by destroying selfhood to bring the user into the dominion of Sauron, to turn him from a being into a wraith. At Weathertop Frodo's use of the Ring to avoid his enemies had the effect of giving him a bare semblance of wraithness. One of the clear evidences of Frodo's increasing greatness of character is his steady will to resist incredible temptation in the face of growing physical weakness. St. Augustine's doctrine of the effective will is well illustrated by Frodo.

Echoes and overtones of a theistic, biblical world appear everywhere. Except for a reversal of the sexes, the marriage of elves and men suggests Genesis 6:4, where we are told that "the sons of God came in to the daughters of men, and they bore children to them." The long lives of certain characters in *The Lord of the Rings* suggest the biblical patriarchs. Elrond performs a miracle at the Ford of Bruinen by causing the waves of water to strike down the Ringwraiths who are upon Frodo,[43] and to further aid Frodo there appears a shining figure, Glorfindel, from "the other side," i.e., the Blessed Realm. There are prayers to "saints" like Elbereth Gilthoniel and Galadriel,[44] and Aragorn calls on the name of Elendil in the thick of the fight with the Balrog.[45] The lembas can easily be taken as a symbol of the Eucharist. The body of Sauron perished in the collapse of Númenor and he returned to Middle-earth as an evil spirit to lead and control other evil spirits,[46] the Ringwraiths, suggesting the "principalities" and "powers" and "the rulers of the darkness of this world" of Ephesians 6:12.

---

43 *The Fellowship of the Ring,* Bk. I, Ch. 12.
44 *The Fellowship of the Ring,* Bk. II, Ch. 1; *The Return of the King,* Bk. VI, Ch. 1.
45 *The Fellowship of the Ring,* Bk. II, Ch. 5.
46 *The Return of the King,* Appendix A, Part 1 (I.).

One clear contrast between Frodo and Sauron is perhaps best understood from a biblical viewpoint. Summing up the account of the people of faith, Hebrews 11:34 (Phillips translation) says, "From being weaklings they became strong men and mighty warriors," not an inept description of Frodo, who is just another hobbit who, like Sarah Smith of Golders Green in *The Great Divorce*, would hardly be noticed but who had greatness within. On the other hand, Sauron's empire, though powerful, has most of its trappings outward and therefore as subject to a total collapse, as was the giant Goliath when struck by the smooth stone of the youthful David.

The eagles that rescue Frodo and Sam at Orodruin must be seen, I think, either as a rather feeble example of the *deus ex machina* or else as a biblical symbol such as that of Exodus 19:4, where God said to Moses, "Have you seen what I did to the Egyptians, and how I bore you on eagles' wings and brought you to myself?" And I do not believe it is an accident that Tolkien in that moving account of the partings of the Fellowship has Arwen Evenstar take "a white gem like a star"[47] and hand it over to Frodo, the symbol of her rights to the Blessed Realm itself. This gem surely suggests Revelation 2:17: "To him that overcometh will I give . . . a white stone, and in the stone a new name written." That the rights of the stone eventuate is clear from that glorious passage in which Galadriel and Frodo's ship passes into the West, "until at last on a night of rain Frodo smelled a sweet fragrance on the air and heard the sound of singing that came over the water. And then it seemed to him that . . . the grey rain-curtain turned all to silver glass and was rolled back, and he beheld white shores and beyond them a far green country under a swift sunrise."[48] The beatific has finally reached a little hobbit who insisted that he was not made for perilous quests but who nevertheless followed the Grail.

47 *The Return of the King*, Bk. VI, Ch. 6.
48 *The Return of the King*, Bk. VI, Ch. 9.

And so we might go on, but now it is necessary to return to Professor Tolkien's insistence that *The Lord of the Rings* has "*no* allegorical intentions, general, particular or topical, moral, religious or political." Let me say a few things that may help to clarify.

First, Professor Tolkien is himself a devout Christian. My summer's experience with him convinced me both of his wide biblical interest and his deep convictions about sin and salvation through Christ. Once he showed me an unpublished paper by a British professor the idea of which was that *The Lord of the Rings* is misunderstood by critics because they failed to see that it is based on the manner of Christ's redemption of the world. To this Tolkien said, "Much of this is true enough—except, of course, the general impression given . . . that I had any such 'schema' in my conscious mind before or during writing." It was against this ticketed didacticism that Tolkien found it necessary to make his disclaimer. I think he was afraid that the allegorical dragon might gobble up the art and the myth.

Both Tolkien and Lewis have suggested their stories began with images of people rather than with ideas. Tolkien says that hobbits first came from nowhere to him as he was reading student papers. The beginning was no moral or sociological or even religious idea, but an image. When I raised the question of motive, Professor Tolkien said simply, "I am a Christian and of course what I write will be from that essential viewpoint." Lewis was sure that "the only moral that is of any value is that which arises inevitably from the whole cast of the author's mind." Many of Tolkien's remarks on the story suggest that, behind the scenes at least, there is a solid theistic world. He told Henry Resnick that the most moving point of the story for him is "when Gollum repents and tries to caress Frodo and he is interfered with by Sam." The tragedy is, he added, that "the good people so often upset the not-so-good people when they try to repent and it's a tragic moment."[49]

Second, one concerned with the possible Christian implications of the story will turn inevitably to Tolkien's famous essay on Faërie and particularly the last part of it in which he discusses the *eucatastrophe* and *evangelium.* "The Birth of Christ," he says, "is the *eucatastrophe* of Man's history. The Resurrection is the *eucatastrophe* of the story of the Incarnation. . . . There is no tale ever told that men would rather find was true, and none which so many skeptical men have accepted as true on its own merits." It is as if one discovered a fairy tale "primarily" true, that is, a real Cinderella in your house or your neighborhood, or, better, the heavenly world made visible before your eyes. The joyful *eucatastrophe* of men's stories in its minor way echoes that of the greatest story of all, the descent of God to redeem men. The *evangelium* in the story, even in the midst of a fallen world, gives "a fleeting glimpse of Joy, Joy beyond the walls of the world, poignant as grief."[50] Thus any story falling into the classification of Faërie, as defined by Tolkien, will be happily freighted with the highest *significatio* and redolent of heaven and eternal joy even if it never once mentions the name of Christ.

Third, I think it not insignificant to take note of some remarks of Professor Tolkien in a publication of 1967 called *The Road Goes Ever On*, which most Tolkien admirers are acquainted with. There he speaks, for the first time I believe, of Elbereth as "a 'divine' or 'angelic' person" and admits that elves and men and hobbits "invoke" her aid in time of trouble and that elves sing hymns to her, and then adds in parentheses the highly significant remark, "These and other references to religion in *The Lord of the Rings* are frequently overlooked." A little later he describes the Valar as

49 *Niekas*, no. 18, 39.
50 *Tree and Leaf*, London, 60.

presenting themselves to physical eyes clothed in "veils" or "raiment," being "self-incarnated" because of "their love and desire for the Children of God."[51] (This is, I think, the first time that the word "God" has ever been used by Tolkien in connection with *The Lord of the Rings*.) It is clear enough that the High Elves may be quite properly regarded as angels in the normal meaning of the term. When we have once acknowledged that fact, then it seems to me that the whole story must be given a strong spiritual or biblical inference.

Thomas de Quincey pointed out that all great literature becomes "a Jacob's ladder from earth to mysterious altitudes above the earth" where a thoughtful reader may find meaning unlimited, and it is this sort of idea that gives credence to Guy Davenport's remark concerning Tolkien's story: "For a generation that can't make head or tail of St. Paul, Mr. Tolkien has got Isaiah and St. Paul back before readers' eyes."[52] He has indeed got the essence of St. Paul and Isaiah and the biblical landscape before our eyes. Yet I for one will vote very strongly with Professor Tolkien against turning the story *simply* into Christian allegory. It is not allegory but myth. It is not a "statement" or a "system." It is a story to be enjoyed, not a sermon to be preached. Yet I think it is clear enough that for many readers the story deeply suggests the sadness of a paradise lost and the glory of one that can be regained.

---

51 *The Road Goes Ever On*, Boston, 1967, 65–66.
52 "The Persistence of Light," *National Review*, April, 1965, 334.

Chapter 15

THE EVOLUTION OF A FRIENDSHIP AND THE WRITING OF *THE SILMARILLION*

Though Kilby was always willing to share impressions of his first meeting with Tolkien, and the amazing summer of friendship that followed, he did not write an account of the experience until asked to do so by Kodon, *the Wheaton College literary magazine (as he had been requested to do after his meeting with Lewis, twenty years earlier). By the time that account was published (as he describes below), Tolkien had died. Shortly after, Luci Shaw began to persuade Kilby to expand his impressions of Tolkien and the as-yet-unpublished* Silmarillion *into a book. The result, published in 1976 by Harold Shaw as* Tolkien and the Silmarillion, *contains some of Kilby's most insightful writing, and remains among the most illuminating things written about Tolkien's whole body of work. The book itself was something of a collage, marred in its first edition by Christopher Tolkien's request to exclude its heart, a chapter outlining* The Silmarillion. *After* The Silmarillion *was published, the chapter was restored as an appendix. Included here is the opening section, which recalls, in some detail, the evolution of Kilby's relationship with Tolkien, and the work that led to the eventual posthumous publication of* The Silmarillion, *in 1977.*

The plan for this piece could hardly be simpler. It originated in a request from the editor of *Kodon*, the literary magazine of Wheaton College, for an article on J. R. R. Tolkien. In the several months intervening between the request and my actual writing of the article we were all shocked and grieved over the news of Professor Tolkien's death on September 2, 1973. This sad event added to my feeling that perhaps a record of my acquaintance with him, and particularly my experience as reader of *The Silmarillion*, might be significant.

This book makes no claim to biography. That must be left to someone far better acquainted with Tolkien than I, perhaps one of his own family. Even there I have the feeling that it will not be a simple matter. Tolkien's son Michael reports being asked innumerable times what kind of person his father was and what took place inside the walls where his great mythological world was engendered and grew up. The son confesses that he finds such questions difficult, if not actually impossible, to answer clearly and definitely.

I felt that Tolkien was like an iceberg, something to be reckoned with above water in both its brilliance and mass and yet with much more below the surface. In his presence one was aware of a single totality but equally aware at various levels of a kind of consistent inconsistency that was both native—perhaps his genius—and developed, almost deliberate, even enjoyed. The word, if there were one, might be *contrasistency*. If my account of him is sketchy and in itself inconsistent, it has the virtue of reflecting my real impression of the man. This, then, is not intended to be a comprehensive introduction to Tolkien. That also would be a large and difficult task. Though I have written as succinctly and honestly as I know how to do, this essay is little more than a straightforward record of my experience of personal contact with him during the assigned task of reading *The Silmarillion*.

FIRST MEETING

I first met J. R. R. Tolkien late on the afternoon of September 1, 1964. His fame was then rapidly on the rise, and he had been forced to escape his public whenever he could. Visitors were more or less constantly at his door and his telephone busy. Phone callers from the United States sometimes forgot the time differential and would get him out of bed at two or three o'clock in the morning. He was paying the price of his sudden emergence from the relative obscurity of a professional scholar to the glare of publicity accorded to any internationally known writer.

Knowing the reported difficulty of getting inside his house, I asked for help from his personal physician, Dr. Robert E. Havard, who then lived at 28 Sandfield Road, not far from the Tolkien home. After an exciting hour of conversation over tea in Dr. Havard's garden, I inquired how I might contrive to get into Tolkien's presence. What I hoped was that Dr. Havard would telephone and introduce me. Instead he said, "Just go down there and ring the door-bell. He isn't doing anything."

With great hopes and some fears I walked to 76 Sanfield Road, opened the gate, nervously approached his door, and rang the bell. I waited what seemed to me a very long time and was on the point of a reluctant departure when the door opened and there stood the man himself.

Tolkien matter-of-factly invited me inside but added that in only a few minutes he had to go out. We went into his downstairs office, remodeled from a one-car garage. Possessing no automobile, he was then using taxis for errands to Oxford, two miles away, and elsewhere. This little office was pretty well filled up with a desk, a couple of chairs, and bookcases along the walls.

After his sober greeting at the door, I found him immediately friendly as we sat down. Tolkien was a most genial man with a steady twinkle in his eyes and a great curiosity—the sort of person one instinctively likes. The main reason that was forcing him to shut out visitors was not his antipathy to them but rather the knowledge that his natural friendliness and love of talking with almost anybody who happened along would seduce him into spending time with visitors while his work languished.

I briefly explained who I was and told him that, like thousands of others, I had come to love his great story and regard it as something of a classic. He laughed at the idea of being a classical author while still alive, but I think he was pleased. He then became a bit apologetic and explained that people sometimes regarded him as a man living in a dream world. This was wholly untrue, he insisted, and described himself as a busy philologist and an ordinary citizen interested in everyday things like anybody else. As an illustration of his practicality he told me of his keen regret that salaries were raised at his college at Oxford the very day after his retirement. He had begun at Oxford as Rawlinson and Bosworth Professor of Anglo-Saxon and later became Professor of English Language and Literature at Merton College, remaining there until his retirement in 1959. Tolkien was happily aware of the increasing popularity his books in the United States and elsewhere and hopeful that sales would continue to increase.

He talked of *The Silmarillion*, commenting that his main trouble with it was the lack of a commanding theme bringing the parts together. He was much aware that he needed to complete the story and spoke of his hope to publish it by 1966. He recounted some of the plot, especially its beginning. At that time I had no idea I should later read the story in manuscript.

He told me, surprisingly, that he and his good friend C. S. Lewis had long before agreed to do narratives dealing with space and time. Lewis wrote *Out of the Silent Planet* and *Perelandra* and thus fulfilled his part of the plan to write on space, but Tolkien said he had never embarked on a story about time.

He and Lewis had begun their careers at Oxford University in the year 1925 and were close friends. Later they were both prominent in the "Inklings," where members read their manuscripts to each other for pleasure and the benefit of criticism. The two men had often taken walks together. Only once had Tolkien been with Lewis on one of the long walking holidays Lewis enjoyed so much. They had hiked in the neighborhood of Minehead in the southwest of England. Tolkien concluded that twenty-five miles a day over rough country with a heavy pack on his shoulders was more than he preferred, so he had confined himself thereafter to shorter jaunts nearer Oxford with his friend.

To my surprise, at the end of our brief visit, Tolkien warmly invited me back for the morning of September 4, the day before I was to fly home to the United States. At that time Mrs. Tolkien greeted me at the door and showed me upstairs to her husband's main office, a room crowded with a large desk, a rotating bookcase, wall bookcases, and a cot. I was received like a longtime friend.

I was by no means unhappy to find him doing nearly all the talking. It was a pleasure to listen as he went easily from one topic to another. Tolkien, himself a Catholic, told anti-Catholic anecdotes with a glow of humor and an utter lack of antagonism. One story was of Lewis's Anglican childhood in North Ireland, where he had been told that the wiggletails in a well at his home were wee popes. Such stories, I later found, did not mean that Tolkien had a casual view of his religion.

While he talked he stood up and walked about or else sat on his cot. Like C. S. Lewis, when I visited him some years earlier, Tolkien continually fiddled with his pipe but actually smoked little. As his talk grew in enthusiasm, he would sometimes come very close to me and put his face almost against mine, as though to make sure the point of some remark was completely understood. One had the feeling that he had thought considerably about whatever opinion he was expressing and simply wanted to state it accurately. While he could not go long without a brightening of his eyes over some anecdote that might tumble out, he could also be very sharp in his antagonism to anything he thought awry in the community or the world. Once he spoke of a certain well-known person in Oxford as "one of God's congenital idiots."

He told me that he was fourteen years writing *The Lord of the Rings*, also that he had typed all of it himself, with many changes, by the three-finger method, in the very room we were in. I asked him how *The Hobbit* was related to *The Lord of the Rings* and whether he had got the idea of the latter while doing the former. He promptly insisted this was not the case. The stories originated, he said, in orbits of their own and neither was necessarily the consequence of the other. He admitted that the manuscript of *The Lord of the Rings* was sold through his agent to Marquette University because he needed money, owing to his having been "retired on a pittance." (Later I learned from Marquette that the manuscripts made a stack seven feet high.)

I asked how he went about inventing the hundreds of names of characters and places, and he said he did it by a "mathematical" system. He meant, I think, that his inventions, including his Elvish languages, arose not simply out of imagination but from his professional knowledge of the origin and growth of languages themselves and particularly from his experience in the worlds of Nordic, Teutonic, and Celtic mythology. He was also aware of an even deeper meaning and origin for his fiction. He said that a member of Parliament had stood in the room we were in and declared, "You did not write *The Lord of the Rings*," meaning that it had been given him from God. It was clear that he favored this remark.

I asked why he did not come to America. He told me that long before our visit Marquette University had invited him to accept an honorary degree, but after he had bought steamship tickets an illness of his wife prevented their departure.

As I prepared to leave, he spoke of getting a letter from a man in London whose name was Sam Gamgee. I asked him what reply he had made and he said he had written that what he really dreaded was getting a communication from S. Gollum. He gave me an autographed copy of *Tree and Leaf* and was about to do the same with another book to which he had contributed but found that he had only one copy of it.

A SUMMER WITH TOLKIEN

When I left Tolkien's home in 1964 I had no idea of ever returning. We carried on a little correspondence. One item of it concerned the possible publication of a manuscript of his called *Mr. Bliss*, a children's story written and illustrated by him somewhat in the Beatrix Potter style. He concluded that, in his words, this story would not "enhance" his reputation, and it still remains among various other writings yet to be published.

Another topic of correspondence concerned a plan developed late in 1964 to establish at Wheaton College a collection, or set of collections, including his works and those of C. S. Lewis, Charles Williams, Dorothy Sayers, G. K. Chesterton, George MacDonald, and Owen Barfield. I wrote him that we planned to bring together "everything you have written and everything written about you, both in books and periodicals." Of course we also desired manuscripts. He told me that with his major manuscript already sold he felt his others should be left to his heirs. Later on he did offer us, after its publication, the manuscript of *Smith of Wootton Major*, and we made the best price we could, but it was less than he anticipated.

Another item of correspondence had to do with my sending him copies of feature articles which from time to time came to my attention. I eventually found that such things so displeased him it was just as well not to send them at all. Reporters, he assured me, always got things wrong. Actually Tolkien was not the sort of person, if indeed anyone is, who could be captured in the oversimplification of the feature article. This was especially true of articles that emphasized him as a cult figure and something more or less than human. This attitude may have been why Tolkien managed so remarkably to keep the events of his actual life hidden from the public. Of some of the features published about him, he remarked that too many people thought him "a gargoyle to be gaped at."

Then in the latter part of 1965 I wrote him that, like many others, I was eager to see *The Silmarillion* published and would therefore come to Oxford during the summer of 1966, if he wished, to assist him with his correspondence or in any other manner that might facilitate the publication of his story of the First Age of Middle-earth. On Christmas Eve I found the following letter in my mail:

> I am very sorry that your letter written on November 19th has not yet been answered. I was deeply touched by it, indeed overwhelmed by your generosity in offering to sacrifice your precious time (and holiday) in helping me. But when your letter came to me I was rather burdened and distracted. My wife's health for more than a month has given me much anxiety (and necessitated my going twice to the Southwest in the interim with much loss of time, but became worse with the sudden early onset of winter). A competent part-time secretary, after giving me much assistance with Ballantine business, departed. And I was suddenly presented with the necessity of revising, and correcting the proofs of, *The Hobbit* for new editions. Each day I thought it would be done, but I only got off the

last material a few days ago. However, the mere burden of correspondence has been eased. Unexpectedly a competent secretary appeared, after 11 years assisting David Cecil. She is brisk and orderly, but has no knowledge of my work. So that I am not in such straits as to allow you to spend your valuable time on mere correspondence. . . .

I have never had much confidence in my own work, and even now when I am assured (still much to my grateful surprise) that it has value for other people, I feel diffident, reluctant as it were, to expose my world of imagination to possibly contemptuous eyes and ears. But for the encouragement of C. S. Lewis I do not think that I should ever have completed or offered for publication *The Lord of the Rings. The Silmarillion* is quite different, and if good at all, good in quite another way, and I do not really know what to make of it. It began in hospital and sick-leave (1916–1917) and has been with me ever since, and is now in a confused state, having been altered, enlarged, and worked out, at intervals between then and now. If I had the assistance of a scholar at once sympathetic and yet critical, such as yourself, I feel I might make some of it publishable. It needs the actual presence of a friend and adviser at one's side, which is just what you offer. As far as I can see, I shall be free soon to return to it, and June, July and August are available. (As at present advised I am booked to take my wife on a cruise in the Mediterranean, to forearm her against winter, on Sept. 15, for about 3 weeks.)

Alas! in my domestic circumstances I cannot offer lodging, entertainment, or any of the normal hospitalities one would desire to offer in such a case. (I have not even a spare bedroom!). But if you were in Oxford you could

> have access to all the files and relevant material, and I should benefit by your opinions and assistance, especially with regard to the main problem: in what mode to present it, discussion would be (for me) a great encouragement and help.
>
> I have, of course, made some money out of my books, though less than legend makes it, especially after the attentions of the tax-gatherers. . . . I could not hope to remunerate you or defray your expenses in any way proper to your value! But I should wish (and insist on it) to ask you to receive some honorarium. That, however, we can go into, if I hear again that you are willing to help. I should call the Job: *editorial and critical assistance*. . . .
>
> With my cordial wishes and very deep gratitude for your generous thought and offer,
>
> Yours very sincerely,
>
> J. R. R. Tolkien.

I began at once to prepare to render him the best service I could. I brushed up on mythology in general and the mythologies of northern Europe in particular. I once again, and now more carefully than ever, read *The Lord of the Rings* looking particularly for allusions to the First and Second Ages of Middle-earth. I assembled this material and gave attention to its chronology and geography.

I reached England on June 16 and called on Mr. Rayner Unwin, Tolkien's publisher, in London. I found him a cordial man with fine eyes and a great interest in Tolkien. He graciously said he hoped I might be the one to put *The Silmarillion* in shape for publication. He had recently been up to Oxford to visit Tolkien and thought that one object of his trip might have been to persuade him to cooperate fully with me. No one knew better than he that a campaign of sorts was needed to get a manuscript out of the famous man.

But first Mr. Unwin urged me to persuade Tolkien to write a brief preface to his translations of *The Pearl* and *Sir Gawain and the Green Knight.* Tolkien wanted it to have a preface, else the translations would already have been in print, but for some years he had failed to write it. Even a very brief preface would do, Mr. Unwin assured me. Actually, in this I failed utterly. My various reminders and coaxings were accepted seriously, yet at the end of the summer Tolkien almost triumphantly said, "Well, I didn't write it!" One day, earlier in the summer, he had said, in some exasperation (and I think mainly to himself), that he *couldn't* write it until the thing came "rightly" to him. Later I was to learn that those translations had been completed at least twenty years before and their publication continuously postponed until he could better perfect what he had undertaken.

And yet he did indeed intend to bring the task to completion. On August 10th I found him with the Gawain translation in hand. He assured me he expected to get it off to London "right away." Again on the 18th he was working on it with intention to complete it. On August 25th he told me that Mr. Unwin expected it by September 15th. His tone was utterly matter-of-fact, and I thought he fully expected within three weeks to have the material ready. One sees a significant element of Tolkien's makeup in the fact that at his death seven years later these translations were still unpublished. Whether that preface was ever written I do not know.

I went up to Oxford and settled in at Pusey House. Then I telephoned the Tolkiens that I was at their service. I was warmly welcomed into the Professor's upstairs quarter. I found the place no less crowded than two years earlier. He was in process of revising *The Two Towers*. He began our new association by showing me boxes of manuscripts—poetic, scholarly, creative. As time went on I discovered him a Barliman Butterbur, looking here and there for portions of *The Silmarillion*. Having had some experience in setting up filing systems, I finally offered to put his papers in order, a proposal he quickly rejected on the ground that *then* he should never find anything.

I was immediately aware that he had much unpublished writing. For instance, he was an expert on the *Ancrene Riwle*, that little book from the thirteenth century offering guidance to three women who had purposed to become nuns. He often mentioned this work and others from its time. He was also an expert in the Middle English period and once told me that he never opened a book written then without finding new things in it. He had serious thoughts of doing a translation of the Anglo-Saxon epic *Beowulf* but felt the task would be difficult because the poem was so concentrated. Coming over to me, he illustrated his concern by putting his torso almost against mine and, pulling back his fist, insisted that the reader must feel the very sword-thrust into the dragon. He said he had written parts of a bestiary, some bits of which had gone into Tom Bombadil. But I was aware also of numerous unmentioned manuscripts. One can imagine the perplexity of a writer with so many ideas and so many incomplete or unperfected writings on hand and with the realization of so little time left. He was then seventy-four.

Two things immediately impressed me. One was that *The Silmarillion* would never be completed. The other was the size of my own task. How could I in a few weeks read, analyze, and give a critical judgment on such a mammoth literary effort? Actually I spent one entire day on a six-page section of the manuscript.

Perhaps I can best give an idea of our sessions together by a seriatim record of one of them. But first I should say that what went on was hardly a conversation. One of my friends had been told by C. S. Lewis that one might ask Tolkien questions but one would not necessarily get the answers expected. One might find him talking on an entirely different topic, to which he had seen a relationship lost to the questioner. I soon found this to be true. Discovering that efforts to discuss portions of the manuscript with him would not succeed, I began to write out my comments and simply attach them to the manuscript.

Here are the notes I made from my first day with him that summer:

1. His fan letters tend to come in waves, and he has three sorts of replies: a) a purely form letter, b) a form letter he personally signs, and infrequently c) a response dictated to his secretary.
2. He had nothing good to say about *The Saturday Evening Post* feature that had just appeared. He said that he had finally hung up on the transatlantic conversation with the author of it. But he did confess that his own mode of speaking was a factor.[53] In point of mystifying circumlocution C. S. Lewis compared Tolkien to his own father, whose conversation often contained non sequiturs that first bothered the hearer and then became so outrageous as to be screamingly funny. Tolkien's deviations from the expected were owing not to preoccupation but rather to his scurry after the quarry across mental fences and quagmires.
3. Looking out of his window at a birch in the front yard, he declared it to be his totem tree.
4. He and Mrs. Tolkien were angry with W. H. Auden for remarks he was reported to have made

53 His obituary mentions him as "the best and worst talker in Oxford—worst for the rapidity and indistinctness of his speech, and best for the penetration, learning, humour and 'race' of what he said." *Times Literary Supplement*, September 3, 1973. His British secretary told me that she herself failed to understand everything he said. He often added to the difficulty by clamping his pipe between his teeth as he talked. One friend reported him "completely unintelligible" as a talker.

at a meeting of the Tolkien Society in Brooklyn, New York, especially his comment that the Tolkien home was "hideous . . . with hideous pictures on the walls."[54] Mrs. Tolkien invited me to come and sit in the same chair Auden had occupied when visiting them and see if I thought the house looked hideous. I readily confessed that it was a nicer house than I had ever lived in myself.

A little earlier Auden had agreed to write a brochure on Tolkien for a series being published in the United States. Tolkien emphatically assured me that Auden would never get his permission. He told the publisher what he had written Auden: "I regret very much to hear that you have contracted to write a book about me. It does meet with my strong disapproval. I regard such things as premature impertinences; and unless undertaken by an intimate friend, or with consultation of the subject (for which I have no time at present), I cannot believe that they have a usefulness to justify the distaste and irritation given to the victim. I wish at any rate that any book could wait until I produce *The Silmarillion.* I am constantly interrupted in this; but nothing interferes more than the present pother about 'me' and my history." It should be said, however, that Tolkien went on to express his gratitude for Auden's ardent commendation of *The Lord of the Rings.*[55] Later in the summer, Tolkien spoke to me of his hope that this disagreement with Auden might be wiped out when they got together in the autumn. Whether it was settled or not I do not know. I had the

54 *The New Yorker,* January 15, 1966.
55 Unpublished letter to Roger Verhulst, March 9, 1966.

opportunity afterwards to talk with Auden and found him most friendly toward the Tolkiens.

5. He spoke of his dislike of the covers on the Ballantine paperbacks. To my surprise, he said he was glad for the Ace Books controversy because it kept Mr. Ballantine on his toes. Actually, Tolkien's general opinion of publishers was not high. He felt that even the U.S. clothback publishers did their business poorly as to distribution. As time went on he repeatedly reminded me that it was actually the Ace edition of *The Lord of the Rings* that first made him widely known, a comment curiously in opposition to the diatribes against Ace current in those days.

The whole controversy arose after Houghton Mifflin had imported unfolded press sheets from George Allen & Unwin for its U.S. edition. The copyright laws allowed this on condition that no more than fifteen hundred copies be imported. When more than the legal number were brought in, Ace Books used this infraction as excuse to issue its paperback. This lower-priced book sold widely. Eventually the word went out that Ace had simply pirated its edition. Young admirers writing in the *Tolkien Journal* and other such periodicals were outraged. Tolkien wrote a letter to his readers in the U.S. denouncing the Ace edition and asking them not to buy it. He repeated the idea in the Foreword of the Ballantine Books paperback. But, as I have said, he told me afterwards that it was actually the Ace edition which first brought him into wide public notice. Of course there was no necessary conflict. Tolkien could appreciate the acclaim and still object to the moral angle and the loss of royalties. Ace

Books had not at that time sent Tolkien any money, though they did later.

The really upsetting aspect of all this lay elsewhere. Tolkien insisted to me and to others that this controversy so occupied his time that it interfered with the completion of *The Silmarillion*. One of the deeply puzzling aspects of Tolkien comes to light in this circumstance, perhaps another a case of "contrasistency." I failed to understand why he could not see instantly that the Ace edition need not usurp even one day of his time. It was a purely legal matter and only needed to be handed over to his lawyer.

6. He was pleased with the Japanese translation of *The Hobbit* and showed me with particular satisfaction the frontispiece which portrayed Smaug falling convulsively over Dale. He had various other translations on his shelves. The Portuguese illustrations he regarded as "horrible."
7. He mentioned Mrs. Tolkien's chronic illness. He spoke proudly of his four children, one by one.
8. I asked him if people had not sought to write his biography. He said they had and went on to discuss the difference between the outward facts and the inward motives of a life, mentioning as an illustration the joys which stirred him as a child in South Africa and at his first glimpse of his "native" English soil.
9. He has the intention of completing a full account of the Second Age of Middle-earth under the title *The Akallabeth*, a word made up of *kalab* meaning "fall down," with the doubled "l" giving it intensity, i.e., the "great fall." The Númenórean language, he informed me, is based on Hebrew.

10. He showed me many manuscripts, most of them old and obviously reworked.

[These recollections] intend to show the variety of subjects that might come up in a visit with Professor Tolkien. I might add here that Mrs. Tolkien would sometimes come in and join the conversation. She was always gracious and friendly.

That summer, I went out to their home on Sanfield Road two or three times a week and was there one to three hours, periods solidly filled with talk, nearly all his.

It was said that C. S. Lewis could make a new suit look old the second time he put it on. Not so with Tolkien. He was always neatly dressed from necktie to shoes. One of his favorite suits was a herringbone with which he wore a green corduroy vest. Always there was a vest, and nearly always a sport coat. He did not mind wearing a very broad necktie which in those days was out of style. Once he spoke admiringly of a tie I was wearing and I rewarded him with it.

The most obvious thing about him was not his clothing but his easy and stately stance and particularly his well-shaped head and ever interesting face. Much of the time there was about him the atmosphere of the actor, yet without any sense of the jack-a-dandy. His conversation bore about it a steady parturiency, like the sort of grass that sends out runners to root in every direction. One often felt that his words could not pour out fast enough—there was a sense of the galloping on of all his ideas at once, along with kaleidoscopic facial changes.

In fact, I have never known anyone who so successfully meshed facial and oral expression. One noticed the built-in humor that seemed to begin around the mouth and eyes and extend back into the brain and down into the solid torso and on indefinitely. His penetrating eyes took possession of his hearer, and his eyebrows lifted instantly to express a point made or the beginning of an idea to be lassoed, tied down, and branded on the spot, or lowered to concentrate while conveying the assurance that behind those eyes something nimble and many-faceted was taking shape and would momentarily erupt. But it also seemed me that at times there was a passing enjoyment over what he was keeping back in the very moment of the eruption.

Sometimes there would appear a pixy face, round and growing up toward what seemed could only end in chuckle, yet never quite did. Or a genial face suddenly shifting into an expression of blazing criticism, soon followed by a repentant warmth. Sometimes a "What!" face and sometimes a "Yes, we can take care of that subject also" face. And always there was an expression of both pose and genuineness revealed like a double exposure. Then again (occasionally) a dead-serious face emerged like the others from deep within him along with a look through the window into nowhere, pipe held stolidly center.

We met generally in his upstairs room but sometimes in the garage office. When the weather was warm, we might go out into the garden. On our first visit there he took me round the garden and gave me the personal history of nearly every plant, and even the grass. He said he had loved trees since childhood and pointed out the trees he had himself planted. One easily understands Michael Tolkien's remark that from his father he "inherited an almost obsessive love of trees" and considered the mass felling of trees "the wanton murder of living beings for very shoddy ends." Tolkien wrote a letter to the editor of the *London Sunday Telegraph* taking exception to what he thought an unfair allusion to his attitude toward trees. "In all my works," he wrote, "I take the part of trees as against all their enemies," and he spoke of "the destruction, torture and murder of trees perpetrated by private individuals and minor official bodies. The savage sound of the electric saw is never silent wherever trees are still found growing."[56] He spoke of birds, saying that a certain blackbird was now tame enough to eat out of Mrs. Tolkien's hand. He recommended to me a particular book on the sparrow. Elsewhere he is reported to have said that his most treasured book was Johns' *Flowers of the Field*.[57]

It would be satisfying to record that I always found him busy at his writing, but that is not true. I did find him sometimes working at his Elvish languages, an activity that seemed endlessly interesting to him. I think he did a good deal of reading of detective stories and science fiction. He told me more than once of his pride in being chosen a member of a science-fiction writers' association in the United States. Yet in *Tree and Leaf* he speaks of science fiction as "that most escapist form of all literature." He said he found Dorothy Sayers a "fair" writer of detective stories but believed he found some "vulgarity" both in them and in her *Man Born to Be King*. He did not care for the detective stories of G. K. Chesterton.

He was happy with what he considered his histrionic talents, saying he had done some stage work in earlier life. He had the script of a British Broadcasting Corporation dramatization of *The Lord of the Rings*, thought it badly done, that he could have acted better than some who took part, but that the BBC had refused him the chance. Those who have heard the Caedmon phonograph

56 Michael Tolkien, "J. R. R. Tolkien—The Wizard Father," *London Sunday Telegraph*, September 9, 1973; J. R. R. Tolkien, *London Daily Telegraph*, July 4, 1972.

57 *Attacks of Taste*, ed. Evelyn B. Byrne and Otto M. Penzler (New York: Gotham Book Mart, 1971), 43.

records in which he reads from *The Hobbit, The Lord of the Rings,* and *Tom Bombadil* know the dramatic quality he sought after. One is also impressed with the melodic beauty of his reading of Elvish and also the recorded Gregorian-chant character of a longer Elvish poem sung by William Elvin to the music of Donald Swann. When I was with him he once began to read me a passage in Elvish, then stopped, came up close, and placing the manuscript before me said that Elvish ought not to be read but sung and then chanted it in a slow and lovely intonation.

Tolkien's skill as an artist is now well known, particularly from the illustrations he did for *The Hobbit.* He spoke of the pleasure he had in doing the tree that appeared on the British edition of *Tree and Leaf,* also of the problem of drawing the many varieties of leaves. His readers can look forward to many other pictures done by him. He also had the mastery of various forms of handwriting. Once he sat down and wrote out my name in thirteenth-century script. His interest in medieval literature and life was more than a profession—it was a love.

He told me more than once how his grandfather, I think it was, could write the Lord's Prayer on a sixpence when he was over ninety. I got the impression that he himself expected to live to a very old age. But both he and Mrs. Tolkien were then in need of some attention from physicians. Both complained of rheumatism, which they felt was accentuated by wet weather. Sometimes he could rise from his chair only with real effort, and then would remain standing rather than sit again. One day the idea arose of our taking a walk over some path he and Lewis had once covered, but he said it was no longer possible for him to walk far. He reminisced about earlier years when he could ride his bicycle up the long, steep Headington Hill between his home and the university.

As readers of Tolkien know, the contrast of light and darkness in *The Lord of the Rings* is always emphasized. In this connection

Tolkien told me of C. S. Lewis's story about the man born with a cataract on each eye. He kept hearing people talk of light but could not understand what they meant. After an operation he had some sight but had not yet come to understand light. Then one day he saw the haze rising from a pond (actually, said Tolkien, the pond at the front of Lewis's home) and thought that at last he was seeing light. In his eagerness to experience real light, he rushed joyfully into it and was drowned.

I greatly hoped that Tolkien would accept an invitation to be present in Cheltenham for a dramatization under the direction of Mrs. E. M. Webster of *The Lord of the Rings*, but almost at the last minute he declined and suggested I go instead. It was one of the finest experiences of my summer, two and a half hours' presentation by ten- and eleven-year-old British children who had spent part of their time for an entire year studying the story and preparing their own dialogue, scenery, and costumes. The play was put on in a small gymnasium. I was given a front seat and sometimes had Gollum crawling over my feet, as the stage was small for the number of youngsters taking part—participating, I should add, with dead seriousness. I was later told that the boy who played Frodo Baggins did not emerge from his role for a month and then only reluctantly. It has occurred to me many times since that perhaps nothing more fitting could be done in the way of a movie version than what I saw in Cheltenham that night. More than once I was moved to tears.

One day toward the end of the summer I found Tolkien in very low spirits. He said he was too tired to think about anything. He had been up during the night with Mrs. Tolkien and said he was going to bed for some rest. But as I rose to return to Oxford he began talking and perked up quickly. Actually gloom had little part in his makeup. Once his doctor prescribed a collar for cervical muscular spasm. When I arrived he grabbed it, put it around his neck, stuck his face into mine, and asked how I would like to wear *that* in the summer heat.

One thing for which Tolkien would stop talking was to hear a good story or joke. He had a fine supply of his own. Once he spoke of getting a letter from a husband whose pregnant wife had fallen in love with Aragorn and what was he to do? Tolkien had no answer for that one. While I was there a bust of him done by his daughter-in-law was being completed. He had picked up both the plaster and bronze casts and was carrying them, one on each side, in a taxicab. It came into his scholarly head that they were like the Dioscuri twins, Castor and Pollux, but he immediately concluded that their real names should be Castor and Plaster.

Sometimes his wit was so close to both humor and reality that it was impossible to decide which he meant. He told me once that women always kill bees, moths, spiders, and such creatures inside the house, but men capture the insect and carry it to a door or window and let it go free. He went on to describe how once in a dining room he had used his matchbox to capture a fly on a stranger's nose and how the man was surprised and a little indignant about it.

It was Mrs. Tolkien's task to stand between Ronald, she called him, and the many visitors who sought to see him. One man showed up at their door saying, "I have traveled six thousand miles to see Professor Tolkien." She politely had told him that her husband was simply not seeing anybody. One reason might have been that he was carrying what she described as a "big covered thing," which she believed to be a tape recorder. One might as well have brought a loaded gun to the door. I felt gratified when he so willingly allowed me to take a picture of him on my earlier visit, also a couple of times on the second.

His attitude toward photographers was similar to that toward feature writers, i.e., that they were people likely do the wrong thing. In this connection he showed me a large, elaborate book of photographs that someone had sent him. The photographer had obviously waited until his subjects could be caught in a grimace or some other unnatural appearance and had made up his book out of such distortions. Tolkien had been asked to pose but on seeing the results congratulated himself that he had refused.

It seemed to me that, perhaps rather naturally, he had mixed and somewhat antithetical feelings about any public image of himself. On the one hand, he was proud of seeing himself as a successful writer. I had the impression that some of his colleagues at the university (and possibly also some of his own relatives) had lifted eyebrows concerning his decades of toil over Elves and Orcs and dragons. Now all but the most cynical were put in their places, and even the cynical could not fail to admit that the work, whether good or bad, had paid off financially. On the other hand, Tolkien took appreciations with a grain of salt. Like Lewis, he held a low opinion of the twentieth century, literary critics and all.[58]

Tolkien spoke of the "terrible twenties" as having laid the foundation for the collapse of later years. He felt that education at all levels was deteriorating. He believed that England's government was going from bad to worse and spoke of the leaders as "donlets," a word that also suggested his feelings about the dons! He had little use for modern gadgets and many modern ideas. He felt nothing but antagonism for "psychological" explanations. "Nobody ever takes to psychology unless there is something wrong with his own 'psychology,'" he used to say. He was amused

58 I was invited to dinner with some of the faculty at Christ Church, and afterward one member asked me if *The Silmarillion* had any sex, in the modern sense. The next day I mentioned this to Tolkien, and to my surprise he said he had written a couple of sex stories, though he did not volunteer to show them to me. Readers of *The Lord of the Rings* know of the moving account of the love between Arwen and Aragorn, and when *The Silmarillion* is published we shall have others of the same sort, but they are vastly different from what we call sex stories today.

by Freudian interpretations of *The Hobbit* in which some of his motives were supposedly explained in terms of his being scared by spiders in his youth. On the contrary, he insisted, he and his boyhood friends scared each other with spiders because they really *liked* to be scared!

I also got the impression that many of the older writers also displeased Tolkien. He said he did not like Russian writers and could not read them. Interviewed by a London newspaper, he is reported to have said of Lewis's comparison of *The Lord of the Rings* to Ariosto, "I don't know Ariosto and I'd loathe him if I did. . . . Cervantes was a weed-killer to romance. . . . Dante doesn't attract me. He's full of spite and malice. I don't care for his petty relations with petty people in petty cities."[59] I was pleasingly surprised at the familiarity he showed with American literature, especially that of Mark Twain.

One antipathy of his struck me oddly. Though elsewhere he had spoken of George MacDonald with real appreciation, at the time I visited Tolkien he was making frequent wholesale attacks on him. He called him an "old grandmother" who preached instead of writing. He thought MacDonald would have done better to retain his native dialect in some of his writings. He did not like the way in which MacDonald wrote of trees, etc. Now there is common agreement that MacDonald's writings have serious shortcomings at their worst but equally great significance at their best. A friend of mine who is well versed in MacDonald and also fond of Tolkien suggests that the dislike of MacDonald may have arisen partly to throw people off the scent of his deep indebtedness. Whatever the real explanation, I think that the indebtedness is clear.

A similar antipathy of Tolkien's was for one of his own characters, Sam Gamgee. I have never known a reader who did not on

59 "The Man Who Understands Hobbits," Charlotte and Dennis Plimmer, *London Daily Telegraph Magazine*, March 22, 1968.

the whole find Sam a person to be admired. Yet Tolkien spoke to me about Sam as "vulgar" and "despicable," and in a letter to Vera Chapman he described Sam as sententious and cocksure. "He was the youngest son of a stupid and conceited old peasant. Together with his loyal master-servant attitude, and his personal love for Frodo, he retains a touch of the contempt of his kind (moderated to tolerant pity) for motives above their reach."[60]

But if Tolkien was critical of others he was even more critical of his own writings. Few authors ever denigrated their own works more than he. In the foreword to the Ballantine paperback of *The Lord of the Rings* he describes the story as containing "many defects, minor and major," and that he might well have produced an accessory volume of explanation and additions. The chief defect is actually the omission of what he obviously intended to put into the story and did not. For instance, he says there were five Wizards but two are never again mentioned and a third is barely named. Again, Cirdan is essentially a nobody, though he held Narya the Great, one of the Three Rings of Power, and we are told "saw further and deeper than any other in Middle-earth" (3:456). Possibly Tolkien, given more time, would have built the other three Wizards and also Cirdan into a truly noteworthy place in his story.

Something of the extent of Tolkien's perfectionism may be sensed by noting that he, like C. S. Lewis, thought a story properly composed only after the author had first done the whole thing in poetry and then turned it back into prose. Some of the manuscript of *The Silmarillion* is in verse form. It is a concept reminiscent of Horace's dictum that an author rework his writings for nine years before giving them to the public.

Yet, as I have said, Tolkien greatly disliked the image of himself as an unsubstantial dreamer. He wanted to be thought of as,

60 *Mythprint*, September 1973.

in Wordsworth's phrase, "a man speaking to men." The truth is that he was sometimes impractical, not in the self-conscious manner but in the everyday one. A problem that was bothering him when I was with him involved an American manufacturer who proposed to exploit the Hobbit image by making dolls, T-shirts, and the like. This manufacturer declared his intention of going ahead with or without permission but offered some remuneration for the privilege. Again I felt it to be simply a legal affair that need not at all trouble Tolkien the writer.

But another somewhat parallel problem might indeed have properly usurped his time. Young people fell in love with his Elvish languages, and some of them began to discover the linguistic principles of their construction. Some in their enthusiasm proceeded to extend the Elvish to its various possible forms, and a dictionary of greater or less proportions seemed inevitable. They would have supposedly been able to copyright the very languages invented by him and thus put a check on his own use of them. I tried to reassure him that the Hobbit images and the extension of his languages were both evidences of his growing reputation and in the case of the languages could do him no real harm. As to the languages, I suggested that he might kill two birds with one stone by simply writing an entire book in Elvish. Not only would many young people love it but he could then copyright his Elvish vocabulary. He made the surprising answer that he would indeed do a story in Elvish if only he knew enough Elvish!

I became convinced that Professor Tolkien was suffering in an accentuated way, because of his genius, from some of the inner conflicts belonging to us all. I found that he had a real measure of "insecurity." As early as 1939 C. S. Lewis wrote his brother that Tolkien's "trials, besides being frequent and severe, are usually of such a complicated nature as to be impenetrable." Now internationally famous, he nevertheless needed assurance concerning himself as a writer and particularly concerning *The Silmarillion*. He had such grave and long-standing doubts about the story that I felt he had done little work on it for years, and had possibly even grown unfamiliar with it.

My own policy in the reading of other people's manuscripts, and particularly when I ask others to read my own, is to give or request negative criticism, the sort that nets the most value toward a revision. But I quickly discovered that sort of criticism was not what Tolkien wanted or needed. Convinced that he could not write a genuinely poor story, I was able conscientiously to be generous with my praise. And this I was. My negative criticism of the manuscript became more or less a footnote to the positive. Afterward I remembered that Lewis also believed that Tolkien could be influenced only by encouragement.[61]

A similar need extended further. I was perfectly willing simply to listen to what Tolkien had to say rather than insist upon a two-way communication. In due course I discovered his need of a genuinely interested listener. Before we had been long together he said one day that, if I would hold it confidential, he would "put more under my hat," more than he had ever told anyone. But as time went on I realized that any discussion of his most deeply private world was simply impossible for him. Indeed, for a period it seemed to me that the very idea generated its contrariety and modified the ordinary generosity of his conversation. As opportunity allowed I encouraged him to speak his deepest feelings, but to no avail. Whatever he might have revealed I have little idea, though I remain certain that he was fundamentally "every inch a man" and a good man at that.

His problem as a writer he stated with great charm and meaning at the beginning of his story "Leaf by Niggle." That story

61 *Letters of C. S. Lewis*, edited by W. H. Lewis (London: Geoffrey Bles Ltd., 1966), 87.

begins, "There was once a little man called Niggle, who had a long journey to make." The journey was into death and the hereafter. Niggle describes himself as a painter, not a very successful one owing not only to interruptions that usurped his time but also to a tendency toward plain laziness. Niggle's real trouble was that his reach exceeded his grasp. He had various paintings that he worked on, and "most of them were too large and ambitious for his skill." Actually he preferred to paint leaves more than trees. "He used to spend a long time on a single leaf, trying to catch its shape, and its sheen, and the glistening of dewdrops on its edges." Yet at the same time he longed to paint a whole tree. Indeed one painting had started with "a single leaf caught in the wind," but it grew, "sending out innumerable branches, and thrusting out the most fantastic roots. Strange birds came and settled on the twigs and had to be attended to." For me it represents both a splendid picture of his perfectionism and the increasing vision of the mythology he was creatively to inhabit.

But then came a larger idea still. Not just a single leaf, nor only a tree, but an entire country began to show up, including high mountains in the far distance. Niggle now turned away from his other paintings "or else he took them and tacked them on to the edges of his great picture." Might this not explain the Tom Bombadil episode and the Bombadil poems that did not quite manage to get into the main story? In due course Niggle's painting got so large he needed a ladder to reach its top. What a perfect insight into the whole creative process, whether Tolkien's or that of a Thomas Wolfe, a Stephen Spender, or any creative mind overwhelmed by the magnitude of its subject.

The time eventually came when Niggle began to take a hard look at what was turning out to be the main activity of his life. He looked and looked and wished for someone who "would tell him what to think." He wondered if he were simply wasting time.

He wondered if he should have dropped all other paintings for this single one. Was it really a painting, or was it just a chimera? Niggle concluded contradictory things about it. "Actually it seemed to him wholly unsatisfactory, and yet very lovely, the only really beautiful picture in the world." Not only do we have here the experience of many a writer or artist, but we have what seems a most faithful description of Tolkien's own creativity.

In the foreword to the Ballantine edition, Tolkien begins by saying, "This tale grew in the telling, until it became a history of the Great War of the Ring and included many glimpses of the yet more ancient history that preceded it." And what a landscape is seen! Yet the greatest defect of *The Lord of the Rings*, said he, is that it is too short. I can easily believe that Tolkien, had he had enough lives, would have written thirty or forty thousand pages, and who knows whether it would not still have been too short for his teeming genius?

I might remark on one apparent difference between Niggle and his counterpart. Niggle was up on his ladder at work when the Inspector in black came to take him away. My own impression was that Tolkien, despite protestations to the contrary, had greatly slowed down at the time of my visit and perhaps seldom climbed the ladder clear to the top at all. I hope I am wrong. And even if I am right, might not a Niggle at seventy-four richly deserve a recess from the heights?

SOME NOTES ON *SMITH OF WOOTTON MAJOR*

Though the reading of *The Silmarillion* was proving about as much as I could handle during that summer of 1966, Tolkien from time to time handed me other shorter pieces and asked me about their publishability. One was called "The Bovadium Fragments," a satire written long before and having as its main point the worship of the *Motores*, i.e., automobiles, and the traffic jams blocking the roads in and around Oxford. It was full of the inventiveness to be expected of Tolkien. Some of the characters are Rotzopny, Dr. Gums, and Sarevelk. I judged that it had two elements that would make it unpublishable. One was the more than liberal use of Latin, and the other the probability that a reader's eye would focus on its playfulness rather than its serious implications. Actually it was an early comment on the commercialization of our world.

The other and far more interesting manuscript was *Smith of Wootton Major*. I assured him it was my notion that it should be published as soon as possible. It actually was published in 1967, but whether my recommendation had anything to do with it I am doubtful.

In order to comment on this story, it is necessary for me to remark once again that while I was with him Tolkien frequently fired verbal cannonades at George MacDonald. Someone had asked Tolkien to consider writing an introduction to a book on MacDonald, and he had for that reason gone back to read again some of his works. He said he had found MacDonald terrible and his broadside criticism of him implied that nothing he had written was worthwhile. I asked Tolkien if *Smith of Wootton Major* referred to MacDonald. No, he said, his aversion had only been the "explosion" that started him off on the story, no more.

I read the story and interpreted it as primarily about the creative process and the special problems of a fantasy writer like Tolkien. He staunchly denied it had any autobiographical meaning. It was, he said, originally intended as "just a story about cake." But it still occurred to me that at the beginning Old Nokes may represent MacDonald. "Fairies and sweets were two of the very few notions he had about the tastes of children." Nokes knew the sort of things that should be outside a cake but had dim notions as to "the inside of a Great Cake" and so went to some old recipe books of former cooks and also hunted up some spices. In this search he found a much tarnished star.

Nokes thought the star "funny" and therefore amusing to children, but his young apprentice, who was actually a far better cook, insisted it was "fa'rie" and a serious business. Here we seem to have a fundamental idea from Tolkien's essay "On Fairy-stories," and if Nokes is meant to be MacDonald we must assume that Tolkien thought his fa'rie simply something pretty and sweet with little notion of *eucatastrophe* and *evangelium.* (I can imagine lovers of MacDonald rising up wrathfully to dispute this conception. I myself would dispute it.)

The star, along with other trinkets, was baked into the cake, and at the winter festival the ten-year-old son of the smith swallowed it unknowingly. But the star possessed fa'rie and so the child sang "high and clear, in strange words that he seemed to know by heart." The child began to be almost the opposite of the stodgy Nokes and even his community. He became a good workman, making useful things but also at times beautiful and substantial ones as well. But because too many people were like Old Nokes, he could speak of fa'rie to few.

Some few at least could understand what was taking place in young Smith, yet no one understood the beauty and terror he experienced on some of his longer journeys. Eventually "possessed," Smith saw "elven mariners tall and terrible." Smith also strayed in gray mists and over wide plains. Finally he found the "King's tree . . . tower upon tower . . . and it bore at once leaves and flowers and fruits uncounted, and not one was the same as any other that grew on the Tree." Though Smith never saw that tree again, he could never forsake the search, and the search led him through "the Vale of Evermorn" and glory where he heard elven voices and found maidens dancing.

It seems to me that the autobiography is unmistakable. The star unconsciously swallowed suggests the manner in which creativity rises in seemingly accidental fashion and without precedent. The useful things he at first made could represent Tolkien's scholarship. Later came his vision of Middle-earth. I suspect that such a vision almost inevitably meets with skepticism, if not outright derision, among the other makers of "useful" things, not to mention the vast multitude who are nonmakers. The beauty and terror seen by Smith on his longer journeys clearly represent, I believe, Tolkien's particular birth into the world of myth and his own "calling" to the myth of Middle-earth, a calling that is intensified by the visits to elvish country and the tree bearing "leaves and flowers and fruits uncounted." (How close this is to *Tree and Leaf*!) This created world is to be as large as the world itself.

In the story Smith, when he returned home, seemed more of an oddity than ever to his neighbors. But he bore a light that had been given him by a fairy queen. She told him not to be too much ashamed of his own folk. And here the story may return to MacDonald. Old Nokes had wanted to stick "a little doll on a pinnacle in the middle of the Cake, dressed all in white, with a little wand in her hand ending in a tinsel star, and Fairy Queen written in pink icing round her feet." Does Tolkien mean that though MacDonald knows nothing about the real inside of a cake, nevertheless he may accomplish something by the saccharine figures he presents? Nokes grew old and skinny and "just made his century: the only memorable thing he ever achieved." MacDonald died in 1905.

But Tolkien may also mean that the little imitation fairy had somehow incited Smith on his perilous way to find the true queen. There is no doubt in my mind that, whatever this story may satirically say of MacDonald, and in spite of Tolkien's several severe attacks on him in my presence, Tolkien was, as I have already said clearly indebted to MacDonald. For instance, there are at least a dozen places in *The Hobbit* or *The Lord of the Rings* that are reminiscent of *The Princess and Curdie.* The most striking of them is the parallel rehabilitation of the king of Gwyntystorm and King Theoden in *The Two Towers* after a close "friend" in the palace had almost destroyed him.

LATE CORRESPONDENCE AND DEATH

I conclude [. . .] with a note on the correspondence between us after I returned home. In October 1966 he wrote me of "nearly seventeen days of unbroken sunshine" on a cruise he and Mrs. Tolkien had completed in the Mediterranean. It was marred, however, by the fact that Mrs. Tolkien had slipped and fallen on the first day and thereafter had been in the hands of the ship's surgeon much of the time, preventing some of the sightseeing they had anticipated. He had returned to England to a large "mound" of correspondence. In December 1967, he wrote me that his work had proceeded "hardly at all" for a year. "I have been so distracted by business and family affairs (interlocked), and my dear wife's health, which doesn't improve, that there seems little time for concentration except at night, and I can no longer burn so much of the wrong end of the candle as I used to." In the same envelope was another letter that, said he, "I began at some date I cannot remember." He told of an illness he had experienced that was serious enough "to require the daily visits of an anxious doctor for a month, and left me an emaciated wreck. It was eight weeks before I could walk about."

Other letters passed between us in 1968, but I shall mention only one in June of that year. "I am now leaving Oxford," he wrote, "and going to live on the south coast. . . . For my own protection I shall remove my address from all books of reference or other lists." He reported that thereafter his correspondence would come through his publisher in London. "I have made up my mind not to see anybody from your country whom I do not already know, nor anybody from any Press in any country." In this letter he made a scathing reference to William Ready, the author of a book about him, and reported that Ready had "the impertinence to send me a personally inscribed copy."

After Mrs. Tolkien's death late in November 1971, he returned to his old haunts in Oxford. The pressure from visitors began to mount again. In February 1973, I wrote him concerning the possibility of his coming to the United States to receive the honorary degree he had been offered. I suggested that if he felt able I would arrange a few speaking engagements for him and meantime do my best to guarantee such privacy as he might wish. He answered that he was unable to accept. "My age alone is I think sufficient reason but I have been in medical hands recently and have had some severe advice with regard to my future conduct." Of his life between that time and September 2, when the Inspector in black came for him, I know little.

POSTSCRIPT

Looking back at my summer with Professor Tolkien, I remember more vividly than anything else his invariable practice of coming downstairs and out to the front gate with me and always with expressions of warmest appreciation. He said that he had wanted an "outsider" to examine *The Silmarillion*, and though he had confessed his own lack of confidence in it, he showed great gratitude for what he described as a renewed interest in completing the story. The correspondence I have just mentioned unhappily suggests that apparently he did little or nothing about it. Let us all hope I am mightily wrong.

Chapter 16

A BRIEF CHRONOLOGY OF THE WRITINGS

In this very rich addendum to his account of his summer with Tolkien, Dr. Kilby added this carefully researched speculation on the process of Tolkien's composition of his whole vast mythology. He also adds some remarkable conjectures as to the relationship between the landscape of the story and the contemporary landscape of Europe and England. Tom Shippey (Tolkien's successor at Oxford) has expanded greatly on Kilby's speculation as to the local correspondences of place in his discussion in Tolkien: Author of the Century. *Shippey argues that Tolkien's very deliberate intention was to re-create an English mythology that he felt had somehow been lost. Kilby adds the intriguing detail that Tolkien told him he had considered dedicating* The Silmarillion *to Queen Elizabeth with the comment, "The only thing in which your country is not rich is mythology."*

At Tolkien's death his story of the First Age of Middle-earth was incomplete—how incomplete nobody will ever know. For him *The Lord of the Rings* was likewise unfinished. We must never fail to recognize that he was not simply "writing a story" but wrestling with a world. There is some parallel between what Tolkien was attempting and the production of Dr. Samuel Johnson's dictionary in the eighteenth century. Imagine the task of sitting down to bring together all the words of the English people and showing their pronunciation, their origin, history, usage, and varied meanings. Both Tolkien and Dr. Johnson had some precedents. There were dictionaries before Johnson and there were mythologies before Tolkien. Johnson had in view the pulling together of the world of words to provide a broad and consistent framework for the English language. Tolkien, having tried to pull together strands from the world of mythology and finding the result uneven, even weak, was endeavoring to construct a more complete pattern. He told me that he had contemplated dedicating *The Silmarillion* to Queen Elizabeth and saying, "The only thing in which your country is not rich is mythology." But perhaps no mythology whatever was as rich as Tolkien wanted it to be.

It was my task to read the typescripts he handed me and give him my judgment of them. But I soon realized that I was doing more. Tolkien needed someone not so much to give him literary criticism as to press him, one way or another, into renewed attention to it. I have mentioned my feeling that he had done relatively little work on this story for a long time. On more than one occasion I found him unable to answer specific questions about the contents of *The Silmarillion.* He seemed happy that I was making records of what the story contained and was comparing its narrative with people and events in *The Lord of the Rings*, feeling that such a record would be valuable in the process, which he described as "writing backwards." For a man of his age it was a superlunary task to set about integrating the three ages of Middle-earth into one whole.

Something of the enormity of his intention is apparent in his plan for a whole series of languages, any one of which might require decades to work out. He planned a Dwarf language. Compared with Elvish it was to sound "cumbrous and unlovely." We know of Tolkien's relish for genealogies, chronologies, and maps, and of course all these were to accompany all three ages. He had drawn a splendid map of Beleriand (though in some minor ways it was incomplete), but whether there were also maps of the region of

Valinor and Eressëa I do not know. I pointed out to him the good effect of poetry in *The Lord of the Rings* and the desirability of poetry in his accounts of the other ages.

What I actually did was carry to my room the portions of the story handed me and endeavor to judge them individually and in relation to each other. All together this amounted to twenty-eight portions from a couple of pages in length up to 132 pages. Sometimes there were overlapping portions. For the most part they were concerned less with the Valar and early history of Middle-earth than with Elves, Dwarves, and Men, particularly Elves and more particularly the curse upon the Noldor.

In my hopes of encouraging him to go on with the composition, I pointed out with serious concern that I had found nothing about Tom Bombadil, the Ents and Entwives, the making of the Palantíri, and other items. We recall, for instance, that Treebeard's eyes were "filled up with ages of memory and long, slow, steady thinking,"[62] and that Tom Bombadil remembered the first raindrop and the first acorn.[63] We are told exactly that the Ents were known to the Eldar "in ancient days."[64] In my working out of a chronology for the First Age, I tried to encourage him by inserting such corollaries at points that seemed to me appropriate.

The most persistent hope among readers of Tolkien is for the publication of *The Silmarillion*. What many of them do not recognize is that much of that story is already scattered through *The Lord of the Rings*. There are over six hundred allusions to the First and Second Ages of Middle-earth in *The Hobbit* and *The Lord of the Rings*, all the way from the times before time when Eru, the One, creator of all things and self-existent, gave a vision of all Arda to the heavenly beings about him, to Eärendil's desperate voyage centuries later to the Blessed Realm to request help from

62 *The Two Towers*, Bk. III, Ch. 4.
63 *The Fellowship of the Ring*, Bk. I, Ch. 7.
64 *The Return of the King*, Appendix F.

the Valar lest Middle-earth be entirely overcome by Morgoth.[65] The appendices to volume 3 are, in places, rich with significant information. In the story proper we may expect to find allusions particularly germane to the Elves in the songs and tales of such places as Rivendell, Lothlorien, and Fangorn. A Dwarf such as Gimli may be expected to allude warmly to the past in locations like Moria and Helm's Deep. Mysterious intuitions of the ancient past may also come from a Hobbit such as Sam Gamgee. Allusions to the Second Age are more likely in such places as Rohan and Gondor. In truth, past history pervades the stories of Tolkien that are already in print, and careful reading of those accounts often reveals not simply the facts but often the poignant joys, sorrows, and significance of those ages.

I must leave my reader the choice either of making his own reconstruction of *The Silmarillion* out of *The Lord of the Rings* and other books by Tolkien or else the easier way of simply awaiting the publication of that story. What I wish to do now is discuss briefly the chronology of the composition of Tolkien's fiction.

Unless one reads with care it is possible to assume that most of Tolkien's creative writing was done in the 1930s and later. In the foreword to the Ballantine paperback of *The Lord of the Rings* Tolkien says that this story was "begun soon after *The Hobbit* was written and before its publication in 1937." He adds that the content of *The Lord of the Rings* was derived in some of its elements from what had been said in *The Hobbit*. Indeed, its main theme, the Ring, was settled with the finding of the ring by Bilbo at the time of his underground riddle-making contest with Gollum and his knowledge of the fact that it made the wearer invisible.

Tolkien goes on to say that after the publication of *The Hobbit* in 1937 he was "encouraged by requests by readers for more

65 *The Fellowship of the Ring*, Bk. II, Ch. 1; *The Return of the King*, Appendix A, 1. The Númenórean Kings.

information concerning hobbits and their adventures," and this caused him to go back to "the older world," i.e., to such characters and places as Gandalf, the High-elves, Durin, Moria, Elrond, and Gondolin. It was the "discovery of the significance of these glimpses and of their relation to the ancient histories [which] revealed the Third Age and its culmination in the War of the Ring."

He continues in this foreword to say that "the composition of *The Lord of the Rings* went on at intervals during the years 1936 to 1949," and he identifies particular portions and the year of their composition. In a letter he reports, "The general idea of *The Lord of the Rings* was certainly in my mind from an early stage; that is from the first draft of Book I, Chapter 2, written in the 1930's. From time to time I made rough sketches or synopses of what was to follow, immediately or far ahead; but these were seldom of much use: the story unfolded itself as it were. The tying-up was achieved, so far as it is achieved, by constant re-writing backwards."[66] Book 1, chapter 2 recounts Gandalf's long talk with Frodo about his search for Gollum and the meaning of the Ring, now vastly larger than in *The Hobbit*, so one can see how very naturally the writing of that portion came first.

But in his article in *Diplomat* Tolkien proposes an entirely different version of the origin and composition of his main creative works. "This business," he said, "began so far back that it might be said to have begun at birth." The mythology "first began to take shape during the 1914–18 war. The Fall of Gondolin (and the birth of Eärendil) was written in Hospital and on leave after surviving the Battle of the Somme in 1916." Very significantly, he speaks of the account of Lúthien Tinúviel and Beren as the "kernel" of the mythology, and says that it arose from a "small woodland glade filled with 'hemocks' (or other white unbellifers)

---

66 Unpublished letter to Caroline W. Everett, in her master's thesis, "The Imaginative Fiction of J.R.R. Tolkien."

near Roos in the Holderness peninsula—to which I occasionally went when free from regimental duties while in the Humber Garrison in 1913."[67] Actually he told one of his closest friends that he had the whole of his mythic world in his mind as early as 1906. He told me that he was writing some of *The Silmarillion* (doubtless yet untitled) about 1910, and he wrote me that the story, meaning possibly the account as a whole, began in 1916–1917 "and has been with me ever since."[68]

I think it unwise to understand anything other than that all three ages of Middle-earth, and indeed *The Hobbit*, have, in some respects at least, a cognate fountainhead in Tolkien's imagination.

As early as January 1930, Lewis identified Tolkien to Arthur Greeves in Ireland as "the writer of the voluminous unpublished metrical romances and of the maps, companions to them, showing the mountains of Dread and Nargothrond the city of the Orcs." If by 1930 it was "voluminous," and if we recall that Tolkien was a busy don, and also that Niggle was a deliberate and painstaking artist, it is easily possible to assume an accumulation reaching back into the 1920s or even earlier.

From a letter by Lewis to Greeves we also know the date at which *The Hobbit* was completed, for he wrote on January 30, 1930, "I have had a delightful time reading a childhood story which Tolkien has just written."[69] By 1939 Lewis reported his and Tolkien's reading together, chapter by chapter, of the "new *Hobbit*," and again in 1946 he reported that the longer story was being read a chapter at a time in the Inklings. Lewis repeatedly pointed out to people that *The Lord of the Rings* was written before the events of World War II and the use of the atomic

67 *Diplomat*, October, 1966, 39.

68 See page 17.

69 Both these letters to Greeves are unpublished. Lewis adds to the second letter: "Whether it is really good (I think it is until the end) is of course another question: still more, whether it will succeed with modern children."

bomb.[70] Likewise, said Lewis, it is wrong to assume that Tolkien's "methodology" grew out of the writing of *The Hobbit.* At some date after 1944, Lewis wrote Charles A. Brady that *The Hobbit* was "merely the adaptation to children of part of a huge private mythology of a most serious kind." Later Lewis called *The Hobbit* a "fragment" of *The Lord of the Rings.*[71]

This second explanation of the period of commencement of Tolkien's myth coincides with the impression I received from him. It appeared to me as we talked together that the whole thing had begun, as he says, at birth. I sometimes felt it was almost prenatal. The distinguishing word in a comparison of the foreword of the Ballantine paperback and his article in *Diplomat* is "composition," i.e., the time of the pulling together of the parts into a publishable whole.

Tolkien told me that some of the poems in *Tom Bombadil* had been written by him "as a boy." He said also that his love of languages began when he was five or six, and we are told that it was his linguistic concern that generated his myth. At the beginning of his essay "On Fairy-stories," he says that he has been a lover of this sort of writing "since I learned to read." At King Edward's School in Birmingham, which he entered in 1903 at the age of eleven, he was introduced to Chaucer and Anglo-Saxon. One reason he was not a top scholar there was because much of his time was spent in private investigations of Gothic, Anglo-Saxon, and Welsh as well as early attempts to invent a language of his own.

In the *Diplomat* article he makes the significant remark that "the mythology (and associated languages) first began to take shape during the 1914–18 war." He told me that he had read "The Fall of Gondolin" to a college group in 1918. When I inquired about "The Lay of Eärendil," he said that there was

70 *Letters of C. S. Lewis,* 14, 273; *Of Other Worlds,* 49, etc.

71 Both letters are unpublished. The second one is to Thomas T. Howard and is dated October 28, 1958.

none; that as an undergraduate he had written a few lines, but that was all.

From these statements we are able to work out a sequence of genesis and composition something like the following:

1. He acknowledged a very early love of Faërie.
2. At five or six he began to appreciate words as words, and before he entered college he was vitally involved with languages and had started to create one of his own.
3. He had written boyhood verse, some of it possibly about Tom Bombadil.
4. By 1906 he had in his mind the outline of his myth as a whole.
5. Some of the adventures of Lúthien Tinúviel were conceived by 1913.
6. By 1930 the story is "voluminous," suggesting perhaps a decade or more of sporadic composition.
7. When the story of the Valar, the earliest part of *The Silmarillion*, was composed we do not know. Yet we have Tolkien's word that as early as 1913 the long episode of Lúthien and Beren was shaping up. If that episode included the wresting of the Silmaril from Morgoth, then the Silmaril suggests the Two Trees and they in turn suggest the Valar and the early history of Middle-earth.
8. Tolkien gave me the impression of having conceived of Hobbits not long before *The Hobbit* was written, about 1929.
9. He identified 1936 to 1945 as the period of the composition of *The Lord of the Rings*. But Lewis's assertion that that story had no connection with Hitler and the atomic

bomb suggests that the essential story was in existence before the beginning of World War II in 1939.

10. In 1939 Tolkien and Lewis were reading the chapters of *The Lord of the Rings* together, perhaps each chapter as it was completed. This writing and revision were going on also in 1945 or 1946 when chapters were read to the Inklings.
11. The three volumes of *The Lord of the Rings* were published in 1954, 1955, and 1956.
12. Tolkien told me that he had "recently" written "The Wanderings of Húrin," a long account of a man captured and held by Morgoth for twenty-eight years, and of his later wanderings, a portion of *The Silmarillion.*

In the future we shall no doubt have a much better record of the chronology of the conception and composition of Tolkien's mythology, but for the present this would appear to be roughly correct.

THE GEOGRAPHY OF MIDDLE-EARTH

There is no doubt at all that by interpretation, i.e., figuratively, Middle-earth represents our own world. We are at home in its struggles and its joys. The size or oddity of its inhabitants, even in the case of the Ents, does not prevent our full, and often intense, understanding of their mortal meaning. But the question is often asked whether Middle-earth is strictly related in a geographical way to our own world. This is something more than a theoretical question, for if it becomes clear that given locations are identifiable as our own then the allegorical flag may promptly begin to wave.

A good many readers believe that the Shire is England or a portion of England, and this Tolkien confirmed when once asked if there were Hobbits in the earlier ages. He plainly answered that there were none because Hobbits were English, a remark that both confirms geographical delineations and has wide temporal implications. As to the geography, we were once driving a few miles east of Oxford on the London Road and Tolkien pointed out little hills to the north of us that, he said, were just right for Hobbit territory. He spoke also about the old mill at Birmingham, where he lived as a boy, as being the Shire mill, and was pleased with the notion that it might for that reason be preserved.

Of course the rural charm of the Shire fits well with Tolkien's love of the English countryside. He says that the dry and barren places he had known in South Africa gave him a special power "to savour the delicate English flowers and grass."[72] The great number of Anglo-Saxon person and place names also fits both Tolkien's scholarship and his loves. Tolkien points out that though the shape of lands was much changed, Hobbits still linger in "the North-West of the Old World, east of the sea."[73]

But if England is indeed Shire country, then what of rest of Middle-earth? In a telephone conversation with Tolkien, Mr. Henry Resnick asked what was east of Rhûn and south of Harad, to which Tolkien replied, "Rhûn is the Elvish word for east. Asia, China, Japan, and all the things which people in the West regard as far away. And south Harad is Africa, the hot countries." Then Mr. Resnick asked, "That makes Middle-earth Europe, doesn't it?" To which Tolkien replied, "Yes, of course—Northwestern Europe . . . where my imagination comes from."[74] Not long afterward, when I mentioned this interview to Tolkien, he denied having ever said these things. Yet later, when in my own efforts to get the geography of *The Silmarillion* straight

72 "The Man Who Understands Hobbits," Charlotte and Denis Plimmer, *London Daily Telegraph Magazine*, March 22, 1968.
73 *The Fellowship of the Ring*, Prologue: 1. Concerning Hobbits.
74 *Niekas*, 18:43.

I asked Tolkien where Númenor was, he promptly responded, "In the middle of the Atlantic." Is this another instance of the Professor's "contrasistency," or is there a logical explanation? He is reported to have said specifically that Mordor "would be roughly in the Balkans."[75]

All this thrusts upon us not simply geography but European history, and the allegorical framework that Tolkien so vociferously denied. For instance, shall we not under these circumstances take a new look at the degradation of the Shire during the absence of the four Hobbits and the cleansing and rehabilitation that became necessary? To localize a story geographically or temporally is always at least a threat that undercuts any larger meaning, certainly a mythic one.

---

75 "The Man Who Understands Hobbits," *op cit.*

Chapter 17

THE LOST MYTH AND LITERARY IMAGINATION

Kilby was delighted and intrigued by the massive interest in Tolkien, and in the following lecture he gives a penetrating analysis of some of the reasons for that interest. "Postmodernism" had not quite been invented yet (and Kilby would have been deeply suspicious of the looseness of the label). Still, inasmuch as the label means anything, it is useful in understanding Kilby's whole approach, and the power his teaching had on some students who were alienated by a world—even within the church—that seemed dominated by the "modern" characteristics of efficiency, analysis, and a reductive rationality. Kilby wrote before the possibility of genetic engineering, the growth of the virtual world, and talk of "posthumanism." But his analysis anticipates those developments, and the growing interest in fantasy that has accompanied it as a kind of reaction. For it is certainly true that the mood of the last thirty years (whether we call the times "late modern" or "postmodern" or nothing at all) shows an increasing longing for myth and story. Whether the popularity of Tolkien's work (and fantasy in general) is a cause or an effect of that longing is impossible to say. In any case the following analysis of Tolkien in light of the "lost myth" of wholeness certainly illuminates our own time. Readers who are interested in pursuing more of Kilby's prescient musings on modernity, art, and the power of myth and imagination will appreciate the companion volume to this work, edited by Bill Dyrness, The Arts and the Christian Imagination: Essays on Art, Literature, and Aesthetics. *We include this lecture here because*

Kilby finds the malaise of his (and our times) nobly answered in The Lord of the Rings, *and the values we find lacking—"hierarchy, the essential mystery of nature, co-inherence, and right imagination"—richly present and accessible there. Hence, argues Kilby, its great importance for our time.*

The background against which I should like to put what I have to say is J. R. R. Tolkien's *Lord of the Rings* and the peculiar fact that in our so-called realistic world there are hundreds of thousands of high-school, college, and university students (not to mention doctors, lawyers, scientists, teachers, etc.) who are reading a story about elves and dwarves, orcs and balrogs, seeing stones and magical rings, and about ordinary Shire-loving hobbits who, having reluctantly accepted a quest involving their own lives and the life of the entire third age of Middle-earth, carry through on that quest in the highest tradition of heroism and in an atmosphere patently free of the hard "realism" that is said to be the archetype of our time. Though I am sure that David Boroff, writing in the *New York Times Book Review* for January 10, 1965, was wrong, one can sympathize with him for supposing the collegiate interest in *The Lord of the Rings* to be a piece of dandyism and mock seriousness. I want to suggest what I think [is] a better explanation of this wide interest in Tolkien.

This explanation might be evidence of the beginning of recovery, or at least the wish to recover, from an old sore. It could be evidence of a desire to recover the Lost Myth.

This Lost Myth, I think, is the myth of man's wholeness.

Even in the fourth century BC, Plato made it clear that man was already sundered. Aristophanes, talking with his friends Socrates, Eryximachus, and others, told how originally men were supposed to have had four legs, four arms, two heads, etc., and how in time these men began to think they were something and dared to try to scale heaven. Instead of annihilating them, Zeus finally hit upon the idea of humbling them by splitting them in two—since when, says Aristophanes, in their loneliness the two halves have longed and searched for one another continuously.

Zeus threatened if necessary to keep on chopping man into pieces to cure his pride. Well, today it seems that man is in about as many pieces as can be imagined, and consequently his loneliness and confusion are more pronounced than ever. Although José Ortega y Gasset's description of twentieth-century man was written a good many years ago, it seems to me fully as true now as then, possibly more true. He said:

> We live at a time when man believes himself fabulously capable of creation, but he does not know what to create. Lord of all things, he is not lord of himself. He feels lost amid his own abundance. With more means at his disposal, more knowledge, more technique than ever, it turns out that the world today goes the same way as the worst of worlds that have been: it simply drifts. Hence the strange combination of a sense of power and a sense of insecurity which has taken up its abode in the soul of modern man. To him is happening what was said of the Regent during the minority of Louis XV: he had all the talents except the talent to make use of them.[76]

This sense of a broken and adrift civilization is, I think, the most apparent thing on our present horizon.

I should like to discuss mainly one possible factor attendant upon even if not fully causal to our atomized world. And I hope I may be excused if, like so many others, I go back to Lord Bacon

76 *The Revolt of the Masses* (New York: W. W. Norton & Company, 1932), 47–48.

and the year 1620. In the preface to his famous *Novum Organum* he says,

> I propose to establish progressive stages of certainty . . . starting directly from the simple sensuous perception . . . (and having) no confidence in the native and spontaneous process of the mind. . . . There remains but one course for the recovery of a sound and healthy condition,—namely, that the entire work of the understanding be commenced afresh, and the mind itself be from the very outset not left to take its own course, but guided at every step; and the business be done as if by machinery.[77]

This was the road, Bacon said, to certainty and health. The thing that had been at fault was "the native and spontaneous process of the mind." The remedy to overcome this outlaw was to destroy, if I may put it so, its mythic tendency. Bacon, with motives that are understandable, wished to have something certain, something men could quietly and surely agree upon, money they could put in the bank and get a receipt for, a golden yardstick that would enable men forever to say that a yard is a yard is a yard.

But how could one begin to establish Bacon's "progressive stages of certainty" and perhaps in time move on to some final glorious climax of finitude and total knowing? Not backward toward metaphysics and theology. These were the realms that had made Bacon and his century dizzy and given them the longing for certainty. Much earlier there had been a period when the universe appeared a splendid unity. Pythagoras and his brotherhood more than twenty centuries before had discovered what they believed to be a cosmos, one world, one whole, inclusive universe, with a great Mathematician at its

77 Preface, Sir Francis Bacon, *Novum Organum*, by Lord Bacon, ed. by Joseph Devey, M.A. (New York: P. F. Collier, 1902).

center and circumference. There are stories to the effect that when Pythagoras discovered the square on the hypotenuse he sacrificed a hundred oxen, also that when irrational numbers were discovered a penalty of death was set for allowing such a heretical idea to escape and work its evil in the world. The Pythagorean spring had welled up into a great river with glorious tributaries such as Socrates, Plato, Aristotle, Plotinus, Augustine, Aquinas, and the like. But after all the centuries there was still not the certainty that Bacon zealously longed for. How could that certainty be attained?

"I propose," he said, "to establish progressive stages of certainty starting directly from the simple sensuous perception." We know the direction that was taken, what today we call science (from *sciens*, knowing). And out of Bacon's century and following there have flowed rivers of knowing. One need only mention such names as those of Galileo, Kepler, Descartes, Newton, Locke, the Encyclopedists, the Royal Society, etc., and remind ourselves how chemistry swallowed up alchemy and astronomy swallowed up (or did It?) astrology. I need not take any time describing the ever-widening river of "progressive stages of certainty" that flowed through the nineteenth century and has become something of an ocean in our time. Bacon's method is far more successful today than perhaps he ever dreamed. Many are wondering if anything at all is beyond the reach of the inductive method, from physics to chemistry, from chemistry to biology, from biology to psychology, from psychology to sociology, etc. In medicine, for instance, we can now do for men what we do for automobiles—we can supply new parts, and there is talk of starting all over again with some sort of brand new manmade model. In *Brave New World Revisited* Aldous Huxley spoke of his shock at finding his imagined world of total scientific control rapidly coming into actuality within his own lifetime. Dr. Philip Siekevitz, biochemist at the Rockefeller Institute, said not long ago:

> There is a golden age ahead on earth. . . . We are approaching the greatest event in human history . . . the deliberate changing by man of many of his biological processes . . . man will be remodeling his own being. . . . Events in biological research are happening so rapidly that we will soon have to answer a new question. No longer, "What creature is man?" but rather "What creature should he become?"[78]

Is ours not indeed a Brave New World? But then one must ask the additional question why people are not filled with deep satisfaction, quiet ecstasy, and great expectations? Why along with Ortega's sense of power do we have an almost overcoming sense of despair? I heard of a man who went down the street and said "Good Morning" to another man that he passed. The second man asked, "In relation to what?"

You recall Sartre's "No Exit" and a group of people discovering they have gone to hell. In the room where they find themselves, one asks: "But, I say, where are the instruments of torture? . . . The racks and red-hot pincers and all the other paraphernalia?" Later, in a frenzy, he shouts: "Open the door! Open, blast you! I'll endure anything, your red-hot tongs and molten lead, your racks and prongs and garrotes—all your fiendish gadgets, everything that burns and flays and tears—I'll put up with any torture you impose. Anything, anything would be better than this agony of mind, this creeping pain that gnaws and fumbles and caresses one and never hurts quite enough." He grabs the doorknob and shouts: "Now will you open?" whereupon the door flies open and he is urged to leave, to which he hesitates and then replies, "I shall not go." In the end all the group remain, tortured and in pain greater than fire and brimstone, because there is nothing to

78 "The Man of the Future," *The Nation* (September 13, 1958), 128.

be free for. You recall a similar pessimistic evaluation in Camus's *The Stranger*, where a man about to shoot another man whom he actually has nothing against says, "One might fire, or not fire—and it would come to the same thing."

One wonders how to explain the winds of nihilism, destructionism, fragmentation, and the death-wish that now sweep across the landscape, a direction perhaps most clearly manifest in the arts. Lewis Mumford says, "The death of the human personality is the message of modern art." Leonard Baskin declares that in avant-garde art "it is man that has been excluded . . . that has been denied." A few weeks ago I sat at table with a professor of art history from the Free University of Amsterdam who, on the basis of his study of modern art, felt there was little to look forward to except brutality and the concentration camp. A good many years ago Mark Van Doren said, "We are not even sure what poetry should be about, if it can be about anything anymore." *Time* magazine recently said, "Nearly every important American writer—Nabokov, Mailer, Barth, Bellow, Malamud, Donleavy, Roth, Friedman, Burroughs, Heller, Pynchon, Willingham—works from an assumption that society is at best malevolent and stupid, at worst wholly lunatic. The gods are dead and their graves untended, [and] morality is a matter of picking one's way between competing absurdities."[79]

A long time ago I read a book that still sticks in my mind. It reported that libraries double their holdings about once every sixteen years and pointed out that should, for instance, Yale library continue to expand at the same rate for another century as it has for the past two, it will then have 200 million volumes occupying over six thousand miles of shelves. The card catalog will require eight acres, and six thousand catalogers will be needed

79 Lewis Mumford, "Dehumanized Nightmares," *Time*, May 1, 1951; Leonard Baskin, "The Necessity for the Image," *Atlantic Monthly* (April, 1961), 76; Mark Van Doren, "The Poetry of Our Day Expresses Our Doubt and the Time's Confusion," *New York Herald Tribune Book Review* (September 25, 1949), 9; Time (April 26, 1968), 68.

to handle material coming in at the rate of 12 million volumes a year. We seem to be like Faustus or Byron's Manfred running everywhere and searching for Something Big but without finding it. Two hundred years ago Voltaire said, "The multitude of books is making us ignorant." How much more ignorant, then, we must be today. Yet we can add that quantity is never properly equated with quality, and a man who sets himself to the task can read most of the truly great books of the world.

Nevertheless the mere quantity and bewildering bulk of things presented to the attention today is no doubt part of what Ortega was thinking about when he spoke of our parallel feeling of power and despair.

But of course the search for certainty ought never to be a thing to cause despair. Whether by sharpness of instrument or depth of perspective, any means of arrival at what is permanent and true must always be commendatory. The despair therefore, insofar as it is related to the progressive stages of certainty described by Bacon, seems to be the result of an oversell that was neither intended by the best practitioners of the method nor indeed inherent in the method. Rather the despair is owing to two popular misunderstandings. One is the supposition that science actually does move "as if by machinery" toward its goals; the other that its reach is endless.

Not infrequently leading scientists have pointed out that believing such an apparently obvious thing as the "simple sensuous perception" is actually an act of faith and that imagination is about as necessary in all real science as in artistic creativity. Warren Weaver, vice president for the natural and medical sciences of the Rockefeller Foundation, declares, "The shocking fact is that science simply does not have detailed and precise access to what we ordinarily call the external world." Instead of dealing with hard, real fact, Weaver insists that science is "playing a subtle game with nature, all based on an unproved and unprovable faith that this procedure is meaningful and rewarding."[80] As to the supposed infinite outreach of science, Dr. Charles Singer of the University of London, writing on the history of science in the latest edition of the *Britannica Encyclopedia*, says that there "cannot be a 'science' of the whole universe; for it is impossible to attain this by adding the sciences together, and there are vast regions of experience, such as art, literature, and philosophy, that are refractory to scientific treatment." It is a popular belief in Science Unlimited, a faith that nothing whatever is beyond the reach of science and that any other approach to truth is as antiquated as an auto graveyard, which has left us, in Matthew Arnold's words, with the feeling of

> Wandering between two worlds, one dead,
> The other powerless to be born.

Another possible cause of our despair is the seeming revelations of science about a mechanistic universe, man's animal origin, psychological behaviorism, and the like, leaving us with the feeling of being hardly more than biological specimens. A minor sign of this, I think, is the increasing frequency of our adoption of words like *react*, *interact*, and *feedback*. The *Broadcaster*, a little sheet of announcements at my college, has more than once read, "Come out this evening at 8:00 and interact with Professor Brown on So-and-So." The suggestion seems to be that no arrival at anything like a truth or even a tenable conclusion is to be reached and that only a kind of low-grade cerebral game on the order of ping-pong will be played. After this little stunt we can drink a bit of coffee, then go on our way as if nothing had really happened. The discovery of any real certainty must be left, apparently, to the computer.

---

80 "A Scientist Ponders Faith," *Saturday Review* (January 3, 1959), 9.

Yet the ancient ideal of Truth, Beauty, and Goodness has never been abrogated. The universe, if we are to believe the majority of the scientists themselves, is more than physical, and its structures, harmonies, and meaning rise above measurement. The universal must precede rather than follow the sensuous perception before any greatly significant meaning can appear, and the effort of man to dispossess himself of a "given," to stand outside himself and act "as if by machinery," is both impossible and, as to any ultimate knowledge, the surest means of falsification. Hence it is possible, if one will, to find readily at hand a vertical as well as a horizontal and at least a working approximation to the absolute and transcendent. "The cosmic religious experience is the strongest and noblest mainspring of scientific research," said Albert Einstein. "The most beautiful and profound emotion we can experience is the sensation of the mystical. It is the sower of all true science. He to whom this emotion is a stranger, who can no longer wonder and stand rapt in awe, is as good as dead. To know that what is impenetrable to us really exists, manifesting itself as the highest wisdom and the most radiant—beauty which our dull faculties can comprehend only in their most primitive forms—this knowledge, this feeling is at the center of true religiousness."[81]

The conclusion seems clear that we must pursue values and truth as wise men have always pursued them, that is, by summoning the whole man to thought within a hierarchical universe. This, then, is my first suggestion for the repossession of our lost myth.

A second suggestion toward wholeness would be the recognition of mystery in nature. Keats talks of a time

> When holy were the haunted forest boughs,
> Holy the air, the water, and the fire.

81 Lincoln Barnett, *The Universe and Dr. Einstein* (New York: William Morrow and Co., 1957), 108.

I have asked myself seriously which of two possible attitudes toward, for instance, the sun is actually more humanly tenable. Is it more truthful, in the long run, to declare the sun to be merely gases, heat, and chemical elements identifiable by spectroscopic analysis or else to declare it, as did the early Greeks, a god? Speaking of that word "merely," C. S. Lewis, in his little book *The Abolition of Man*, discusses the "conquering" of nature by reducing it to smaller and smaller bits of less and less living reality and concluding that it is merely this or that. He ends his study with the remarkable sentence, "To 'see through' all things is the same as not to see at all." Some of our best physicists think that Shelley may be right in asserting

. . . Every grain
Is sentient both in unity and part,
And the minutest atom comprehends
A world of loves and hatreds.

More and more it looks as if those things we call atoms may have a will of their own and may be playing a far subtler game with man than he realizes.

I think it would be helpful if we went back and read some of the medieval bestiaries and herbals. Beyond their quaintness we might find in them real values. In those times the most therapeutically useful plants were considered sacred and symbolically assumed to have first grown on the hill of Calvary, a place itself looked upon as the center of the world. Is there the least touch of this kind of thing in our present view of nature? Most of us, I suppose, would think an antivivisectionist in this century little short of a boob, but men like Bernard Shaw, C. E. M. Joad, C. S. Lewis, and Albert Schweitzer believed that vivisectionism in our time marks "a great advance in the triumph of ruthless, non-moral utilitarianism over the old world of ethical law."[82] I think most of us would be shocked beyond measure if we knew how many thousands of animals suffer torture every day in laboratories—perhaps a great many more than need be. If any objection is raised to this, or to such things as cutting a four-lane highway through a forest preserve or despoiling a beauty spot such as Glen Canyon, the answer always is that man must be served. But which part of man? I myself have practiced for many years looking upon the morning light as an unmerited and mysterious gift and on life in flora and fauna as worthy of a daily salute and even a bow. Years ago I heard somebody say that all our political and diplomatic conferences ought to be moved out of smoke-filled rooms and held underneath trees. It seemed to me excellent. I wonder if under those circumstances the conclusions reached might not be quite different from what they are at present.

I have a good friend in the South with whom I have often walked through the woods. He has the uncanny ability to estimate the number of board-feet in standing trees and has made a small fortune through the gift. For myself, the walks are as Wordsworthian as my limited sensitivity will permit. Between the two, though of course they are not mutually exclusive, I choose my appreciation to his money. More recognition of mystery and symbol in nature would, I think, contribute to our reacquisition of wholeness. And the effort will by no means be simply a sentimental one.

The third suggestion I make about wholeness has to do with what Charles Williams calls co-inherence and exchange, doctrines in part growing out of Williams's inability, because of his eyes, to take part in the military and his realization that simply by being alive he is necessarily involved in other lives and sacrifice. Dr. Donne said, "One man's death diminishes me

82 "Vivisection," Boston, New England Anti-Vivisection Society, 7 (further details unavailable).

because I am a part of mankind." We are members one of another. I am not talking of banners and marches. These practices have come into existence because of the loss of a deeper sense of man as a mysterious creature walking about on a mysterious thing in stellar space called a planet, and man filled, as Mark Van Doren says, with the realization that "he is more than he need be and less than he would be."[83] Much is said now about the necessity of self-fulfillment. But the question is which of two selves to fulfill. I have never ceased to be amazed at the popularity for years of a book called *How to Win Friends and Influence People.* Was a more truly selfish title ever hatched up? Later Daniel J. Boorstin wrote a book called *The Image* in which he discusses a world more and more filled with pseudo-events and artificial ways of life. What sort of world is so dominated by the need for "fun" that an entertainer can make more money in a week than we pay the president of our country for his services for an entire year? Anyway, fun is no substitute, as we all well know, for the deeper need called joy, an effect that results from a living sense of co-inherence, exchange, and substitution.

A fourth avenue toward wholeness is imagination. Imagination was deliberately excluded from Bacon's prescription. You remember Charles Darwin's description of himself not long before he died. "My mind," he wrote, "seems to have become a kind of machine for grinding general laws out of large collections of facts, but why this should have caused the atrophy of that part of the brain alone, on which the higher tastes depend, I cannot conceive." He remarked that if he had his life to live over again he would follow the rule of reading some poetry and listening to some music at least once a week. Because "the loss of these tastes is a loss of happiness, and may possibly be injurious to the

83 Mark Van Doren, *Liberal Education* (New York: Henry Holt and Company, 1943), 19.

intellect, and more probably to the moral character, by enfeebling the emotional part of our nature."[84] Earlier in this century a president said that what was needed in his time was a great poet who would tell us who we are and where we are. That need grows more urgent as disparity and fragmentation increases: The great secret of poetry is the metaphor, and the secret of metaphor is imagination. Imagination enables us to reach up and touch sky and embrace trees and talk to birds and animals and to communicate meaningfully with other humans. Imagination lets us know that man is himself an image, a mystery, a symbol, and indeed a myth.

No doubt there are other avenues looking to man's wholeness than the four I have mentioned—hierarchy, the essential mystery of nature, co-inherence, and right imagination. I have suggested these as ones that appear important to me.

Now I should like to return to J. R. R. Tolkien's *The Lord of the Rings* and the fact that this story is now being widely read and proving deeply meaningful to thousands. Let me briefly identify in this work the four types of wholeness I have mentioned.

In the *Rings* we have an unfailing hierarchy whose most obvious element is so completely a moral one that even to mention it seems a little out of place. Edmund Wilson insists that Tolkien's villains are too black and his heroes too white. But he overlooks the fact that in every instance evil is shown to be a corruption of the good. Morgoth and Sauron were in the beginning among those given a celestial vision of the right and who volunteered to help turn that potential good into actual good. The Ringwraiths were formerly good men who were seduced into Sauron's service. Saruman was once a member of the White Council and had long withstood evil before he came finally under the domination of Sauron. If some of the Elvish leaders seem too good, they also

84 *Life and Letters of Charles Darwin* (New York: Appleton Century Crafts, 1901), vol. 1, 81–92.

have an all but eternal background of good and evil against which their conduct must be seen. If Middle-earth history is overlooked, Mr. Wilson's assertion has truth in it, but to overlook that history means to have misread Tolkien.

Divine right is a subject I think I have never heard commended, but the conception of a man divinely given that right to rule and fully accepting the responsibility of ruling as a mediator between higher and lower is one of the finest things possible in the blind alleys of this world. All of the "high" characters in the *Rings*, and especially Aragorn, who is literally a king, represent truly the principle of divine right. Aragorn for long went about as servant and protector of the people and preserved the same excellent relationship when he came to his throne.

In the *Rings*, history is not only present but also warmly alive to promote and even sanctify actions. Hardly anything is more characteristic of elves than their long look at their past, a past that is congenitally rooted and in which consciousness and conscience are coeval.

Then can one fail to breathe deeply of the glory and mystery of nature in the story? Just to mention Lothlorien is to evoke beatitude. Nature there and elsewhere is "inhabited." This is especially true of trees. The talking trees called Ents become characters in their own right. Frodo put his hand on one of the great mallorn trees in Lothlorien and suddenly realized that he had never before understood "the feel and texture of a tree's skin and of the life within it. He felt delight in wood and the touch of it, neither as forester nor as carpenter; it was the delight of the living tree itself." The mystery of seeds and of growth are represented by Galadriel's gift of a mallorn seed and the soft gray dust that caused all other trees quickly to repossess the Shire after Frodo and Sam's return. Lewis points out that reading about enchanted trees gives real trees an enchanted quality. It is so in this story.

The fragrant grass filled with star-shaped yellow elanor and the pale niphredil in timeless Lothlorien works its own magic, as does Aragorn's discovery in the darkness, by its sweet and pungent odor, of the herb athelas for the healing of Frodo's wound from the Ringwraiths. This herb, we are told, had been brought to Middle-earth from Númenor. Its existence was known to very few people, a suggestion perhaps that the essential contact with the perduring good earth is now mostly lost to men. The great horse Shadowfax bears almost a talking relation with Gandalf, and in many other ways the substantial existence of nature in its own right is manifest in the *Rings*.

And again, how thoroughly the principle of co-inherence is exemplified in Tolkien's story. One of the elves in Lothlorien remarks that "in nothing is the power of the Dark Lord more clearly shown than in the estrangement that divides those who still oppose him." The fellowship of the Ring consists of a wizard, an elf, a dwarf, four hobbits, and two men, each with his own peculiarities and strengths yet all moving together in the accomplishment of a single good purpose. It is a case, I think, suggesting the truth of Lewis's remark that democracy is not a process of making people equal but enabling clearly unequal people to live amicably together. One of the finest touches, I think, occurs upon the demand that Gimli the dwarf be blindfolded as he walks through Lothlorien. When Gimli refuses and an impasse seems upon them, Aragorn suggests that all be blindfolded and it is done. All suffer for one, and later when the blindfolds are removed they are repaid by a great burst of glory. Williams's co-inherence and exchange are thus illustrated.

At a time when ancient customs of courtesy and ceremony are about as obsolete as dinosaurs, one of the most appealing elements of the *Rings* is the practice of such customs. We recall the order of the gatherings at Rivendell and Minas Tirith as well as the epochal custom of gift-giving as exemplified in Galadriel's gifts to the fellowship. Gift-giving when the gift contains the giver, as in Galadriel's case, is still one of the significances of our lives, though shoddiness of sentiment and commercialism have trepanned the larger portion of it. The courtesy of King Aragorn to his lowly friends Frodo and Sam in seating them beside him on his throne becomes more than a simple incident in the story.

There is also in the *Rings* a courtesy of sex that, though often noted by its absence today, nevertheless still echoes resonantly at some deep level of our being. Aragorn waited a fantastically long time for Arwen Evenstar, but then their marriage bore all the more meaning and depth for it. Both Sam and Gimli found in Galadriel not simply a beautiful woman but a deeply impelling symbol of courtesy and dignity.

Last we can say that the *Rings* appears to be one of the genuinely imaginative works of mankind. Its 1,200 pages, including over a hundred pages of footnotes which are themselves imaginatively integral, is less an example of imagination than it simply is imagination. Paul Ricoeur says that by means of imagination man recognizes his real existence and exercises a metaphysical prophecy of things possible to him. Imagination, said Einstein, is "more important than knowledge." I believe the *Rings* reminds us of some country we knew and loved in a sort of previous incarnation, a channel opening on the foam of perilous seas in lands longed for in the depth of the psyche, lands never traveled yet always traveled, never visited yet from which we have never really been parted, lands where the light is bright, the colors unmuddied, and where our everyday longing for joy is constantly pointing us.

The three books most popular among college students during the past seventeen years are, in order, *The Catcher in the Rye*, *Lord of the Flies*, and Tolkien's *Lord of the Rings*. In the first a sensitive and lonely boy finds that it is impossible for him to learn anything from the phony adult world in which he lives. The second symbolizes the shallowness of our present civilization and attempts to show that it is only a step back to the jungle. Both these books are negative, even at times bitter, in their inferences. Tolkien's story is utterly different.

A generation boasting of its realistic outlook finds multitudes not only reading of dwarfs and elves and talking trees but also finding such things pertinent to everyday life. A generation the young of which have been accused of an inner malaise and indifference to human values reads a story replete with dignity, courtesy, heroism in the knightly pattern and of fulfillment not through indulgence but through sacrifice. A generation brought up on Cartesian doubt, alienation, the logic of suicide, the notion that God is dead, of newness for its own sake, and only a quasi-belief in religion while its real one is in supposed pragmatic realities, finds that hobbits give more intestinal fortitude than Nietzsche, Sartre, and the bishop of Woolwich.

No one is less "alienated" than J. R. R. Tolkien. In complete contrast with some of the most admired writers of our time, he has a world of certainties. In a time of slackened values he maintains a sure hierarchy. His morals are solidly traditional. He is a thousand miles from the sex angle of much of our current writing, movies, and advertising. Though he is not optimistic about our age, he has no existential angst. In a time when the cult of personality dominates the scene, Tolkien belongs to the tradition of medieval art where the created object completely sublimated the creator of it.

The great majority of discussions of the *Rings* emphasize its continuous moral resonance. In a recent dissertation at the University of Michigan, Dorothy K. Barber says that the real significance of the story is Christian and its basic metaphor is "God is light."[85] A graduate student at the University of Wisconsin

85 "The Structure of *The Lord of the Rings,*" 1965.

wrote that he had found the *Rings* the best reading of his entire life and wished he had discovered it in his teens and had then the experience of what he described as its "therapeutic values." A mother wrote of first devouring the story while recuperating from the birth of a son and bewildering her doctor and family by strange references to black riders, elves, and orcs. She went on to say that for her the story illumined "the nature of Reality, the glorious and tragic dimensions of the struggle between good and evil." "You," she wrote the author, "have made courage and commitment and honor more meaningful." A young businessman in Oxford told me that he regarded the *Rings* as his "Bible," and that when confused and discouraged he went home and read from the story and was restored in mind and spirit.

I conclude with the question whether the wide reading of *The Lord of the Rings* marks a trend. Utopian books reached a peak about the turn of the century and were succeeded by dystopias or anti-utopias. Now there is evidence, a little at least, of a more optimistic turn of things. In his *Books with Men Behind Them*, Edmund Fuller describes the works of contemporary writers with "a round vision of man," and Mark Hillegas, in his *The Future as Nightmare*, suggests some little signs of a possible movement not nightmarish. One of the most emphatic statements is that of Arnold Gingrich, publisher of *Esquire*, who, speaking at the Sorbonne in 1959, declared that the "point of vomit" in writing has been reached and predicted a Puritan revival in literature. Three years later he repeated this conviction that total revulsion and reversal were somewhere in the offing and that the reversal would be total—"hardbound, softbound, periodical and permanent."[86] Gingrich was writing not from a religious view but simply on the assumption that the world has exploited sex and its new liberty to the point of license.

86 "Arnold Gingrich's Prediction: A Puritan Revolution in Literature," *Chicago Daily News* (December 1, 1962).

Is it not possible that J. R. R. Tolkien has portrayed by story, image, symbol, and mythic depth the sources of our often satirized or ignored, yet real, longings? The actuality of a past that is more than the mere passage of time, a past in which there is lively meaning for the present because meaning is a "given," which we could not escape if we tried. That history is not bunk and the *Tao* is still operative? That time is more than the ticking of the clock? That things, yes even atoms themselves, have "innards" and that inwardness is both inescapable and positively desirable? That dignity is not absurd nor antiquity a thing either to be ignored or belittled? And, perhaps best of all, that there is both a *eucatastrophe* and an *evangelium* at the heart of the cosmos?

Chapter 18

LITERARY FORM, BIBLICAL NARRATIVE, AND THEOLOGICAL THEMES

To my mind the richest part of Tolkien and the Silmarillion *is Kilby's extended reflection on the thorough Christian vision at the core of Tolkien's whole mythology. Kilby brings a lifetime of thinking and writing as a Christian teacher to this task, and I think it is one of his most valuable achievements. Its value is perhaps even greater now after Peter Jackson's great but (inevitably) flawed film version of the story, which continues to address a vast audience with a subtle and persuasive gospel, for which the books themselves are the best amplification, with Kilby's commentary a priceless addition. In the postscript to Tolkien's original letter to Kilby inviting him to come and help with* The Silmarillion, *Tolkien links the whole story to the Anglo-Saxon poet Cynewulf's poem on the Incarnation. Tolkien referred to the poem as that "from which ultimately sprang the whole of my mythology." (In retelling the Christian story, Cynewulf mentions an angel named Eärendel.)*

Interestingly (perhaps because it so thoroughly violates Tolkien's own insistence that his work contains no allegorical elements) Kilby does not include here something he recalled in conversation with me: Tolkien's confident linking of the elvish lembas, or "waybread," with the Host at Communion, and the vial of light given by Galadriel to Frodo with the Holy Spirit. Perhaps this is another example of what Kilby calls Tolkien's "contrasistency," but it certainly reinforces Kilby's argument here that his great story has an even greater story at its core.

TOLKIEN AS CHRISTIAN WRITER

A publisher's list speaks of Tolkien as "a retired Oxford Theologist." The error suggests a truth. I do not recall a single visit I made to Tolkien's home in which the conversation did not at some point fall easily into a discussion of religion, or rather Christianity. He told me that he had many times been given a story as an answer to prayer. Mrs. Tolkien joined him in remarking that one of their children had been cured, as they firmly believed, of a heart ailment through prayer. He commonly referred to Christ as "our Lord" and was much upset when he heard others address God as though he were the Lord Mayor. C. S. Lewis says that his talks with Tolkien were a large factor in his conversion to Christianity.[87] Tolkien was a staunchly conservative Tridentine Roman Catholic.

Tolkien did indeed have a special reverence for the Virgin Mary. One of his observations was that she must have jealously guarded her pregnancy since had it been discovered Mary would either have been stoned as an adulteress or, if she had tried to explain, stoned for blasphemy. He thought Mary must have been eager to leave Nazareth for Bethlehem and would have urged Joseph on as fast as possible. He was moved by the degradation of the birth of Christ in a stable with its filth and manure and saw it as a symbol of the real nature of holy things in a fallen world. He spoke of his special regard for the book of Luke because that writer included so much about women.

It is known that Tolkien collaborated in the preparation of the Jerusalem Bible by translating the book of Job into English from what he called a bad literal French version. His keen sense of rightness led him to learn a considerable amount of Hebrew

87 *Letters of C. S. Lewis*, 197.

preparatory to his task. Mrs. Mary Cawte reports attending a seminar of four pupils taught by Tolkien on the Anglo-Saxon text of the book of Exodus on which he was working in the early 1940s.

When I spoke of his success as teacher, scholar, and creative writer, he responded that he had been blessed with a sense of the human, i.e., a "blessing" had preceded and entered into any real value in his life. Like Lewis, he held that theories of man's origin, physiology, and mentality did not go back far enough. Psychologists, he said, sometimes explain spiritual things simply as a result of the function of the glands, failing to realize that God also made the glands.

He believed that creativity itself is a gift of God. After years of teaching aesthetics, I cannot but conclude that the whole of that difficult subject is comprehended in a single line from Tolkien's "On Fairy-stories": *we make still by the law in which we're made.* That he was thinking not of a merely natural origin is evidenced by the same essay where he says that "God redeemed the corrupt making-creatures" and that the Gospels resemble fairy-stories in their far-flung intimations of an unearthly Joy. "The Birth of Christ is the eucatastrophe of Man's history. The Resurrection is the eucatastrophe of the story of the Incarnation. This story begins and ends in joy." The successful fairy-story has "the very taste of primary truth" and symbolizes God's gift to man of creativity. The "Great Eucatastrophe" is the final redemption of man as declared in the Scriptures. Man is called to Joy, and his ability to create "Faërie" confirms that calling. "God is the Lord, of angels, and of man—and of Elves. Legend and History have met and fused."[88] If we recall that by Tolkien's definition his own major creative writings fall within his category of fairy-stories, then it is wrong to describe them, as some have done, as pagan, pre-Christian, or anything else than what he himself held them to be.

88 *Tree and Leaf*, 49, 60–61. Compare C. S. Lewis's "Myth Became Fact," in *God in the Dock* (Grand Rapids, MI: Wm. B. Eerdmans Publishing Company, 1970), 63–67.

It is true that the word *God* never appears in any of Tolkien's stories, not even in *Leaf by Niggle*, where some Christian implications are overwhelming, including a conversation between God and Christ. We recall Tolkien's insistence that his story had no allegorical meaning, religious or otherwise, but contrariwise, at a later time, he spoke of invocations to Elbereth Gilthoniel and added, "These and other references to religion in *The Lord of the Rings* are frequently overlooked."[89] It seems to be another case of Tolkien's "contrasistency." Of course it is equally true that Lewis omits the use of the name of God in books that nobody can doubt as being straightforwardly Christian. I think we shall be near the truth if we conclude that the fiction of both Tolkien and Lewis is Christian, even though we recall a clear difference of opinion between them as to how explicit that meaning should be.

Not long after I began my work with Professor Tolkien, he and Mrs. Tolkien went away for a short vacation, during which he sent me a paper called "Kingship, Priesthood and Prophecy in *The Lord of the Rings*," written by a professor in New South Wales. This paper proposed that Tolkien's story was one of the most misunderstood works of modern fiction because its critics were so often unacquainted with the Bible. The writer insisted that the story is based on the manner of Christ's redemption of the world. Middle-earth is saved, he argued, through the priestly self-sacrifice of the hobbit Frodo, "the Lamb whose only real strength is his capacity to make an offering of himself." It is saved also by the wisdom of Gandalf, "the major prophet figure," as well as by the mastery of Aragorn, who begins despised and ends as King. As each agent responds to his "calling," he grows in power and grace. This essay concluded: "At every point, the human dynamics of *The Lord of the Rings* are drawn from the tradition ascribed to Christ's redemptive activity, and once this is perceived, the way is

89 *The Road Goes Ever On*, 65.

opened to an informed critical approach to the work in question." I suspect this is the sort of interpretation upon which some readers of Tolkien might look with horror.

Tolkien wrote me his own opinion: "Much of this is true enough—except, of course, the general impression given (almost irresistibly in articles having this analytical approach, whether by Christians or not) that I had any such 'schema' in my conscious mind before or during the writing." No doubt Tolkien would have agreed with C. S. Lewis's conclusion that the deeper meaning of a story must rise from the writer's lifetime spiritual roots rather than be consciously inserted.[90]

Responding to a letter from Father Robert Murray suggesting Tolkien's story impressed him as entirely about grace, Tolkien wrote:

> I know exactly what you mean by the order of grace; and of course by your references to Our Lady, upon which all my own small perception of beauty both in majesty and simplicity is founded. *The Lord of the Rings* is of course a fundamentally religious and Catholic work; unconsciously so at first but consciously in the revision. I . . . have cut out practically all references to anything like "religion," to cults and practices in the imaginary world. For the religious element is absorbed into the story and the symbolism. However that is very clumsily put, and sounds more self-important than I feel. I should chiefly be grateful for having been brought up since I was eight in a faith that has nourished me and taught me all the little that I know; and that I owe my mother, who clung to her conversion and died young, largely through the hardships of poverty resulting from it.[91]

90 *Of Other Worlds* (London: Geoffrey Bles Ltd., 1966), 33.
91 Letter to Father Robert Murray, SJ, quoted by him in *The Tablet* (Sept. 15, 1973).

In *The Pilgrim's Regress,* Lewis depicts the universality of sin through the fiction of a farmer and his wife who come to enjoy the taste of wild apples so much that they graft branches from the original tree onto all other trees and finally all edibles whatever. Tolkien's imagery of fallen man is much the same, i.e., that the devil is in the very earth under our feet, and some of him gets into the cauliflower and everything else that grows. Tolkien also believed in the *anima naturaliter christiana,* the sense of God and responsibility to him inborn in mankind. He was greatly disturbed by the decline of Christian belief in England and elsewhere. While I was with him the news came of the murder of fourteen people by a demented student shooting from the top of a building in Texas. He said he heard this news while at breakfast and that it upset his stomach.

In the early part of this book I quoted a letter from Professor Tolkien that happened to reach me on Christmas Eve. But I did not there include a footnote to that letter, which reads as follows: "I hope that perhaps this may reach you at or about Christmas. '*Lux fulgebat super nos. Ëalä Eärendel engla beorhtast ofer middengeard monnum sended.*' Cynewulf's words." Professor Colin Hardie tells me that the Latin phrase may have come from a medieval hymn or the like or else may simply be Tolkien's own. The meaning of it is similar to the meaning of the Anglo-Saxon from Cynewulf's *Christ,* a poem about the Advent, the Ascension, and the Last Judgment, and a work with which Tolkien would have been intimately familiar. Later, at my request, Tolkien gave me his own literal translation as "Here Eärendel, brightest of angels, sent from God to men." That the full meaning of the passage may be clear, I cite the following translated passage from Cynewulf's poem, beginning with Tolkien's quotation.

> Lo! Thou Splendor of the dayspring, fairest of angels sent to men upon earth, Thou Radiance of the Sun of Righteousness, bright beyond the stars, Thou of Thy very self dost illumine all the tides of time! Even as Thou, God begotten of God, Son of the true Father, didst ever dwell without beginning in the glory of heaven, so Thine own handiwork in its present need imploreth Thee with confidence that Thou send us the bright sun, and come in Thy very person to enlighten those who have long been covered with murky cloud, and sitting here in darkness and eternal night, shrouded in sins, have been forced to endure the shadow of death . . . God appeared among us without sin; the mighty Son of God and the Son of Man dwelt together in harmony among mankind.[92]

The word *Eärendel* (now spelled *Eärendil*) is well known to Tolkien readers as the brightest star in the heavens of Middle-earth. Its counterpart in our world is Venus, the Morning Star. Cynewulf's "dayspring" comes from a biblical allusion to the birth of Christ (Luke 1:78). Knowing that it was from such a context that "the whole" of Tolkien's mythology rose, can we any longer doubt its profound Christian associations?

I have elsewhere discussed some of the Christian implications of *The Lord of the Rings*—such as descriptions of paradisal peace and splendor, the contrast between darkness and light, the sense of the ongoing of evil, Frodo's calling and dedication, the place of the human will in goodness, Christ images, the apocalyptic ending, and what Tolkien calls the Eucatastrophe and Evangelium—and shall not repeat them here.[93] But there does seem abundant evidence for W. H. Auden's statement that the "unstated presuppositions"

92 Translation of Albert S. Cook (Boston: Ginn and Company, 1900).

93 *Myth, Allegory and Gospel*, edited by John Warwick Montgomery (Minneapolis: Bethany Fellowship Press, 1974).

of *The Lord of the Rings* are Christian; also Edmund Fuller's conviction that "a theology contains the narrative rather than being contained by it. Grace is at work abundantly in the story," and all the way "a thread of prophecy is being fulfilled"; also W. D. Norwood's remark in his interpretation of Tolkien's aesthetic theory that this writer "sees in the story of Christ a record of absolute reality incarnate in history."[94] Various other interpreters, though by no means all, express similar opinions.

Professor Tolkien talked to me at some length about the use of the word *holy* in *The Silmarillion*. Very specifically he told me that the "Secret Fire sent to burn at the heart of the World" in the beginning was the Holy Spirit.[95] He described his problem in depicting the fall of mankind near the beginning of the story. "How far we have fallen!" he exclaimed—so far, he felt, that it would seem impossible even to find an adequate prototype or to imagine the contrast between Eden and the disaster that followed.

I only wish that at this point I felt able to discuss the pattern of Tolkien's myth in relation to the whole of mythology. There is no doubt of its general similarity in such archetypes as a creator, a creation, a "high" race and a hierarchy, protagonists and antagonists, a sense of doom, heroic undertakings, conduct measured in terms of moral law, and an ending with a new earth and heaven. There are many discussions that endeavor to decide whether myth originates in history, religion, nature, the imaginations of men, or all of these.

My impression is that *The Silmarillion* is oriented as much on a biblical pattern as it is on that of Norse and other mythologies. One interesting instance of this is the depiction of light in Middle-earth before the creation of sun and moon, following the

94 "The Quest Hero," *Tolkien and His Critics*, 53; *Books with Men Behind Them*, p. 184; "Tolkien's Intentions in *The Lord of the Rings*," *Mankato State College Studies in English*, 18.

95 Facing the Balrog in their close combat at the end of the journey through Moria, Gandalf said, "I am a servant of the Secret Fire" (I, 429).

model of the early verses of Genesis. Many believe there was, as in *The Silmarillion*, a long period of time between the two kinds of light. Milton's explanation in *Paradise Lost* is an example:

> "Let there be Light!" said God; and forthwith Light
> Ethereal, first of things, quintessence pure,
> Sprung from the Deep, and from her native East
> To journey through the aery gloom began,
> Sphered in a radiant cloud—for yet the Sun
> Was not; she in a cloudy tabernacle
> Sojourned the while.[96]

The Two Trees in *The Silmarillion* are at first the source of light. After the destruction of the Two Trees there is a long period of twilight in Middle-earth, and it is during this time that first Elves and then Dwarves awaken. It is only long afterward, with the rising of sun and moon, that Men awaken.

We are told that God saw his labors of creation to be "very good" and that on the seventh day he rested (Gen. 2:2). In a quite similar fashion the Valar enjoyed the splendor of their work, and when it was completed they also rested and celebrated with a great feast.

In the beginning Eru gave the Valar a vision in heaven of Arda and required them to make it according to that vision. A parallel may be seen in God's command to Moses concerning the Jewish Tabernacle: "See that you make everything according to the pattern which was shown you on the mountain" (Exod. 25:40).

Again, the marriage of three High Elves with Men is in some ways like the biblical account of how "the sons of God saw the daughters of men that they were fair; and they took them wives" (Gen. 6:2). Except for a reversal in sex, this is very similar to the marriage of King Thingol the Elf to Melian the Vala.[97]

96 VII, 243, 249.
97 *The Return of the King*, Appendix A, 1. The Númenórean Kings.

A major parallel between the Bible and *The Silmarillion* is a great Fall, in both cases premeditated if not actually begun in heaven and descending finally to a vast and devilish opposition against everything heavenly. The curse and its aftermath upon the Noldor suggests the Old Testament motif of disobedience and its dire results. Likewise, I think there may be something of a parallel between Eärendil's desperate voyage to Valinor for aid from the destruction of Beleriand (and the consequent succor and warm invitation to return to that protected and lovely land) and the record of the Hebrews returning to their own land after long exile in Persia, rebuilding the temple, and, after years of neglect, reaffirming the laws of Moses and sobbing out their repentance (Neh. 8). There are those, indeed, who believe the Jews are still fighting "the long defeat" and have yet to face their eucatastrophe.

If one presses the matter, he may find other significant parallels. The life span of some of the Edain in Tolkien is suggestive of the longevity of the early biblical patriarchs. Much longer of course is the life of some of the Elves. Galadriel in particular stands out. It is clear that she was among those present early in the history of the First Age, that is, thousands of years before the reader comes upon her, strong and beautiful in Lothlórien. Christ, we are told, was alive when the world began, yet, says John, "I myself have seen him with my own eyes and listened to him speak" (1 John 1:1, The Living Bible). Is one of Tolkien's intentions in giving us Galadriel to remind us not simply of vast time but even the eternality of Christ?

It is also possible that there is some parallel between the division of the Hebrews, as time went on, into tribes, and the migrations and settlements into small kingdoms of Elves, Dwarves, and Men. We are told that the Elves "made all the old words,"[98] and the

98 *The Two Towers*, Bk. III, Ch. 4.

Bible says that "Adam gave names to all cattle, and to the fowl of the air, and to every beast of the field" (Gen. 2:20). Other correspondences are possible.

In this connection I should mention a lengthy account that Tolkien asked me to read. It was in the form of a Job-like conversation on soul and body and the possible purpose of God in allowing the Fall so that he could manifest his own sovereignty over Satan all the more, of Christ's incarnation, the spread of his light from one person to another, and the final consummation at Christ's return. He said he was not certain whether to include this in *The Silmarillion* or publish it separately.

If I am correct about the extent of this biblical orientation, we may be able to conclude that the Valar (angels) are still executing the will of Eru and that our earth will not always experience change and decay but have its own final eucatastrophe. And it is possible that Tolkien is also suggesting that Elves, "a race now abandoned to folk-tales,"[99] where only a shadow of truth is preserved, but who once had close affiliations with Men, will then arise from their long concealment and live with us again in some Lothlórien. After all, we have been told that Lúthien's line is never to fail.

The tree, so much loved by Tolkien, is a persistent image both in his writings and also in the Bible, particularly as a symbol of beginnings and endings, of significant people and of highly historical events. The opening chapters of the Bible present a garden containing the tree of life, and it closes with the same tree in the re-created new Jerusalem. In the early history of Middle-earth, two trees, Telperion and Laurelin, white and golden, gave glorious light to Valinor,[100] and millennia afterward the flowering of the scion of Telperion in Minas Tirith marked both the victory over Sauron and the restoration of the kingdom of Gondor under

99 *The Return of the King*, Appendix F.
100 *The Return of the King*, Appendix A, 1. The Númenórean Kings.

its newly crowned King Elessar. The ancient lineage of that scion is clear. "There in the courts of the King grew a white tree, from the seed of that tree which Isildur brought over the deep waters, and the seed of that tree before came from Eressëa, and before that out of the Uttermost West in the Day before days when the world was young."[101]

Minas Tirith is itself is not unlike the new Jerusalem, both being dominated by the splendor of light. Gandalf took Aragorn up Mount Mindolluin in the early morning, and they looked down and saw "the towers of the City far below them like white pencils touched by the sunlight, and all the Vale of Anduin was like a garden, and the Mountains of Shadow were veiled in a golden mist."[102] In the next to the last chapter of the Bible, an angel came to John and carried him to a high mountain and showed him "that great city, the holy Jerusalem, descending out of heaven from God, having the glory of God. . . . And the city had no need of the sun . . . for the glory of God did lighten it" (Rev. 21:10–11, 23).

Glorious as Minas Tirith appeared below them, and splendid as the victory over Sauron had been, Aragorn reminded Gandalf that he would die and inquired who would be king over Gondor after him. What he wanted was the assurance of something permanent. He reminded Gandalf that below them the scion of Telperion was still withered and barren, and he asked him for "a sign that it would ever be otherwise." The history of mankind and the history of Middle-earth are similar—a perfect beginning followed by centuries of struggle between evil and good with occasional triumphs on one side or the other and no sign of the hoped-for ideal.

What Aragorn asked for was a permanent victory over all such as Sauron and a permanent glory such as he saw by the early

101 *The Fellowship of the Ring*, Bk. II, Ch. 2.
102 *The Return of the King*, Bk. VI, Ch. 5.

morning light. The parallel I am trying to draw might be greatly advanced by what followed Aragorn's question, but actually it is not. Gandalf asked Aragorn to turn away from the beauty below and look "where all seems barren and cold." It was there, to Aragorn's surprise, that he saw the sapling in the rocks near the snow. The natural parallel here is Isaiah's prophecy of Christ as "a tender plant . . . a root out of a dry ground" (Isa. 53:2). This seems confirmed by Gandalf's question, "Who shall say how it comes here in the appointed hour?"[103] He adds that the life within the tree may "lie sleeping through many long years." So if our efforts to draw parallels is valid, it would appear logical at this point to suggest that Elessar's kingdom would be as permanent as that predicted for Christ. Tolkien's *eucatastrophe* would eventuate and all would be well forever after.

Yet we know this to be out of keeping with Tolkien's frequent realistic assurances that the whole of history of Middle-earth after its "Fall" is mainly one of wars and rumors of wars. There is no evidence to suggest that the Fourth Age of Middle-earth is to be different from the other three.

To explain the seeming discrepancy, the biblical parallel of the tree with its saplings must be noted. Isaiah speaks of King David as "a shoot . . . and a branch out of the stock of Jesse" (Isa. 11:1), and David was himself in turn to be a shoot from which God would raise up "a righteous Branch" and would be called "The Lord our Righteousness" (Jer. 23:6). Jesus spoke of himself as "the root and the offspring of David" (Rev. 22:16). So here we have a succession of scions covering a long period of time and seeming to carry us back to Gandalf's question as to how these mysteriously but surely appear in their appointed times.

Thus I think we may assume King Elessar not as the final and undying ruler of Middle-earth but only as one heroic victor in

103 *The Return of the King*, Bk. VI, Ch. 5.

a seemingly endless conflict. He is a David called up from the barrens of sheepherding to lead the kingdom. But like Elessar, David died. Neither was the tree the real Telperion. They were only saplings—very like but also very unlike.

But Tolkien was too pronounced a believer in Christ as the Sovereign Ruler who was to come to leave the matter thus. There is evidence that, had his story continued to its full and concluding end, the ubiquitous evil of such as Morgoth and Sauron would have ceased. He intended a final glorious eventuality similar to the one described in the book of Revelation with the true Telperion reappearing, the earth remade, the lands lying under the waves lifted up, the Silmarils recovered, Eärendil returned to earth, the Two Trees rekindled in their original light and life-giving power, and the mountains of the Pelori leveled so that the light should go out over all the earth—yes, and the dead be raised and the original purposes of Eru executed.

Chapter 19

DEATH AND AFTERLIFE

When Tolkien died, Dr. Kilby drew on his own brief but deep friendship with Tolkien, his wide knowledge of the huge impact his work had had on so many lives, and above all Tolkien's own eloquent writings on death and immortality to write this moving tribute.

TOLKIEN IS DEAD

John Ronald Reuel Tolkien is dead. He had the life of a mortal man, a little more than threescore years and ten. Yet he had Elvish immortality too, as thousands know from acquiring a measure of it themselves through his works. Tolkien was "otherworldly" in the best sense of that term. Since the news media are overwhelmingly concerned with worldly things, his death received little front-page attention. It is a sign of our sad estate that the most meaningful things are the ones we pay the least public attention to. But those who loved Tolkien knew the true value of the good life, not its mere titillations.

Whether Tolkien will survive as a significant literary figure is a question no man can presently answer. What many of us know now with great assurance is that he survives deeply and joyously in us. A college student wrote, "*The Lord of the Rings* was and will probably be the most significant book of my life." A physician said that the highlight of his four years in medical college was reading Tolkien in his senior year. Another suggested that Tolkien's words say more than words can really say. Still, we cannot prophesy how other generations will receive him.

After Glen Good Knight telephoned me from California of Tolkien's death, I picked up *The Return of the King* and read of Theoden's funeral rites. As the Riders of the King's House rode about the barrow they sang of the king's renown, and I thought some of their words appropriate to Tolkien himself.

> Out of doubt, out of dark, to the day's rising
> he rode singing into the sun, sword unsheathing.
> Hope rekindled, and in hope ended;
> over death, over dread, over doom lifted
> out of loss, out of life, unto long glory.

After the burial and the weeping of the women and Theoden left alone in his barrow, the folk gathered to put away sorrow in a great feast in the Golden Hall of the palace. We who loved Tolkien now bear our period of sorrow, but it is tempered already with the joy of knowing that Tolkien's words outlive him, not only in the pages of a book but in our flesh and spirit.

I read also the tale of Aragorn and Arwen, and I recalled, as I came to Aragorn's last words before his death, that some of them are also appropriate to their creator. Aragorn told his beloved wife, "Behold! We are not bound for ever to the circles of the world, and beyond them is more than memory." My experience with Tolkien made it clear to me that he was a devout Christian and very sure of a larger fulfillment beyond the grave. So there is reason for us to rejoice in his double immortality both as a Christian believer and as the creator of Hobbits and Elves and Dwarves and Ents, of true beauty and proper terror, of golden localities such as Rivendell and Lothlorien, of a good that properly triumphs and an evil that falls, and of a depth of experience appropriate to a need that cries out in us from the roots of our being.

SECTION 3

THE INKLINGS AS SHAPERS OF A NEW CHRISTIAN IMAGINATION

Chapter 20

PORTRAITS OF DAMNATION, PICTURES OF GLORY: INTRODUCING CHARLES WILLIAMS

Kilby clearly responded much more thoroughly and intuitively to the work and the personality of both Lewis and Tolkien than to that of Charles Williams (perhaps, as he explains in his article on the three, because Williams, unlike Lewis, Tolkien, and Kilby himself, was a city lover with little appreciation for nature). Nevertheless, his appreciation for the profundity of Williams's work grew steadily. One way to note that is through his increasing use of Williams's exposition of the basic Christian doctrines of "co-inherence" and "substitution" to illuminate passages in both Lewis and Tolkien. The piece that follows combines two that Kilby wrote on Williams, several years apart. The introduction, "portraits of the unregenerate," is little more than summary; in the second, Kilby is clearly deeply moved by Williams's fiction, especially Descent into Hell. *In fact it was through Kilby's advocacy that Eerdmans acquired the rights to five of Williams's seven novels and brought them back into print. So the many readers who have been terrified, troubled, or transformed (or all three) by Williams's works have Kilby to thank for their availability.*

PORTRAITS OF THE UNREGENERATE

The publisher of these paperback reprints of five of Williams's novels and *The Descent of the Dove* is to be congratulated for bringing before the evangelical world one of the finest Christian minds of this century.

Williams, who died twenty years ago, wrote almost forty books, including literary criticism, biography, drama, poetry, and novels. He was a member of the remarkable group in Oxford that included such men as C. S. Lewis and J. R. R. Tolkien, and he produced books no less original and significant than they. I know a pastor who is convinced that Charles Williams broke through into a new spiritual dimension. There is no doubt about the profundity or brilliance of his insights.

THE NOVELS: BIZARRE BUT PROFOUND

Williams's novels, seven in all, are a strange amalgam of extraordinary and at times horrifying adventure and profound Christian ideas. A deck of Tarot cards creates an indoor cyclone, people are transformed into animals, they meet their own doubles, and men survive undecayed for centuries. Yet all of this is made to serve Williams's keen insight concerning God and man. *War in Heaven* opens with a wildly ringing telephone in the office of a London newspaper while the legs of a corpse stick out from under an editor's desk, but the main theme of the novel is the effort of a devilishly evil man to gain possession of a cup supposed to be the Holy Grail.

Commonly the frenzied ambition of Williams's villains is unlimited power. W. H. Auden says, "I know of no other writer, living or dead, who has given us so convincing and terrifying portraits of damned souls as has Charles Williams."

Perhaps I can best indicate the significance of *The Descent of the Dove* by again citing Auden, who said, in 1956, that he had been reading and rereading the book for sixteen years and had found it "a source of intellectual delight and spiritual nourishment which remains inexhaustible." The subtitle of this book indicates its contents: "A Short History of the Holy Spirit in the Church."

Williams saw history, both good and bad, as the careful working out of God's purpose in the world. He believed that all parts of life belong to God, and the way to hell is the rejection of the real world and the creation of one's own. As in all his other books, Williams here puts imagination to work in the interest of holiness.

Mrs. Alice Mary Hadfield, who worked at the Oxford Press with Williams, said, "I have felt changes in my spirit take place in 20 minutes in his office as definite as if I had grown a foot taller—accompanied by the related growing-pains." Any reader who stays with Williams long enough will feel himself growing taller, but he must not expect to avoid the growing pains. Charles Williams did not know the meaning of the cliché.

HIS SUPERNATURAL WORLD

A few weeks before his death Charles Williams told his wife he intended to write one more novel. But in this one, said he, there would be "no black magic, no dancing figures, and no supernatural beings wandering through its pages."

The seven novels Williams produced between 1930 and 1945 are filled with these very elements. The stories often explore the workings of the universe itself as well as the mysterious innards of man. Most of them center on a search for power and people intent on achieving power at any cost. This power is not simply political, economic, or scientific control, but the very maneuvering of nature and the elements to serve the private ends of world domination.

War in Heaven, the first novel, begins with a corpse lying under a desk in a busy newspaper office. The story deals with three men who seek the Grail cup, each for his own private reasons. Gregory Persimmons, for instance, wants to test out the cup's supernatural power by using it for the Black Mass and the murder of an innocent child. If that proves successful, he wants to extend his canny manipulation and completely annihilate the universe he despises. In *Many Dimensions*, the second novel, similar powers operate through a sacred Islamic stone that enables its owner to gain both wealth and pleasure and to turn people into experimental guinea pigs suited to his own sadistic ends.

In *The Place of the Lion*, a preternatural world breaks fearfully upon a woman named Damaris Tighe. At one point a serpent suddenly enters a club room where Damaris is speaking. This not only scares the wits out of those present but also projects its characteristics into one club member (noted for her deceptive manner), who then coils, writhes, and hisses. Power resides in a set of Tarot cards sought by different people in *The Greater Trumps*. The four hands in the deck can, under the right circumstances, control earth, air, fire, and water, and they have a mysterious connection with a set of dancing golden figures on a table. The principal characters again experiment with the Tarots, hoping to realize their selfish ends and dreams of power.

Shadows of Ecstasy comes close to some of today's motifs. Nigel Considine has conquered death by a heroic control of mind over matter, like the latent potential many see today in the so-called steady march of science toward a golden horizon. One phase of this story is an African invasion calculated to save the West by joining emotion to the unadulterated reason that has enervated the more "civilized" but actually decadent world. There is hatred of minority groups that results in the same kind of trouble we have today.

In the last novel, *All Hallows' Eve*, recently dead people try to orient themselves to their ghostly world while actually walking the murky streets of London. We also find Simon the Clerk, who anticipates becoming a new and more successful Christ through his occult powers.

Williams's stories are becoming increasingly popular in the student world. Why? Is it the combination of, on the one hand, an avid search for Power and, on the other, a willingness to try any means to such an end, whether public riots, private drugs, or whatever?

But what will students say about the real heart of Charles Williams's novels, the part I have not mentioned thus far? That heart is Jesus Christ the Lord, though none of these novels ever forsakes story for sermon. I have seen several students knocked off their feet by Charles Williams's unique view of self, sin, and transformation into the image of Jesus Christ.

In my brief summaries I deliberately omitted *Descent into Hell*, perhaps the best of Williams's novels. It most clearly reveals how Williams welds events and Christian meaning together. Like the others it is filled with bizarre and fearful happenings—the patter of dead feet, a living man and a dead man looking out of the same upstairs window together, phantasms, the drugs of Lilith, a doppelgänger, a suicide and his posthumous life, concurrent residence in the world of the dead and the living, and a slide down a bright rope of infinite length. All these happenings take place in a rather normal residential development on a hill north of London, a hill where from time immemorial battles or portions of battles have been fought and martyrs have been burned. On Battle Hill the busy, everyday world of socialites, intellectuals, and construction workers suffers a double exposure with the world of the dead, both hellish and angelic. In this setting, one of the story's two principal characters moves upward, and the other downward.

Downward-moving Lawrence Wentworth is a prominent military historian who in the beginning has the same assortment of private weaknesses as most people. Two of his are envy of another historian and jealousy of Adela Hunt. Both flaws might have been overcome by a modest act of the will, but instead of destroying them Wentworth first rationalizes them and later tries to erase them in a dream world of his own making.

The main cause of Wentworth's descent involves Adela. Instead of a manly and wholesome effort to win her, he turns to easy and untroubling substitutes. He turns to a fantasy world with an Adela who is unfailingly obedient to all his wishes. Once launched into that world, Wentworth finds that it is not without its own peculiar troubles. From a thimbleful of unquashed evil an ocean of loss eventually comes. Wentworth occasionally recognizes the blackness ahead, but the self-created sensual dream existence is too appealing for him to turn back. He comes to hate every glimpse of the world of problems where he is expected to will and do rather than simply give in. This manufactured world eventually begins to collapse, and Wentworth, like an addict who suspects that soon he will put the needle into his arm for the last time, sees that his "Adela" has finally taken on the face of an imbecile. From then on he sleepily slides down into the black void.

The other principal character is Pauline Anstruther. Like Wentworth, she starts out with common human foibles and hopes. She might have taken Wentworth's road. In fact, she was offered the chance to hear some "comforting tale" and have what she wanted without trouble. But her great trouble was her doppelgänger, the ghostly double of her own self she would see going ahead of or else coming toward her. She had such a deadly fear of the two selves meeting some day that she hardly dared go outdoors. Contrary to Wentworth, who gets rid of the portion of him that gives any trouble, Pauline wants above everything else a genuine solution. Finally she mounts, slowly and painfully to be sure, toward joy. Pauline moves through Reality into a glorious freedom, while Wentworth (also desiring freedom but choosing the unreal way) sees that he is heading for the dark and bitter maw that will swallow him forever.

The first of Pauline's breathtaking discoveries in this process is that her friend Peter Stanhope can actually become her substitute by fearing her doppelgänger and fully relieving her of all fear. The time comes when Pauline can walk to or from her home without even a thought of her doppelgänger. But her final ascent to Reality can only come when, overwhelmed with fears, she herself goes up a dark and lonely way in the middle of the night and meets a stranger in the shadow of Wentworth's house. She discovers there that she must also become a substitute. Among numerous other terrors, the old terror of her doppelgänger suddenly returns. She can feel its presence just behind her. By taking on herself the fears of another, she has learned that she can turn about and face her doppelgänger. When she does so, she doesn't find the horrible other self that had destroyed her peace for years, but a glorious creature. The old self, now transformed by Pauline's discovery of the whole meaning of substitution, becomes indivisibly one with her new self. She understands that true liberty lies in moving straight through one's problems to an everlasting Reality.

Wentworth looked falsely inward and, as someone has said, slid down his own intestine and was cast out into the void. Pauline looked outward toward true humanity, and upward toward God. In facing them and giving up herself, she found a sublimely glorious self that would then have all joy in substituting for the fears and ills of others. Charles Williams's friend C. S. Lewis said, "Self exists to become abdicated and, by that abdication, becomes the more truly self, to be thereupon yet the more abdicated."

Some years ago Arnold Gingrich, publisher of *Esquire*, expressed his conviction that the vomit point had been reached in much modern fiction and that the inevitable revulsion from it would bring on a Puritan (by which I think he meant an essentially Christian) literature. The renewed interest in Charles Williams's novels may be nothing more than the curiosity of experiencing his freakish, whirligig, and psychedelic worlds, and toying with vast power. Or it may involve these things plus a curiosity about the worlds of greatly good and greatly bad toward which he points. A third and hopeful possibility is that in Charles Williams many people are taking a new and wondering look at the greatest instance of substitution that ever was. Instead of wishing to gain some selfish control of power, may they, like Pauline Anstruther, see the desirability of committing themselves unfailingly and forever to that divine Power.

Chapter 21

AN ARDENT APOLOGIST FOR THE FAITH: INTRODUCING DOROTHY L. SAYERS

Dr. Kilby wrote very little on the other four of the "seven" who make up the Wade Collection, but this appreciative review of Dorothy Sayers's essays reveals his understanding of her thought, and its deep resonance with that of Lewis in particular (though it is probably to Williams, especially his work on Dante, The Figure of Beatrice, *that Sayers owes the greatest debt).*

Best known among casual readers as the creator of Detective Lord Peter Wimsey and among scholars as a translator of Dante, Dorothy Sayers was also an outstanding follower and defender of the Christian faith. One critic who despised her and C. S. Lewis endeavored to demolish them at one blow with the epithet "fundamentalists." Lewis and Dorothy Sayers did indeed belong together. They were friends and thought along the same lines, and in these essays Lewis is mentioned perhaps as often as anyone.

But, contrary to the present implication of "fundamentalist" as one who harks back to a dead theology and practice, the very first essay in this volume begins with the remark that the Christian faith is "the most exciting drama that ever staggered the imagination of man." And it is the dogma of Christianity, not some practice of the church, that she finds dramatic. "That Jesus Bar-Joseph, the carpenter of Nazareth, was in fact, and in truth, and in the most exact and literal sense of the words, the God 'by whom all things were made,'" is what Dorothy Sayers believes Christians should think of Jesus Christ.

Although Mr. Jellema, the astute editor of the book, has divided the essays into five categories, it seems to me that the dominant theme is that of God as creator, maker, and artist, and of man as most like God when he also becomes creator. "Our worst trouble today," she says, "is our feeble hold on creation."

Since I fully agree with this position, it is a pleasure for me enthusiastically to recommend the book. Even if one completely disagreed with Miss Sayers, the book would be worth reading for its wit, humor, and sense of paradox. "Christianity," says Miss Sayers, "outrages the tidy-minded by occupying a paradoxical position."

It is noteworthy that both Dorothy Sayers and G. K. Chesterton, each an effective Christian apologist, were famous as detective-story writers, where a sense of paradox is essential. Maybe our seminaries should have courses in the detective story. If so, then the first item studied might be a chapter in this book called "The Dates in 'The Red-Headed League,'" in which, with deadpan humor, Miss Sayers satirizes the specious methods of certain biblical "scholarship."

With great breadth of knowledge, Miss Sayers discusses such significant topics as an aesthetic based on the Christian principles of dogma rather than on the Greek principle of ethics. She insists that there is a poetic as well as a scientific truth and points out, as C. S. Lewis has also done, that it is as difficult for the scientist as for the poet to escape metaphoric concepts in his thought. Even such a concept as "tree" involves a great act of the creative imagination. Even more significantly, one can think of six trees, but to think six apart from trees or apples or other objects is to enter the realm of metaphysics. To the old notion that man has made God in his own image, she notes that man has no choice but to make, by way of analogy, everything in his own image.

Again like Lewis, she points out what the editor calls the disreputable ethics of Christianity in emphasizing "immorality" at the expense of the other six deadly sins. "Perhaps the bitterest commentary on the way in which Christian doctrine has been taught in the last few centuries is the fact that to the majority of people the word 'immorality' has come to mean one thing and one thing only. . . . A man may be greedy and selfish; spiteful, cruel, jealous and unjust; violent and brutal; grasping, unscrupulous and a liar, stubborn and arrogant; stupid, morose and dead to every noble instinct—and still we are ready to say of him that he is not an immoral man." We have, she believes, mistaken acquisitiveness as a virtue and concluded that value is represented simply in terms of profit and cost.

Dorothy Sayers is always likely to say the unexpected, provocative, and sometimes shocking thing. This careful selection of her essays will prove a fine tonic to the doldrums in which orthodox Christians find themselves today.

Chapter 22

THE FORMING OF A NEW FRIENDSHIP

About the time of Clyde Kilby's first meeting with Tolkien in the summer of 1954, Kilby was conceiving the idea that would lead to perhaps his greatest contribution, the collection of letters, manuscripts, books, and other critical materials that came eventually to be known as the Marion E. Wade Center. Kilby was well aware that the core of such a collection would be not only Lewis and Tolkien but also the quite different work of Charles Williams. Kilby wrote little directly on Williams, but he was aware of his profound impact on Lewis, and the fact that some considered Williams, difficult as his work sometimes is, to be the greatest theological genius of the three. Kilby wrote this insightful study of the relationships among the three writers, drawing extensively on resources (especially letters) that he himself was assembling. Though he does not speak of the "wedge" that some later biographers allege that Lewis's friendship with Williams drove into the older Lewis-Tolkien friendship, he does not downplay the considerable differences and tensions between Tolkien and Williams.

The Inklings, in which J. R. R. Tolkien, C. S. Lewis, and Charles Williams were prominent members, was primarily a friendship. The last thing they anticipated was the forming of a "school." The Inklings as an organization is more our conception after the fact than it ever was a reality.

The particular caliber of its members far more than any formal organization justifies us, as we look backward, in our view that a certain sort of history was being made.

I want to discuss the relationships of these three members of the Inklings and to suggest three things about them: (1) their personal relationships, (2) their literary relationships, and (3) what I believe to be the basic elements common to them.

PERSONAL RELATIONSHIPS

Let me take a given year for a vignette of the three, the year 1940, when all were residents of the city of Oxford. In 1940 Lewis was forty-one, Tolkien forty-eight, and Williams fifty-four. By then, Lewis and Tolkien were both well-known specialists in medieval and Renaissance literature at Oxford University. Lewis had published his first book twenty-one years earlier and was the author of eight books. His *Allegory of Love* had given him an international reputation as a medievalist. He had also published two books of poetry, a fictionalized autobiography, and a book called *The Problem of Pain*, the last growing out of his conversion to Christianity about 1930.

J. R. R. Tolkien by 1940 had made himself famous as a philologist and authority on Anglo-Saxon and Middle English. In 1922 he had published *A Middle English Vocabulary* and in 1937 "Beowulf: The Monsters and the Critics," an essay of singular insight. In that same year he had brought out a book of a very different sort. It was called *The Hobbit, or There and Back Again.*

[By] 1940 Charles Williams, along with his routine labors as an employee of the Oxford University Press, had published twenty-seven books, including volumes of poetry, biography, criticism, and six of his seven strange and profound novels.

So when Lewis, Tolkien, and Williams gathered together as Inklings in the year 1940, they were by no means amateur writers, having nearly forty books among them, together with many periodical essays, poems, reviews, and the like. Lewis and Tolkien were university men, and Williams was soon to be awarded the honorary MA because of his brilliant lectures on writers such as Milton, Shakespeare, and Dante, and had himself become a university tutor and lecturer.

Actually the Inklings might have met once, twice, or not at all in any given week. Or some of them might have gathered in a pub or any other place that suited their liking. Lewis describes the conditions under which Williams read aloud to him and Tolkien the first two chapters of his Arthurian poem on Taliessin. "Picture to yourself," he said, "an upstairs sitting-room with windows looking north in the 'grove' of Magdalen College on a sunshiny Monday morning in vacation at about ten o'clock. The Prof and I, both on the chesterfield, lit our pipes and stretched out our legs. Williams in the arm-chair opposite to us threw his cigarette into the grate, took up a pile of extremely small, loose sheets on which he habitually wrote—they came, I think, from a twopenny pad for memoranda—and began."[1] The really noteworthy thing about this meeting is its pleasure, not its formality.

More usually, the Inklings met on Thursday evenings. Lewis wrote his brother, then in Shanghai, of one gathering when there was read "a section of the new *Hobbit* book from Tolkien, a nativity play from Charles Williams (unusually intelligible for him, and approved by all), and a chapter out of the book on the Problem of Pain from me."[2] Again Lewis wrote his brother of a meeting in which Dr. Havard read a short paper on clinical experience with effects of pain. It was an evening "almost equally compounded of merriment, piety, and literature." Lewis added that the Inklings is "now really very well provided, with Adam Fox as chaplain, you as

1 *Arthurian Torso,* 1–2.
2 *Letters of C. S. Lewis,* 170. The "new Hobbit" was of course *The Lord of the Rings,* and the nativity play was *Seed of Adam.*

army, Barfield as lawyer, Havard as doctor—almost all the estate—except of course anyone who could actually produce a single necessity of life—a loaf, a boot, or a hut."[3] If the beginning of the Inklings is rather obscure, the end is not, for the gatherings ceased at Lewis's death in 1963.

Tolkien and Lewis were at least casually acquainted by the middle of the 1920s, being both members of Oxford University. By 1929 they were close friends. Lewis wrote Arthur Greeves late that year that he had been up until 2:30 AM talking to Tolkien, "the Anglo-Saxon professor . . . who came back with me to College from a society and sat discoursing of the gods and giants and Asgard for three hours, then departing in the wind and rain—who could turn him out, for the fire was bright and the talk good." On another occasion it was 4:00 AM when Lewis finally got to bed.[4] To his surprise Lewis discovered that Tolkien was descended from Saxon nobility. His forebears had come to England when Frederick the Great captured Saxony and offered the natives the alternatives of submission or exile. The ancestors of Tolkien had chosen the latter. "Tolkien," Lewis wrote, "is the very last of my friends whom I should have suspected of being *geboren*."[5]

In another of their early meetings Tolkien expounded on the home and how the atmosphere of it must have been different "in the days when a family had fed on the produce of the same few miles of country for six generations, and that perhaps this was why they saw nymphs in the fountains and dryads in the wood—they were not mistaken for there was in a sense *real* (not metaphorical) connections between them and the countryside. What had been earth and air and later corn, and later still bread, really was *in* them. We of course who live on a standardized international diet . . . are

3 *Letters of C. S. Lewis*, 176.

4 Unpublished letters to Arthur Greeves, December 3, 1929, and September 22, 1931.

5 Unpublished letter to W. H. Lewis, September 10, 1939.

artificial beings and have no connection (save in sentiment) with any place on earth. We are synthetic men, uprooted. The strength of the hills is not ours."[6] One can imagine the excitement of such a subject between men of their caliber.

By 1931 Tolkien made it a habit to drop in on Lewis on Monday mornings for a drink and talk. "This is one of the pleasantest spots in the week," wrote Lewis.[7] To Greeves he wrote that Tolkien's likes were so similar to their own that he would have fitted perfectly into their boyhood loves. Reading *The Hobbit* had turned out "uncanny" because it was "so exactly like what we would both have longed to write (or read) in 1916." One reason suggested was that Tolkien "grew up" on William Morris and George MacDonald.[8]

The friendship between Lewis and Tolkien meant not only talking but also walking and swimming together. By 1930 Lewis had moved to The Kilns, the home he was to occupy the rest of his life. Immediately in front of the house was a pond left where clay had been excavated for brick making. Lewis loved this pond and swam in it once or twice a day when the weather allowed. He and Tolkien would paddle a boat out to the middle of the pond, tie it to a snag there, and dive from it into the water.[9] Any close friend of Lewis's in those days was certain to be invited on one of his lengthy walking tours, and Tolkien made at least one such excursion. These cordial relations continued up to the time of Lewis's death in 1963. He and Tolkien lived on the same bus line running east from Oxford, Tolkien being about two miles from the center of Oxford and Lewis about four miles.

Tolkien reported that after the coming of Charles Williams to Oxford he spent a great deal of time with him—"I enjoyed

---

6 Unpublished letter to Arthur Greeves, June 22, 1930.
7 *Letters of C. S. Lewis*, 145.
8 Unpublished letter to Arthur Greeves, February 4, 1933.
9 Unpublished letter to Arthur Greeves, June 26, 1930.

his company: he was gay and amusing." He described Williams as "a comet that appeared out of the blue, passed through the little 'provincial' Oxford solar system, and went out again into the unknown."[10] Tolkien addressed to Charles Williams a long, humorous poem in rhymed couplets with objections to his obscurity and commendations of his genuineness as man and Christian writer almost equally mixed. He speaks of

> . . . that dark flux of symbol and event,
> where fable, faith, and faërie are blent
> with half-guessed meanings to some great intent
> I cannot grasp.[11]

The poem sees Williams taking the chair to read, maybe for hours, in the Inklings, and Tolkien adds his sincere wish to be there on such occasions. Charles Williams's letters to his wife are quite constant in their mention of his being with Lewis and Tolkien. "Tolkien has run up to ask me to speak to the naval cadets," or Tolkien had telephoned to suggest that the two of them go to a nursing home to see Lewis during a spell of illness.[12]

LITERARY RELATIONSHIPS

Although both R. W. Chapman and Nevill Coghill told Lewis of Charles Williams, it was not until early in 1936 that Lewis read one of Williams's books. He wrote his friend Greeves of the experience:

> I have just read what I think a really great book, *The Place of the Lion*. . . . It is based on the Platonic theory of the

10 Unpublished letter to Roger Verhulst, March 9, 1966.

11 A copy of this unpublished poem is among Charles Williams's papers in the Marion E. Wade Collection. The whereabouts of the original is not known.

12 Unpublished letters of January 14, 1944, and July 12, 1944.

> other world in which the archetypes of all earthly qualities exist; and in the novel . . . these archetypes begin sucking our world back. The lion of strength appears in the world and strength starts going out of the houses and things into him. The archetypal butterfly (enormous) appears and all the butterflies of the world fly back into him. . . . It is not only a most exciting fantasy, but a deeply religious and (unobtrusively) a profoundly learned book. . . . It deserves reading over and over again."[13]

It happened that Williams almost at the same time was discovering Lewis, and so there was an exchange of letters.

Lewis and Williams apparently met a time or two thereafter, but it was not until September 1939 that they got together regularly, the Oxford University Press having removed from London because of the war. Just after his arrival in Oxford, Williams wrote his wife, "I have fled to C. S. Lewis's rooms. . . . He is a great tea-drinker at any hour of night or day, and left a tray for me with milk and tea, and an electric kettle at hand." Thereafter they were together as much as their work and their war services would allow.

Lewis saw and promoted Williams's great talents whenever possible. He helped, for instance, to arrange for Williams to speak on John Milton at the university. As a result, other lectures followed, both inside and outside the university, and in due course an honorary degree was conferred on Williams. Lewis described him as "an ugly man with a rather cockney voice. But no one ever thinks of this for five minutes after he has begun speaking. His face becomes almost angelic. Both in public and in private he is of nearly all the men I have met, the one whose address most overflows with love. It is simply irresistible."[14]

---

13 Unpublished letter of February 26, 1936.
14 *Letters of C. S. Lewis*, 196–97.

Lewis tells how he, his brother Warren, Tolkien (Warren Lewis called him "Tollar"), and Williams would meet at times in a pub on Broad Street, Oxford, when "our fun is often so fast and furious that the company probably thinks we're talking bawdy when in fact we're very likely talking theology."[15] The triumvirate [of Lewis, Tolkien, and Williams] was to cease on May 15, 1945. At that time Lewis wrote of his grief for "the death of my great friend Charles Williams, my friend of friends, and comforter of all our little set, the most angelic man."[16] Tolkien also felt the loss and wrote Mrs. Williams, "I have grown to admire and love your husband deeply, and I am more grieved than I can express."[17]

Of course this friendship did not mean that they necessarily approved of each other's writings. Tolkien reported that he and Williams never spoke directly to each other about their authorship. Before they became acquainted he had read some of Williams's books, and in the Inklings he heard Williams read parts of *All Hallows' Eve*, *The Figure of Beatrice*, and "the Arthurian matter" but believed that Williams's connection with the Inklings was "in fact an astronomical accident that had no effect on his work, and probably no effect on any of the members except Lewis.[18] In an interview with Henry S. Resnick, Tolkien is reported to have said bluntly, "I have read a good many of his books but I don't like them," and in the same conversation seemingly contradicted his remark to Mrs. Williams at the time of her husband's death by saying, "I didn't know Charles Williams very well."[19]

Lewis apparently thought the least of Williams as a dramatist. Of his novels Lewis's adverse criticism is mainly pointed at their obscurity. Otherwise he liked them. He described Williams's *Many Dimensions* as "the very fine working out of the logical

15 Unpublished letter to Arthur Greeves, January 11, 1944.
16 *Letters of C. S. Lewis*, 206.
17 Unpublished letter of May 15, 1945.
18 Unpublished letter to Roger Verhulst, March 9, 1966.
19 *Niekas*, 18:43.

consequences of time-travel."[20] Williams wrote his wife that Lewis had a higher opinion than his own of *All Hallows' Eve*.[21]

Lewis's main encomium is reserved for some of Williams's literary criticism and especially for his poetry. Concerning the criticism, one remark is eminently sufficient. "After Blake," wrote Lewis, "Milton criticism is lost in misunderstanding, and the true line is hardly found again until Mr. Charles Williams's preface."[22] Lewis had no particular enthusiasm for Williams's early poetry but believed his later Arthurian poems "produced word music equaled by only two or three in this century and surpassed by none . . . jeweled with internal rhymes," and on the whole evocative of "a perilous world full of ecstasies and terrors, full of things that gleam and dart," a world of "pomp and ritual," of "strong, roaring, and resonant music." Lewis placed Williams as poet, when at his best, in a class with Spenser.[23]

In a broadcast at the time of Williams's death, Lewis summed up his opinion of Williams as a writer.

> I think he gave something I had never seen done before. When I first heard of him I realised this was an author unlike any I had ever met before. And when I started reading him this was entirely borne out. . . . What he has, I think, is a very deep and profound understanding of the moment at which a man departs from the ordinary this-worldly life in either direction of this frontier, what he could call Broceliande, the land of shapes through which you pass either to heaven or hell and that is why some people have found that the characters who embody good in his novels are to them almost as disquieting and

20 *Letters of C. S. Lewis*, 162–63; *Of Other Worlds*, 69.
21 Unpublished letter of February 28, 1944.
22 *A Preface to Paradise Lost*, 129. The same idea also occurs in Lewis's dedication of this work.
23 *Arthurian Torso*, 192ff.; *English Literature in the Sixteenth Century*, 372.

> repellant as the ones that embody evil, because they are both equally characters departing from the ordinary—well, merry Middle-earth, as the Middle Ages would have called it. I don't agree at all myself. I think his good characters are a triumph and he shares this with very few authors, because his good characters are more convincing than his bad ones, more real. He knew more about good than about evil.

Lewis was lavish in his enthusiasm for the genius of Tolkien. He felt that his essay "On Fairy-stories" was the best of its kind.[24] He wrote a close friend of having received the first volume of *The Lord of the Rings* and "gluttonously read two chapters instead of saving it all for the weekend. Wouldn't it be wonderful if it really succeeded (In selling, I mean)? It would inaugurate a new age. Dare we hope?"[25] Lewis's review of this first volume began by saying, "This book is lightning from a clear sky." He went on:

> Perhaps no book yet written in the world is quite such a radical instance of what its author has elsewhere called 'sub-creation!' The direct debt . . . which every author must owe to the universe, is here deliberately reduced to the minimum. Not content to create his own story, he creates, with an almost insolent prodigality, the whole world in which it is to move, with its own theology, myths, geography, history, palaeography, languages, and orders of being. . . . The names alone are a feast, whether redolent of quiet countryside (Michael Delving, South Farthing), tall and kingly (Boromir, Faramir, Elendil), loathsome like Smeagol who is also Gollum, or frowning in the evil strength of Barad Dûr or Gorgoroth: yet best of

24 *Of Other Worlds*, 26.
25 Unpublished letter to Mrs. Austin Farrer, December 4, 1953.

> all (Lothlórien, Gilthoniel, Galadriel) when they embody that piercing, high, Elvish beauty of which no other prose writer has captured so much . . . here are beauties which pierce like swords or burn like cold iron; here is a book that will break your heart.[26]

Lewis told one of my friends who was visiting him that *The Lord of the Rings* was as long as the Bible and not a word too long.

Lewis regarded *The Hobbit* as more than plot and exciting adventure. He thought the humorous flurry of the early part shifted into what he called epic. "It is as if the battle of Toad Hall had become a serious *heimsohn* and Badger had begun to talk Njal." He recommended this book to his friend Sister Penelope as "a good fairy story by a Christian for a 12-year old."[27]

Surprisingly, Lewis and Tolkien talked of doing a book together, but Lewis felt it was not very likely to be written since "any book in collaboration with that great, but dilatory and unmethodical man . . . is dated I fear to appear on the Greek Calends."[28]

To a correspondent who thought he saw great similarities between the creative writings of Lewis and Tolkien and wondered about mutual influences, Lewis wrote, "I don't think Tolkien influenced me, and I am certain I didn't influence him. That is, I didn't influence what he wrote. My continued encouragement, carried to the point of nagging, influenced him very much to write at all with that gravity and at that length. In other words, I acted as a midwife, not as a father. The similarities between his work and mine are due, I think (a) To nature—temperament, (b) To common sources. We are both soaked in Norse mythology, Geo. MacDonald's fairytales, Homer, Beowulf, and medieval romance. Also, of course, we are both Christians (he, as R. C.)."[29]

---

26 *Time and Tide*, August, 1954, 1082.
27 *Of Other Worlds*, 19; unpublished letter of August 24, 1939.
28 *Letters of C. S. Lewis*, 287.
29 To Professor Francis Anderson, September 23, 1963. Used by kind permission

I have as yet found no record of Charles Williams's opinion of Tolkien as writer. Williams's letters often mention Tolkien. "Tomorrow I go to Magdalen at 10:45," he wrote, "where Lewis and Tolkien will put on their gowns and take me to the Divinity Schools."[30] There Williams was to deliver his first lecture at Oxford University. Since Williams was a prolific reviewer of books, it probably means simply that there was nothing by Tolkien for him to comment on in the period of Williams's residency in Oxford. How interesting it would be to see what Williams might have said about *The Lord of the Rings*!

Although Tolkien spoke to me warmly of his long and happy association with Lewis, he also sometimes found fault with him. He mentioned that Lewis "borrowed" from him. I pointed out that Lewis had acknowledged the borrowing of the word "Númenor," but Tolkien insisted there were unacknowledged "echoes" in Lewis. In a letter to Jared C. Lobdell, Tolkien mentioned *eldil* as one example, also *Tinidril* as a composite of his *Idril* and *Tinúviel*.[31] A copy of *Perelandra* given by Tolkien to friends contains one of those equivocal notes characteristic of him. On the jacket he has written: "A bottle of sound vintage (?) I hope!"[32] Tolkien wrote me that he found Lewis's *Letters to an American Lady* "deeply interesting and very moving." I have cited earlier in this volume Tolkien's remark that except for Lewis's encouragement *The Lord of the Rings* might never have been published—warm praise indeed.

Williams reviewed some of Lewis's books. Of *The Problem of Pain* he said, "The great pattern of the book wrought too deeply into Christian dogma and the name of man . . . for one

---

of its present owner, Robert H. Baylis.

30 Unpublished letter to his wife, January 29, 1940.

31 Unpublished letter of July 31, 1964. It is interesting to note an unexpected source apparently used by both Lewis and Tolkien, i.e., place names from the Fertile Crescent (now the region of Turkey and the lands south and east of it) such as "Arslan-Tash" and also "Warka-Uruk-Erech," "Lagash," and "Uzun."

32 This volume is in the Marion E. Wade Collection at Wheaton College.

to disagree." He found Lewis's *Beyond Personality* to contain some original thoughts and "as new as the Christian Church." Williams's review of *The Screwtape Letters* took the form of a letter from hell. "If many of the wretches read them, we must be prepared for a serious increase in virtue. They give everything away. In explaining our modes of attack, Screwtape has shown men their best defense. . . . We must certainly discover how these letters got out and we must prevent them from ever being re-read. . . . You will send someone to see after Lewis?—some very clever fiend?"[33]

There was at least one clear difference of personal taste among these three men. Both Tolkien and Lewis were avid lovers of nature. It is impossible, for instance, to read *The Lord of the Rings* or Lewis's *Perelandra* without noting an enormous sensitivity to the glory of water, wood, and sky. On the other hand, Charles Williams had all but an aversion to the world of nature. He was a Londoner by birth and preference and, like Charles Lamb, loved the great city. Perhaps we can also note a difference in Tolkien and Lewis from Williams in respect to a love of Faërie. The first two find no hesitation in writing of dwarves, elves, humanized trees, and the like, and their stories often take place in faraway, numinous places. On the other hand, Williams's characters and situations are commonplace, even though visited by the occult, the magical, and the horrible. It is hard to imagine a Hobbit or an Elf slipping into the pages of a Williams story.

THE COMMON ELEMENTS

It seems clear that there are two important elements common to these three men, manifest both in their personal lives and in their

33 *Theology*, January, 1941; *Time and Tide* (June 16, 1945); Ibid. (March 21, 1942).

works. These are a deep-seated Christianity and a vivid imagination.

Imagination, of course, is an element in all creativity, but in our times it is not usual to find a far-flung imagination combined with orthodox Christianity. In Lewis's *Perelandra*, for instance, we have not simply a "science-fiction" voyage to the planet Venus but also a profound metaphor that suggests what may have been the temptation in the Garden of Eden. In *The Lion, the Witch and the Wardrobe* we have both a delightful set of adventures by children in the land of Narnia and also a moving recall of the death and resurrection of Jesus Christ. In Charles Williams's *Descent into Hell* we find not only human and ghostly characters (once a living man and a ghost look through the same window together) but we also see Pauline Anstruther emerging from the haze of worldly social life into the calm clarity of godliness.

It is not necessary to labor this quality in Williams and Lewis. Readers are clearly aware of its existence. Chad Walsh says that in *Perelandra* he "got the taste and the smell of Christian truth. My senses as well as my soul were baptized. It was as though an intellectual abstraction or speculation had become flesh and dwelt in its solid bodily glory among us."[34] Edmund Fuller describes Charles Williams as a "wholly committed writer. He interprets all of natural or familiar life, plus all of its other extraordinary and mysterious dimensions, in terms of Christian theology."[35] Similar comments might be cited at length.

It is the recognition of Tolkien with Lewis and Williams as a Christian writer that may cause a raising of eyebrows. I have already discussed this matter and endeavored to show that his main works possess not only religious but also strongly Christian overtones. To be sure, no real lover of Tolkien's fiction would want it turned into sermons, no matter how cleverly preached. What

---

34 *Light on C. S. Lewis*, 107.
35 *Books with Men Behind Them*, 203.

he, and also Lewis and Williams, have done in all their best things is mythic. They have discovered a dimension as large as life, indeed as large as eternal life. Nevill Coghill described his friend Lewis as having a "hunger for magnitude," a remark equally applicable to Tolkien and Williams.

It is inevitable that any three writers in close friendship who have read their works to each other, and read them open to criticism and suggestions for improvement, should have an influence on each other. What that influence amounted to is quite another matter. Lewis several times warned that the more specific the claim the more likely it was to be wrong. Our intention here has been simply to identify the nature of the friendship.

A bookseller told me of asking a college girl just why she liked *The Lord of the Rings*. She replied that she liked the story because it had black and white meanings. (Oddly, this is the element that is adversely criticized by Edmund Wilson and certain others.) Certainly it is strange that a story of Elves, orcs, and talking trees and of no uncertain moral conduct should have become one of the popular books of our time. When this bookseller asked me for an explanation of such a phenomenon, I said I thought our present world had been so drained of elemental qualities such as the numinous, the supernatural, and the wonderful that it had been consequently drained of much—perhaps most—of its natural and religious meaning. Someone wrote me of a sixth-grade pupil who, after reading *The Lord of the Rings*, had cried for two days. I think it must have been a cry for life and meaning and joy from the wasteland that had somehow already managed to capture this boy.

Chapter 23

UNDERSTANDING THE OXFORD GROUP

Dr. Kilby was always eager to introduce Christians to the group of writers whose works he was assembling, and the following lecture is a helpful introduction to all of them (with the exception of G. K. Chesterton, who had not yet been added to the authors then comprising the Marion E. Wade Collection at Wheaton College).

I should like to tell you about six people. Many of you are familiar with one or more, but I suspect not many of you know all six. A. W. Tozer believed that in our contemporary world, perhaps during the last thirty years, evangelicals have not produced a single really significant book. A tremendous accusation. But there is a happy response, and that's what I'd like to discuss. Not more than one small step away from the evangelical world we find some of the most significant people of our time. It's a tragedy that many of us have been willing—and sometimes glad—to exclude them.

Isn't it tragic? I've seen people literally throw out C. S. Lewis, in spite of the fact that he, for all of his life, tried to state in every way possible, "I'm nothing but an orthodox Christian. I believe in the Apostles' Creed. I believe in the great doctrines of the church. I believe the Bible. I believe in Heaven and Hell." Ask yourself whether you believe in hell. I suspect that most evangelicals don't. I've been asking myself specifically, "Do I believe in hell?" Here is a man who came on the scene, and has taught us tremendous things. More than that, he made us *feel* the meaning of heaven and hell. Nobody—*nobody*—since St. John on Patmos has so presented heaven as to genuinely inspire one to be there as did C. S. Lewis. After reading his books many times, I discovered that he can't even finish his scholarly books without discussing heaven, let alone his specifically Christian work. This doesn't happen in every book, but it's amazing how close to unanimity it appears.

These writers are our friends. Kathleen Knott, a British novelist and poet, wrote a book against C. S. Lewis, Dorothy Sayers, and about ten others. She jumped on Lewis and Sayers in particular. Her word for them was "fundamentalists." That's about as orthodox as one could get. These six people are Anglicans, except Tolkien, a Roman Catholic. They belong to serious writing, to our century. Only one of the six, George MacDonald, who died in 1905, is not contemporary. In a sense, he is a father to several of these writers. Readers who didn't like their Christianity were compelled to respect their other accomplishments. This is something toward which all of us should strive.

First on my list is C. S. Lewis. He wrote between forty and fifty books, with some still coming. He was a medieval and Renaissance scholar. I possess a letter from a former student who attended Duke University. She wrote: "My Lewis shelf is almost single-handedly sustaining me in the midst of a monumentally demanding situation." I could relate many other such tales, wherein Lewis is the mainstay of a student attending a secular university. He has been called the "apostle to the skeptics" by Chad Walsh, who wrote a book on this subject in 1948. There is a scarce book about intellectuals who turned to Christ. In fact, five of these refer to C. S. Lewis as the main reason for their turning to Christ. For me, he has been a considerable influence.

Lewis regarded *Perelandra* as his best book. If you would like to visit the Garden of Eden and see precisely what the sin was, I don't believe you could read fifty books of theology that would teach you more—and make you *feel* more explicitly—than this book. He has not misrepresented the Garden at all. He has shown how the human will, the selfhood, is involved—you're just as guilty as Adam and Eve. *The Great Divorce* is a bus trip from Hell to Heaven, where people who've been in Hell are allowed to board a bus for Heaven. People in Heaven approach and warmly invite them in; but only one person enters. Some, such as the Anglican minister, who's been in Hell a long time, refuse, remembering that at the last minute he has an important paper to deliver to his club. So he returns on his bus. *Surprised by Joy* is Lewis's autobiography, covering half of his life. We wished he'd published further autobiographical material, but did not. It is a very great book to give somebody who is wondering about Christianity, having doubts. In *The Problem of Pain*, you have the finest argument for atheism I've ever encountered. I've read Bertrand Russell, and he's a dumb cluck beside Lewis. Russell's case for atheism is shallow. However, C. S. Lewis's is excellent. But then he takes a tremendous whack at the argument. He wrote one book, *The Abolition of Man*, about sixty-five pages, and I don't know any pages more significant than this. I've seen many young people discover Lewis, and a great change occurs in the depths of their spiritual lives.

The second writer is Professor Tolkien. His great book, the three-volume fairy tale of 1,100 pages, is *The Lord of the Rings*, with one hundred pages of footnotes. One of the happiest of his other works is a poem called "Tom Bombadil," which I like very much. One matter that I've not mentioned elsewhere: Professor Tolkien told me that more than once he'd been given a story in answer to prayer. Readers wonder if there really is a Christian slant to his books. After that statement, you would not doubt, would you?

On to Charles Williams. I've known more than one student who has started on Lewis, moved to Tolkien, and finally to Williams; and who has commented that after reading many of the works of these three, Williams is the greatest. He was connected with Oxford University Press, almost a handyman, doing work he shouldn't have been asked to do. He's still being discovered. One day we will recognize him as one of the significant writers of our time. He wrote all kinds of books: biographies, plays, criticism, theology, and novels. One, *The Descent of the Dove*, is a most unusual history of the church; or rather, as he says, a history of the Holy Spirit in the church. He wrote seven novels, which have been called supernatural thrillers. For instance, *War in Heaven* begins with the discovery of a dead body underneath the editor's desk at a newspaper office. But actually the book is about the Holy Grail, the apparent discovery of the cup used at the Last Supper. He uses detective stories, and some of the most sublime accounts of true poems you could possibly imagine.

In his novels there is always a struggle between good and evil. He has pages that describe with a frightful clarity the deterioration and damnation of a human soul. On the other hand, there are other pages that describe the triumphant struggle toward salvation. He is known for inventing one or two expressions. One is *co-inherence*. The more I learn of this, the more exciting it is to me. The notion is that the Universe has a great unity given it by the Creator himself; and thus every part of the Universe is dependent upon every other part. When you apply this notion, you increase in fellowship toward every person, not merely toward Christians but toward people, because it is one world: God's world, says Charles Williams. And this co-inherence is observable in nature and human society, but it is much deeper. It is a relationship of souls. You see this in many of his books. This is a fine antidote, this idea which runs through Charles

Williams's books, to what I call the utter loneliness of every one of us. The world has never been so lonely. We cannot come into contact with each other, I'm increasingly convinced. He encourages people in this direction.

The fourth person I want to mention is Owen Barfield. He was an attorney in London, now retired. Some of us have got to know this man very intimately. He is one of the most brilliant men alive, in my opinion. *The Gordon Review* published an address of his originally presented at Wheaton. It was called "Philology and the Incarnation." Can you contemplate how difficult it is to imagine a subject like that? Let me tell you what he said. Suppose a man lived three hundred years before Christ to three hundred years after Christ; and was a philologist, a student of language. Suppose he'd never once heard the least whisper of Christ, but simply studied the language of the time, its word meanings, he would be forced to declare that some great event happened during that period. The best word to describe it would be "incarnation." How do you like that for an idea?

We recently hosted him at Wheaton College, where he offered an address, "The Harp and the Camera." Before he spoke, I wondered what in the world this meant. I can't tell you. It would take too long. It was one of the most profound things I've ever heard. Men from the philosophy department came up afterward and said, "This is the most brilliant address I've ever heard in my life." I felt the same way. This man has written eight or ten books, which I've been trying to read for several years, and have been attempting to discover the basic meaning of; and I think, at last, I've begun to unravel the thread. I'm reading *Romanticism Comes of Age*, just reissued. Recently I wrote Barfield, stating, "I wish you would change the titles of some of your books!" He published two earlier books, still to be discovered by Christians and scholars in the secular world. It seems to me they have very dull titles, but they are very exciting books. The first is called *Poetic Diction*. The other is called *History in English Words*.

I'll attempt to explain his theory in one sentence: In the beginning there was a vast and glorious, almost unconscious relationship between nature and man and God. The whole history of the Western world has been the history of the abstraction from this great, vital composite. Today we have the most abstract world possible. And this is why we're so lonely. We can't get together because we're all in billions of little pieces. It is impossible to consider a unified world.

Now a word about Dorothy Sayers, who died eleven years ago. Most of you know her as a detective-story writer. She refused to write detective stories for the last twenty years of her life, partly because she hated to pay the enormous income tax. She wanted to be known as a serious writer. She was one of the world's great detective-story writers. Also, she was a wonderful Christian who wrote profound things. She wrote Christian dramas and many fine Christian essays. I might mention *The Mind of the Maker*. If you're interested in becoming a creative writer, you should not miss this book. In it she draws a lengthy parallel between the Trinity and the technique of writing. How's that for a thesis?

And just a word about George MacDonald, who died in 1905. He was a great influence on C. S. Lewis, and to some extent on one or two of these other writers. He wrote over fifty books. I'll mention two or three that might interest you. This one might shock you a little bit. He wrote a book called *Lilith*. You may not know, but Lilith was the first wife of Adam. I was so shocked when I first heard this that I thought I'd misunderstood. Then I investigated, and discovered that there's a great deal of writing about Lilith. MacDonald's best works are children's books. He published one called *At the Back of the North Wind*. You Bible students certainly know that the word *pneuma* is the word for "spirit." It's also the word for "wind." Here the north wind is the Holy Spirit. MacDonald tells the story of how the wind visits a little boy. The Holy Spirit is completely personified here, a living thing, helping this boy.

Another book is *The Princess and the Goblin.* In this book, the princess is able to move about in a dark cave. She's able to do so with an invisible string on the ground. You can see what MacDonald is portraying: the Holy Spirit leads us. God is leading, and she can see the string. She has a friend, and they go up into an attic where an old woman lives. The princess finds this room, and takes her little boyfriend there to see, but he can't see anything. C. S. Lewis does this in two of his books. In *The Last Battle*, he has some dwarves who can't see the glorious sight before them. And in *Till We Have Faces*, we encounter a similar image. We talk about Christians possessing a newer way, a better way. But somehow it doesn't work out in our lives. These books offer a real image, a real feeling, that these two ways are really present. And unsaved people can't or don't see the glory that is everywhere apparent.

Elijah under the juniper tree said, "Lord, let me die. I'm discouraged." The Lord replied, "Don't forget, I've got seven thousand people here who haven't bowed the knee to Baal." Sometimes we evangelicals think, "We're in a corner. We're doing the best we can. But we can't do very much." We have allies in these writers. They are our friends and we ought to claim them. They don't belong to the world. I hope that what little I've said this morning will encourage you to accept these writers and their great suggestions.

Chapter 24

THE WADE COLLECTION AND THE PRESERVATION OF A LEGACY

Dr. Kilby began the important collection of books, letters, and manuscripts now known as the Marion E. Wade Center with no outside funding or encouragement beyond his conviction of the great importance of these writers. The first piece in this chapter expresses the sense of excitement, satisfaction, and sheer delight he had in the process of persuading the writers—or their heirs, friends, and relatives—to part with the documents that eventually became the core of this collection. On my occasional visits with him during those years in the late 60s, I first heard some of the stories he tells here, and can still see the sparkle in his eye.

The second part of this chapter, "A Note on the Wade Collection," written in 1981, five years before his death, is a more factually informative account of the Wade Center—though it is somewhat less lively. Perhaps the lack of personal involvement in the essay reflects the fact that by this time the aging Kilby was no longer directly in charge of the collection, and he undoubtedly felt the loss of that severance from what was clearly his own child.

It should be noted that there are certain inaccuracies in the following accounts (e.g., Dorothy Sayers's "foster" son was in fact her own biological son). However, I have not made an attempt to correct these errors as they reflect Kilby's own understanding and perspective as he built the collection as well as the biographical information that was then available. In this way, the recollection provides a more accurate and personal portrait of the fledgling Wade Collection from that era.

Those reading this account of the early struggles and successes of the Wade Collection may be interested to know that the handful of books and manuscripts first gathered together by Dr. Kilby in those early days has now grown to a collection of thousands of books, manuscripts, letters, photographs, recordings, and various other resources, used annually by hundreds of scholars from all over the world who come to the Marion E. Wade Center to conduct research on the seven authors included in these archival holdings.

Clyde Kilby would be delighted that the collection he founded in 1965 has now celebrated more than fifty years serving as an internationally recognized research facility with a museum, spacious reading room (named in honor of Clyde and Martha Kilby), and an extensive archive and library of literary resources. As part of its fiftieth-anniversary commemoration, the Marion E. Wade Center dedicated the Bakke Auditorium, a lovely new space in which to provide increased programming on the seven authors.[36]

In no small part due to Dr. Kilby's original vision, interest in these seven British authors—Owen Barfield, G. K. Chesterton, C. S. Lewis, George MacDonald, Dorothy L. Sayers, J. R. R. Tolkien, and Charles Williams—and their work continues to grow, introducing a new generation of readers worldwide to the transformative power of their thought and imagination.

---

36 More on the history of the Wade Center, as well as a fifteen-minute video that includes Dr. Kilby describing the establishment of the collection, can be found at http://www.wheaton.edu/wadecenter.

TRAVELS IN ENGLAND AND THE GROWTH OF THE WADE COLLECTION

I thought you might like to hear something about my recent trip to England. Our first four-page bulletin about the Lewis Collection is dated February 1, 1965, so we're nearing the end of the sixth year of the collection. People ask me how it came into existence. The more I work with it, the more I am convinced that God brought it into existence. I mean that precisely.

I confess that we didn't ask anybody. We were a little afraid that if we consulted a committee, that would be the end of it. At any rate, we decided on seven people: Lewis, Tolkien, Charles Williams, Dorothy Sayers, George MacDonald, Owen Barfield, and G. K. Chesterton. We gave up Chesterton a little bit later because he had published, as I recall, 125 books. We thought that would disproportionate our budget. We supposed that his manuscripts had been acquired. From the very first we thought in terms of a serious collection; and no collection is true, as far as I'm concerned, unless it possesses manuscripts.

The class of 1966 appointed a committee to pose a recommendation for what they would donate their money to. It was $2600 or thereabouts to be given to the college. Everybody was pretty well in favor of the Lewis project. There was one skeptic in the group who said: "I'm in favor of this, but how could a little college like Wheaton ever acquire any manuscripts from England?" None of us knew anybody in England except evangelists who occasionally came to speak in college chapel. At any rate, this skeptic caused them to postpone their meeting. In the meantime I had been in touch with a Charles Williams man. I discovered that he had some little sheets on which Charles Williams had written in his own hand some sonnets. I think there were ten or twelve. When I heard this, I was so happy that I wrote right back and made him an offer. And he accepted the offer. I didn't ask anybody. It was sudden, and got me so excited that I'm not sure what I did, except that I sent him a check, offering a guess as to what he might accept. He announced that he was sending the material. Then this committee met, and the skeptical question arose again. Somebody happened to know about this and stood up with glee, stating: "Well, this little Midwestern college has already got some manuscripts!" I didn't feel then nearly so much as now that it was the Lord's affair. I've grown in the conviction that this is of the Lord.

We have steadily improved the collection. This was my fourth trip to England. I went in '64, '66, '69, and again in '71, generally for the summer. We've been looking for first editions. Ideally we will possess all editions, but we don't have the money. We have had very little money, as a matter of fact. My guess is that we haven't invested much more than $25,000 into this collection. We discovered that Sotheby's, the great auction house in London, was going to sell some C. S. Lewis letters. Excited, I went down to Sotheby's and got the catalog listing the letters, but it turned out there were only three letters by Lewis. I could hardly believe my eyes. I was shocked and a bit disappointed. I hoped there'd be more of them for sale. We didn't get them, finally. But I became acquainted with a rather important London agent, who asked, "Well, how much should I bid for you?" I said, "Seven or eight pounds, eight pounds at twenty dollars." I thought that was a very sufficient price. He said, "Oh, I'm sure these three letters will sell." There were four pages, two of them of very small pieces of paper, and one a little larger. Three letters, a total of four pages. One of them was typed and postscripted in Lewis's hand.

We let it stand for a few days. Just as I leaving we talked again, and he said, "Well, I'll go down there to Sotheby's and find out what they think, whether they've got any bids, and write you." I received a letter from him stating that Sotheby's expected thirty to forty pounds. Forty pounds is $100. Well, I simply couldn't believe it. I went around for several days trying to believe that this price is possible for three little letters. We'd had hundreds and hundreds of letters given to us. I finally cabled him to bid thirty-six pounds—that's $90—as a top, not knowing which way to jump, to tell the truth. I'd just received a letter from him in the last few days saying those letters sold for $100, those three little letters of C. S. Lewis. We have at least 850 of his letters in our collection, I think it was $28,330 worth of letters at that rate. We have almost as many letters by Charles Williams.

My second trip was the summer of 1966. I was invited to visit by J. R. R. Tolkien, who, at that time, was the most read author in the world. More people read *The Lord of the Rings*, his most famous work. There's the suggestion that the world is divided into those who've read *The Lord of the Rings* and those who haven't. But I did enjoy the great honor of working with this man for an entire summer. People couldn't get into his house. His wife stood at the front door and told them no. She said, "Yesterday a man came and said, 'I came six thousand miles to see Professor Tolkien.'" I asked her the $64 question: Did he get in? She said, "No, I didn't let him in." I remember one of the reasons he didn't get in was because he had a concealed tape recorder. This was like carrying a double-barred, cocked shotgun into the house. I brought my camera, and I bought a little fifty-cent shopping bag over there. I've taken it on all my trips since, so I look very British, nothing American about it. I slipped my camera in with the manuscripts that I was carrying for him back and forth, and sometimes I was able to take pictures of him. He's complaining all the time about how journalists call him up during American time and rouse him out of bed at two or three in the morning, asking questions about his life. He didn't like questions about his life at 9:00 AM, let alone 3:00 AM!

As I said, this is an endless story. I was reading *The Lord of the Rings*, the story of the Third Age of Middle-earth, and I was reading the story of the First Age of Middle-earth. It's called *The Silmarillion*, the story of the three silmarils and their adventures. It's quite a story. I think that I was probably one of less than a half dozen people who've ever seen this manuscript. But I was taking it a portion at time, carrying it to Oxford where I lived. I was reading it, trying to estimate its value, its relation to other parts of this story, and so on. This story will not be published, will never be finished, I'm absolutely sure. When I go to London, I always talk to Tolkien's publisher, Raynor Unwin.

I met C. S. Lewis one time in 1953—Martha and I were over there for only a little while—thirty or forty minutes. I left thinking I had done him an injustice to impose upon him at all. If everybody who liked his works went to see him, there'd be no more works. That's the point, you see. Charles Williams died in 1945, and I'd never heard of him. I got to know his wife several years ago, and always visited with her when I was in England. She died about two years ago. This summer I was with his son, his only child, who is almost fifty now, and we are well acquainted; and I harbor great hopes that the Lord is going to give us the great bulk of Charles Williams manuscripts, which are now owned by the son.

George MacDonald died in 1905. We'll never be able to build a set of his manuscripts. To my absolute astonishment, we've discovered that Yale University found over three thousand of George MacDonald's letters somewhere. They've been opening them during Christmastime.

Dorothy Sayers died fifteen years ago or so. We tried our very dead-level best to contact her foster son. She married an older man who had a son. Both of them, husband and wife, were getting along. He lives in Switzerland. We'd tried our best, we tried every way to get in touch with them. One thing I did was to write to Billy Graham's daughter up in Switzerland to see if she happened to know this particular man. None of this worked. But Dorothy Sayers's papers have just appeared for sale in the last few months in London, and this man who was bidding for me on the three Lewis letters is the man who has them. They want only $62,500 for them. When we get the Williams items, if we do, I'm going to become excited about those Dorothy Sayers items. I've written the agent, asking him once again whether the Dorothy Sayers material might be split up.

On the one hand, she wrote her detective stories. On the other hand, there were her Christian writings. She was a Christian and wrote a very considerable amount of apologetic material. She wrote that fine title, *The Mind of the Maker*, a most exciting book. She uses the Trinity to illustrate the writing technique through an entire book. Anybody that's got $62,500 will be glad to get those papers. I think we can buy them for something less than that. But I didn't press the agent on that point. I think it was understood between us.

I know of possibly fifty Lewis letters, two little batches. One is way up the mountains—well, I shouldn't tell you about that. There's one in the United States, anyway. Now that they're high-priced, I think we must do everything we can to get them. But they're not more than fifty letters of Lewis's. The Bodleian Library [Oxford University, started collecting] . . . in the twelfth century. And here's little Wheaton out in the prairies of Illinois! We have the best collection of Lewis in the world. . . .

Major Lewis, C. S. Lewis's brother, has willed us some very valuable things. He keeps them in a bureau drawer in his bedroom. I've seen it, marked: *PROPERTY OF CLYDE S. KILBY*. We'll possess the best collection in the United States forever and ever. No way to change it. We have an arrangement with the Bodleian of exchanging microfilm of our manuscript material. Microfilm is not handed out easily to anybody, and they are never handed out to another institution, by the way. They are loaned to research workers, but not to another institution.

The weather was just fine, lovely, sunshine and warmish weather most of the time. Once it was twenty-six degrees at Pusey House in Oxford where I lived. We had radiators, but the heat never was turned on. I got up three different nights and put on my fleece-lined overcoat and went back to bed, that's how cold it was! Pusey House is a Gothic building with very thick walls, but the wind blew right through the windows, blowing the curtains around. I got up and put one of my blankets over the window to stop the wind.

I visited with Major Lewis many times. He has told me, very graciously, that I'm a member of the family. I've been in the bedroom where Lewis died, up in his regular bedroom. In his last days he couldn't go upstairs; he had heart trouble and various other serious ailments. I'd sometimes sit with Major Lewis at night and watch television. He is seventy-six, the only brother of C. S. Lewis. There were only the two boys in the family, the parents long since dead.

Owen Barfield is a very interesting person. Did you hear him the last time he was here? We hosted him at our writer's conference to talk about Lewis. Barfield was Lewis's closest friend for about forty-five years. Barfield is retired, a London solicitor. I don't see how he did any law work. He's one of the brainiest men alive, in my opinion; a man to be reckoned with. He's recognized more and more as a scholar, a thinker. It's a joy knowing him. I've been in his home. To make a long story short, we were able by the Lord's grace to bring all of his manuscripts back. He'd just published a book on Coleridge. He has a big unpublished novel of two volumes, a total of seven or eight hundred pages. It's a typescript, not a published work. We've got all his other papers. I kept sending my clothes home because, otherwise, it's hard carrying manuscripts back in my suitcase!

Shall I tell this tale? A Wheaton girl visiting England wanted to talk with me awhile. I said, "Well, I'm awfully busy, but can you call me next Tuesday at 3:30. We can have tea at 4:00 if I'm here at 3:30." I took a bath about 2:30, and I washed my socks. You do your own laundry when you're abroad. I had just got them good and wet when I realized I'd sent all my socks home! So this girl called up at 3:30 and I said, "Okay, come over here to the hotel where I am, and you slip back here to my room. Don't let anybody see. They might not let you come." I told her how to find me, and she arrived. Fortunately the radiator was good and hot, so after an hour my socks were dry. I walked her down to the London Underground so she could go home.

I was twelve pounds overweight on my suitcase. Fortunately the airlines don't charge for overweight now, at least Pan Am didn't. But I did bring home a heavy suitcase, almost entirely manuscripts. Most of them were Owen Barfield's manuscripts. So really, we possess every Barfield manuscript. I think he saved one small piece, I forget what. Barfield is really "ours" now, and I think he enjoys visiting Wheaton. He's taught one semester at the University of Missouri. He's lectured mostly in eastern part of the United States. I won't try to tell you about Barfield's theory of life and the world, but it's a very substantial idea called "anthroposophy." He claims that he's a Christian, and I think he is a Christian. Anyway, a fine man. He's sixty-five. Two of our six writers are alive, Tolkien and Barfield. The others are gone.

Again, it seems to me that for a little college like Wheaton, it's a miracle for us to acquire anything, especially when we have no money. If we had plenty of money, it wouldn't be a problem. But we have made friends all over England. I added them up before

I went on this trip, and it seems to me there were around 120 people that I knew, a few by rather lengthy correspondence rather than personally. We added to the list considerably on this trip. Among people that I went to see: Pauline Baynes. If you know C. S. Lewis, you know something about Pauline Baynes. She was the illustrator of his Narnia books, and illustrator of some of Tolkien's books. She illustrated *A Year for All of England.* She's a charming, delightful woman living in Surrey.

I visited Lord David Cecil, who taught at Oxford during the years that Lewis was there. He told me that he believed that C. S. Lewis was the greatest man at Oxford University in the years that he was there. A great compliment from a man who is himself a great man, the author of many fine books. One of my former students, Bob Siegel, wanted me to go up in the Lake Country. Well, I told him I couldn't do it. I didn't have time. Finally I was persuaded. I wanted to see a man to whom I had written, but who had not answered. I possessed a list from Major Lewis listing all of C. S. Lewis's correspondents, and I wrote to all of them. A few didn't respond.

So we went. We thought we would be two people walking through the Lake Country, but we ended up with eight. Six were from this country, and two were Britishers. One was a pastor from the famous Round Church in Cambridge. I attended the church once, standing room only, which I was glad to see.

While we were up there, we had two cars, and drove to this village called Little Langdale, way out in the mountains. We asked at the post office where this man, Delmar Banner, lived. So we went farther out in the mountains, and finally found the place, a beautiful house. There were sheep in the front yard. A fine-looking old man met us at the door and said, "Come in and have tea. What do you want? What are you here for?" It turned out that this man, Delmar Banner, was one of the famous modern painters of England. He has a portrait, for instance, of Beatrix Potter, who was his good friend, hanging in the National Gallery in London. His wife came in, and I saw that she was really a sculptress. Later I looked her up in *Who's Who*, and she received nearly an entire column, which practically nobody gets. They were friends of C. S. Lewis. I was excited about this house, this lovely, antique, very ancient house, I suppose Tudor or earlier. They took us all over, showed us the studios and pictures and so on. Then he showed us his C. S. Lewis books. He had been friends with Lewis. He'd write Lewis, and the reply would be pasted into the front of the book very securely, unfortunately for us. So I didn't say anything; except, of course, to explain the connection. We always say, "Lewis!" That's the first thing to say. Once we shouted up to a woman up on a hillside in South England. We just said, "We know C. S. Lewis!" The man and woman both practically hugged me. They'd never seen me before, and I'd never seen them.

I wondered how on earth I'd ever approach the matter again. Lo and behold, I received a letter from this man that says, "I think you came up here to try to get my Lewis letters! I've got 20 of them and I'll sell them for $500." We'd never paid anything like that for a Lewis letter. We paid around $6 a page for Barfield, extremely valuable letters. The second-best collection of Lewis's letters were sent to Barfield. We have both the best collection, and the second most important collection here, as well as many other collections. I wrote back and told him we never pay more than $6 a page; but we'd pay him $7.50 a page. He had already given me one typed letter as a starter, enclosed with the letter stating, "I suppose you want my letter." He was able to dig up three others, and for some reason he gave us a copy of *The Problem of Pain* with the letter pasted in. We're very hopeful that there will be a way to remove it without destroying either the letter or the book, in which case that book will be sent airmail to Mr. Delmar Banner.

A NOTE ON THE WADE COLLECTION

The Marion E. Wade Collection holds the best array anywhere of books and papers on C. S. Lewis, Charles Williams, Dorothy L. Sayers, and Owen Barfield. It has more than 1,100 original letters by Lewis and over 850 pages of his manuscripts. It also contains such accessory writings as twenty-three volumes of Warren H. Lewis' lifetime diaries, original letters by him, and eleven volumes prepared by him and known as the "Lewis Papers"; these are family journals, correspondence, and the like going back to 1850. Among the manuscripts are Lewis's boyhood "Boxen" stories, written and illustrated when he was about thirteen.

The collection has over 8,000 pages of Dorothy L. Sayers's manuscripts, including the detective stories, *The Man Born to Be King, The Mind of the Maker, Busman's Honeymoon*, and many essays, along with first editions of her books.

The majority of the manuscripts of Charles Williams are located here along with some 850 of his original letters. The manuscripts include *The Figure of Beatrice, Descent into Hell, All Hallows' Eve*, and a large array of essays, both literary and religious, as well as first editions of his books, many of them autographed, including such scarce items as *The Masque of the Manuscript* and *The Masque of Perusal.*

Although the Wade Collection holds a complete collection of the books of G. K. Chesterton, and many about him, as well as a complete set of *G. K.'s Weekly*, it is limited otherwise to a few original letters and manuscripts. It holds some thirty original letters by Tolkien and has first and other editions of his books and books about him. It has some twenty letters by George MacDonald and has an unusually large collection of his books, including, for instance, twenty-two editions of *At the Back of the North Wind.*

At present by far the best collection of Tolkien's papers is at Marquette University in Milwaukee, "a seven-foot stack" I was informed some years ago. I understand that the Bodleian at Oxford will receive most of the others, presumably to be delivered some years hence when Christopher Tolkien has completed the task of editing and publishing the great array left by his father.

The Bodleian has an excellent collection of original letters and manuscripts by Lewis, along with copies of those in the Wade Collection received through mutual arrangement.

The University of Texas owns many letters and manuscripts by Dorothy L. Sayers, including those concerned with Wilkie Collins, as well as many by Charles Williams. There are various Chesterton collections around the country and a splendid one owned by John Sullivan in England. I believe that Yale University has the best available collection of the manuscripts and letters of George MacDonald. Harvard is also rich in MacDonald materials.

My own experience suggests that the British still prefer the pen to the typewriter. These seven authors came on the scene just when one might type his own manuscripts or have them typed. In Tolkien's case it seems that he first did holographs and then typed them out himself, doing which he added so many corrections that another typing was necessary, and then more corrections, etc. Lewis's early handwriting was very readable but grew steadily more unclear. Lewis says he wrote his manuscripts once, then after corrections made a single fair copy for the editor. No doubt at some point they were finally typed out. The holographs of Dorothy L. Sayers, without exception as far as I have noticed, are pretty well sprinkled with corrections. Charles Williams's manuscripts are quite clean, though in a very small hand difficult to read. Chesterton dictated some of his essays and wrote others in longhand himself.[37] He seems to have made it a habit to sign even his typescripts in his own bold hand.

In 1980, the Wade Collection at Wheaton College was successful in establishing an Anglo-American Literary Review that drew its title from the seven authors in the Collection—C. S. Lewis, J. R. R. Tolkien, Charles Williams, Dorothy L. Sayers, G. K. Chesterton, George MacDonald, and Owen Barfield. The journal, titled *Seven,* is edited by Dr. Barbara Reynolds, long a lecturer at Cambridge University and chief editor of the two-volume *Cambridge Italian Dictionary.*[38] She was a close friend of Dorothy L. Sayers and at Sayers's death completed the translation of *The Divine Comedy. Seven* is designed and printed by Heffers of Cambridge and published by Wheaton College in Illinois. There are equal numbers of American and British members of the advisory board.

A study surveying the period between 1965 and 1980 indicates that master's theses or doctoral dissertations on these writers were done in seventy colleges and universities in the United States, including Chicago, Columbia, Cornell, Fordham, Massachusetts, Michigan, Notre Dame, Pennsylvania, Temple, and Texas; also in the universities of Aberdeen, Auckland, Cambridge, Gakushuin, Leicester, Münster, Oxford, The Gregorian in Rome, Reading, Toronto, Toulouse, and Victoria. In this same period some 120 books were published about the seven authors, the great majority in the United States.

I am not able to speak at any length about research elsewhere except to say that in the latest twelve-month period the Wade Collection has welcomed eight hundred visitors (including a good many children and others to Lewis's Narnia wardrobe). Of these, three hundred were our own college students. There were

37 Letter from Barbara Davis, the Lorette Wilmot Library, Nazareth College of Rochester, January 7, 1981.

38 For further information: http://www.wheaton.edu/wadecenter/Journal-VII.

at least twenty off-campus researchers working on books and academic studies, some staying with us for as long as a month. Among these were Charles Malik of the United Nations; Roma King, the Robert Browning expert; the chairman of English at Baylor University; and a scholar from the University of California engaged in writing a dissertation.

At this writing I know of a biography on C. S. Lewis that is underway by his former student and friend George Sayer. Mrs. Youngberg has contracted to publish an annotated checklist of literature on Dorothy L. Sayers. Mrs. Mary Jordan is working on a very elaborate bibliography of the works of George MacDonald. The Marion E. Wade Collection has prepared a record of dissertations on C. S. Lewis showing, in brief, the substance of the study and the works of his covered, together with title, date, and institution. It plans to prepare similar records on the other six writers.

Chapter 25

A CONVERSATION ON THE IMPORTANCE OF LITERATURE

John Kenyon, associate editor of Christian Herald *magazine, conducted this interview, published in March 1978. It sparkles with details about the early days of the Wade Collection. More important, it places that history within Kilby's larger vision and goal: that evangelical Christians recover their imagination. He sees several hopeful signs of such a recovery, partly through the influence of the English writers he championed so effectively.*

Kenyon: The Wade Collection is becoming a kind of literary crossroads, isn't it?

Kilby: The Collection is attracting increasing attention, and it has done exactly what we had in mind: to establish Wheaton College as a place of serious, scholarly work, second to none in this chosen field. We've been collecting for twelve and a half years. For half that time we had few books and fewer manuscripts or anything anybody would especially want to see. But in the last six years, this thing has been flying high. It seems impossible for me to believe this, but for three of the seven authors, we have the best collection in the world, forever and ever. On C. S. Lewis, we think we have the best collection, considering all things. We have more than one thousand of his original letters. Even the Bodleian Library at Oxford has fewer than five hundred C. S. Lewis letters.

Kenyon: How did you get into this?

Kilby: The very peculiar thing is that I don't know. The more I think about it—and I don't like to use the clichés—there's no question in my mind that the Lord ordered it. In 1964 I had been to England, and after my return was talking about my trip with Bob Golter, who was then our college librarian. Suddenly we were both convinced we ought to begin this collection, and we were convinced that these were the seven authors. We've never wanted to change—add or subtract. For about the first five or six years we didn't have any money from the college. Now we have three full-time people, and we still can't keep up with the work. At the beginning, I had about fifteen letters from Lewis, and handed those over. We got a donation of $500, and that was big money at the beginning. We began to buy Lewis books, and at the beginning called it the Lewis Collection. But we had all these authors in mind. In 1964, the year after the death of C. S. Lewis, I got acquainted with Major W. H. Lewis, his brother. Major Lewis and I became real friends, and he willed us all his own papers, as well as those of his brother that he had in his possession at that time. The collection was housed here in a little wire cage about the size of an ordinary room door, a little square space, and anyone wanting to see the collection got into the cage and the door was shut behind him. When he wanted out he shook the door like a chimpanzee. The collection for about three years was small enough to be housed in the cage. Later, after meeting Major Lewis, I met Mrs. Charles Williams and her son Charles, and we became friends. I met Owen Barfield and was able to help him in his first traveling itinerary in the United States. The collection began to grow as a result of these friendships. Ruth Cording, the wife of a Wheaton faculty member, volunteered at first to come over to do what needed to be done. Our original $500 lasted quite a while; there weren't so many books coming out on C. S. Lewis, and he had passed away. Now, the books on him pour out. Last week I received a new book, a collection of essays on Lewis's fiction, and in the same mail I received a big manuscript on Lewis's fiction from a publisher who wanted me to read it.

Kenyon: What were the characteristics that you saw in these writers that attracted you to them and that commend their writing today?

Kilby: I don't need to tell you that evangelical writing has left something to be desired. But here are people who had Christian testimonies and who could write—all of them. We thought there was no need for us to start collecting Shakespeare or Robert Browning or Tennyson or Wordsworth; they are already collected. Here with these seven modern writers were authors we had a chance to collect. At the same time, many of them are making a mark, especially somebody like C. S. Lewis, on the public as Christian apologists and as stylists. I can't prove things about writing style, but I think Lewis has an almost perfect style. It is so perfect that you don't notice it. I had a wise old teacher who said that's what real style is like. I used to try to be an amateur painter, and I can still go to a big art museum and come home thinking I've got to paint several masterpieces. It all looks so easy. That's part of the whole trick. And these authors were scholarly. We tried to get people who were also known for accomplishments in fields not directly related to religion. Owen Barfield was an attorney, a solicitor in London. Tolkien and Lewis and Charles Williams were university lecturers and experts in their given fields. Lewis's scholarly works are recognized everywhere; even those who don't like his books have to acknowledge that they're remarkable. His book on Milton is I suppose read in every college and university; his history of sixteenth-century English literature is a standard work. Then, they were friends. There was an amazing set of relationships among them.

Kenyon: They met together, didn't they?

Kilby: Yes, the ones who were contemporaries. George MacDonald died in 1905; that left him out. And it was put in print that Dorothy Sayers was one of the "Inklings" who got together at Oxford for discussions and mutual criticism, but she wasn't. But that's only because she wasn't around. One of the things that puzzled me was why Lewis, who liked Chesterton so much, didn't ever try to meet him. Chesterton died in 1936, when Lewis would have been thirty-seven years old. Lewis had been considerably influenced by Chesterton. There were many connections among these seven authors.

Kenyon: It's an amazing thing that C. S. Lewis's books continue to sell in such volume.

Kilby: Would you like to have the latest figure? I just had a letter from Macmillan saying that they have sold 12 million copies of his books, and expect to sell two million this year.

Kenyon: Why is that?

Kilby: They're good!

Kenyon: What do they say that other books don't?

Kilby: Lewis knows how to take the philosophical and especially theological things that other people make dull, and turn them into very simple statements. I spoke once at the University of Illinois on Lewis as a logician and imaginer. He has that tremendous combination of being a past master in logic—he learned his logic as a young atheist, from the old atheist Kirkpatrick—and it was this logic that he says brought him to God, very much against his personal will. He couldn't help it. On the other hand, he has this other quality that so many evangelicals lack in any really tangible way: his tremendous imagination. Just a couple of weeks ago a young preacher, a graduate of our college now going to a pastorate in Hamburg, New York, and who wants to be the very best pastor he can, asked me about this over a period of about two hours. One of the things I said was, "You've got to try to get a metaphoric mind." I suggested he read some poetry, and read it seriously. So many people feel that's an alley they are not going to travel. They don't know what you mean. But C. S. Lewis had an amazing way of getting an illustration, a metaphor, which was perfect. With some writers this shows up as a contrived or forced cleverness. Not so with Lewis. There is an immediacy, a directness in what he had to say, as if it was all there, and all he needed was a question to bring it out. Growing out of his literary life, I've recently had two brilliant young men, both graduates of Wheaton, who told me that they had an edge on other men in seminary because they had been literature majors. I do think that the study of literature gives you this metaphoric way of looking at things. Yet a good many Christians think of imagination as foxfire of some sort.

Kenyon: Lewis's imagination is most clearly seen in his children's books, such as the Narnia series, isn't it?

Kilby: But there you have another aspect of it—you have things like marsh-wiggles and that famous mouse Reepicheep. I think Lewis created two characters in the full sense, the way Charles Dickens did. Reepicheep and Puddleglum, the two characters, are the genuine article, based upon his literary study. Our college kids pick this up in a hurry. But most Christians don't know much about the mythic; the notion of talking trees is just nothing for them. Dryads and centaurs and dragons make them smile condescendingly. Lewis was drawing on a vast reservoir of reading that most of us know nothing about, and out of that he wrote. And of course he had the mythic view. Students spend a quarter or a semester in a course I called the Modern Myth, to grasp the fact that there's something very real here. When they get it, you ought to see what happens to them. A revolution takes place in their lives. Sometimes on my final exams I asked them which of the books they had read were most appropriate to our modern times. They would take it to heart, and talk about what happened to them in reading a given book or in the whole course. The brighter they were and the deeper their Christian commitment, the harder they were hit. I think I saw Christian development take place in my one-semester class that a preacher would be glad to see in a year of preaching. Students said, "My life is changed. I see everything clearly now. I know a direction I'm to take."

Kenyon: What you're saying is that this literature really grips the young people.

Kilby: As nothing ever did before. It's like falling in love. And by the way, this thing spreads. One of our graduates, a woman who majored in chemistry and went on to take her doctorate in that field, is teaching at a community university in the state of Ohio. She wrote me, "What do you know? I'm in the English department here, teaching literature." And it turns out that she has sort of rehabilitated the whole English department. She has sixty-seven people in her class—something unheard of; they usually expect about ten in a class—and she had to turn about thirty away. When the English department there put in its first graduate-level course they asked her to teach it, and it was a seminar on C. S. Lewis. Her classes fill up. So do Tom Howard's at Gordon College. The class here at Wheaton runs about a hundred students. One of our young men went over to teach at Aurora High School, and after a year or two they asked the teachers if they'd like to teach some elective course they'd enjoy, thinking it would be something like stamp collecting. He said yes, he'd like to teach a course on these British authors. He nearly knocked me off my feet when he told me that 350 high-school kids signed up to take the course.

Kenyon: Then the popularity of these authors isn't likely to decline.

Kilby: Not at all. I saw a printout of the best sellers in the Logos stores, located near college campuses, and out of the three hundred top books, C. S. Lewis is on the list twenty-eight times. His books ranked first, second, third, sixth, eighth, tenth, eleventh, and so on, topped by his *Mere Christianity*, *The Lion, the Witch and the Wardrobe*, and *The Screwtape Letters.*

Kenyon: Are you impressed with the quality of the Christian books being published now?

Kilby: I'm happy to say that in the forty years that I've been at Wheaton College, there has been a very great improvement in everything, down to the quality of paper. We've learned how to use white space, and how to use color. The quality has improved. Christian novels were notoriously bad, almost without exception. But evangelical taste is going up, clearly, and we are doing better. I believe our writers' conference at Wheaton has had something to do with that. It's now twenty-two years old. Poetry has greatly improved. As an example, Bob Siegel, a Wheaton man, has two books of poems, and they have been reviewed in glowing terms by the most erudite poetry journals—a thing unheard of years ago. Luci Shaw is going all over the country giving readings of her poetry; that tickles me. John Leax at Houghton is doing well as a poet. In drama, little is happening as far as writing is concerned, but there's a lot of dramatic production going on, and writing will follow.

Kenyon: In this electronic age, with television claiming so much attention, are young people willing to discipline themselves for serious writing?

Kilby: A writer in *U.S. News & World Report* recently said that it is now obvious that only about 30 percent of the population is going to be "liberally educated" in the future, and he concluded that they will be the ones to run the country. I hope that's true. I have staunchly stood up for liberal education. I used to have to calm the literature majors down a little, and say, "Don't get your education in terms of graduating in June and getting a job in July.

After all, you're going to live several years. Don't worry; you'll get a job." I ask them what they would like with all their hearts to be doing twenty years from now. If they tell me they'd like to be writing, or in publishing, I suggest that they borrow a little money if necessary, go to a Christian publisher, and say, "I'll work for you free of charge for six months," and mean it. Chances are, he'll take them on, and they'll get the experience they need.

Kenyon: What qualities should people look for in books for their own enjoyment?

Kilby: One thing they've got to do is somehow pry themselves loose from the TV set. I keep hearing—and it's a joyful thing—of parents who read books to their children. Often it's the Lewis *Narnia* series. It's easy to get started, because there are paperbacks of a great deal of Lewis and Tolkien and these others. Lists of the best novels in the world do exist. But I don't think the problem of most Christians is a list of books; it's an attitude that has to be created, that books are really valuable. The real problem is that life catches us all, and we don't have the will to [choose] the right priorities. I'm guilty of this myself: I promise myself that I'll take a long walk every day, and more than half the time I don't do it. It's our priorities, and the blasted television set, that keep our will weak. One book I recommend to people is *How to Read a Book,* by Mortimer Adler. He gives characteristics of a great book. I often quote one thing he says: "A great book is one that will not let you down if you try to read it well." Isn't that beautiful?

Chapter 26

ON READING AND WRITING FICTION

The intense interest in Tolkien gave rise to a number of "little" magazines and journals. One of the most important of these was Arkenstone, *which published the first part of this interview with Kilby, conducted by Katherine Langan, in the May/June 1978 issue. It reveals important details about Kilby's love of books from childhood on, and the path that led him to become such an important voice for the writers in the Wade Collection.*

Some people are born with a love for books. Clyde S. Kilby, founder and curator of the Marion E. Wade Collection at Wheaton College, was one of them. It was the growth of this love, along with many other related topics, that was explored in a three-hour interview with Dr. Kilby, conducted at his office in the Wade Collection. With the affability of a true gentleman, Kilby begins these remarks reminiscing about his early days as a bibliophile growing up in the mountains of eastern Tennessee.

We had a little public library in my hometown that must not have been much larger than my office here. As I recall, it opened twice a week and they let you take out three books at a time. I went and got my six books a week. Sometimes I can remember the very smell of those books from over sixty years ago, and the texture, I guess. Sometimes I feel a tremendous closeness to those books. My family members weren't readers. They didn't take much to reading, but I did. I had a yen to read, right from my earliest life.

This little library provided Kilby with Hawthorne's Twice Told Tales, *The Rover Boys, Tom Swift, and "all the usual stuff." One book that became particularly dear to Kilby was Frances Hodgson Burnett's* The Secret Garden.

I was given the book when I was a little boy, I imagine in the second or third grade. I've read it many times since. I was given that book because Burnett lived in Knoxville. I lived about a hundred miles from there; in those days it would be something to have a Britisher living there in the mountains. I didn't read it for some years, but I did come to love it and I love it more as years pass.

When Kilby was fifteen or sixteen years old he spent $100 and carried home, one winter's evening, four boxes containing the Harvard Classics.

It was not long after they were published. I saw that they were far beyond my understanding, but I read in those things. It still seems a total mystery to me. They were far above me, but I read them and kept reading them.

Seemingly in contradiction to his love of books and learning, Kilby quit high school in order to work in a dry goods and notions wholesale house, and later went to business school to learn advanced shorthand. He aspired to become a court reporter and actually hung out his shingle for a while in that profession.

I was active though I didn't intend to go back to college, which is a silly thing. But in due course I got some sense. When I entered college I was twenty-two. And I had a tremendous yen to know everything. I really did.

Kilby was so intent on learning that he went to the University of Arkansas, "quite deliberately" to take a course from the head of the philosophy department, who was an avowed atheist: "I had heard lots about evangelical Christianity, so I thought I ought to hear the other side." This endeavor had a surprise ending. Finding that he could not get into a class taught by the head of the department, he signed up for another course with another instructor, expecting "a lot of wild stuff." Kilby was surprised:

One of the first things I remember was that the teacher attacked the theory of evolution. I couldn't believe this would happen in a big university. To make a long story short, we nearly hired him, years later, here at Wheaton. The man was from Calvin College and a thorough Christian. In fact, I think the one reason we didn't hire him was that he was, like all good Calvinists, smoking his pipe. This is who I ran into while intending to get the other side.

Despite this unsuccessful attempt to learn what the other side had to say, Kilby did not lose interest in finding out. He continued to read all that he could from both Christian and non-Christian authors.

I think I've learned, in my later years, as much about Christianity from the anti-Christian writers as from the Christian ones.

Among the non-Christian writers that Kilby mentioned were Bertrand Russell, Voltaire, Camus . . .

. . . and Sartre [who] wrote that book on hell. I can never get that out of my mind. No preacher ever taught me more about the terror of hell than he did. It isn't flames. It couldn't be further away from flames; it's a fantastic thing.

One of the more momentous occasions embedded in Dr. Kilby's past, among the influence of other major literary figures such as Milton,

Shakespeare, and Browning, was his first encounter with William Wordsworth more than fifty years ago.

I still remember him having a tremendous influence on me. I can remember my first discovery of Wordsworth, I thought he was as good as the Bible, I don't know why, I just flipped.

In keeping with his bent to Wordsworth, Kilby's college career was marked by an intense appreciation of nature, such that it included general courses in all the sciences except geology. He cites the years he spent thoroughly reading the scientific philosophers as one of the best things that happened to him.

They are humble, genuine people for the most part. They are willing to acknowledge that a very great deal of our knowledge is still to be acquired on any subject that counts.

He still enjoys general reading in the areas of science and nature and calls them "one of my favorite worlds." Yet he is conscious of a change in the quality of his appreciation.

I have to work very hard now to get the same experience out of nature that I got naturally earlier in my life. I have to look sharply and hard, I have to make it a part of my life to look up at the sky and to look at the trees and to listen to the birds and to thank God that they're there. This is what Wordsworth spoke of in *Ode on Intimations of Immortality* when he talked about the glory tending to disappear.

No discussion of literature with Dr. Kilby can go for very long without shifting to focus on the writers in the Wade Collection, who are often, though incorrectly, collectively called the Inklings (i.e., Owen Barfield, C. S. Lewis, Charles Williams, and J. R. R. Tolkien). The Wade Collection includes papers of these three along with those of three others: G. K. Chesterton, George MacDonald, and Dorothy L. Sayers. Kilby's first reading of these writers, when he first came to Wheaton, was G. K. Chesterton's Orthodoxy.

I got the book and it was one of the really great influences on my life. The other book (that Lewis thinks is even better), *The Everlasting Man*, didn't hit me quite as hard.

Kilby commented further on others of the Wade Collection writers:

Lewis has certainly been a great influence in my life. In my early days I jumped on the expository works with great joy, and somehow omitted the fiction. I don't think I even took that much to Screwtape, but I ate up *Miracles* and *Mere Christianity* and those works. I think that is partly because when I first began to read Lewis, thirty-five years ago, there was a great deal more need to defend the gospel. Charles Williams is always difficult to describe. I've seen people who have fallen more for Williams than they have for Lewis or Tolkien. He is unique in his own way. There is just no way to get him down to a category. He has a way of knocking you cold. Lewis and Williams had written their congratulations to each other before they met. They discovered each other and loved each other. So they had a great time together in those last six years of Williams's life. I wish very much that MacDonald were read more. He's too good. MacDonald is one of the best writers in the world, at his best. But he can't keep it up, so you can find weaknesses in every piece of fiction that he wrote. I do remember that awful ending in *The Princess and Curdie*. Unbelievably bad. Nobody with good sense could have written a final chapter such as his. That's his flaw, but I wish people would see the good in his writing.

Kilby describes his experience with Tolkien as "one of the biggest events of my life." Kilby had many contacts with Tolkien, and still maintains very cordial relations with the Tolkien family, but the most exciting was undoubtedly the summer of 1966, when he worked with Tolkien on the manuscript of The Silmarillion.

Tolkien was a good and great man. I am very fond of him, in spite of his idiosyncrasies, which grew out of his genius. I don't think you could call Lewis a genius: he had too thorough a control over his works and his life. Tolkien couldn't handle it, his vision was too big. Lewis had the big vision, but he was always pulling it down to our level. Tolkien couldn't pull it down.

The television production of The Hobbit *offered, in Dr. Kilby's estimation, a regrettable portrayal of Tolkien's work.*

I hated every minute of it. It was awful in every way. The only thing that I thought was good about it was an occasional backdrop or a landscape that I liked. . . . Of course, they exaggerated everything. Lightning alone, by itself, just ordinary, straightforward lightning is something everybody respects. But why in the world do you have to make lightning four feet broad? That's Saturday morning stuff. It's terrible in a serious film. Another thing that I thought was pretty good was Bilbo's trip down to the dragon. The worst thing about the film, among other bad things, was that they crowded too much into it. At least the trip down to the dragon was spread out enough that you began to feel a little something. They used Tolkien's own words quite properly.

Because of the responsibilities of curating the Wade Collection, Kilby has found that his reading time has been sharply curtailed. He retains the joy of reading imaginative fiction and evangelical books. He says:

My real pleasure is in the old books. I'm very fond of Pooh and *Wind in the Willows*—those classics, you know, that tend to be in the direction of children's books. They're not children's books. Lewis said that any book not readable by both children and adults was not a good children's book. This I agree with, if you go beyond grade one or two.

Dr. Kilby confesses, among his other great loves, to having a tremendous inclination toward children.

I have a great yen for children. I have no children, but I love children. Some people say it's because I'm not around them long enough. I love children and nature. I've never checked this, but I've heard that Martin Buber in his later years said that he couldn't learn anything more from adults, and he tried to stay around children. I've felt that kind of thing. It's amazing how many masks we acquire. Children, I know, acquire them very young. But still, I think you can see more reality in them (of a certain kind) than you can ever see again in adults.

A friend of Kilby's and one of his favorite people was the author of several excellent children's books, Madeleine L' Engle.

She comes here frequently; she even cooked breakfast at my house one morning when my wife was in the hospital. She went into my kitchen, without asking one word, and started cooking. She seemed to know where everything was. . . . I think she is one of the most amazing people I've seen in a while. If I had to pick the five most significant people I've ever met, I'm sure she would be on the list. The interesting thing is that there is nothing put-on about her. She is amazingly who she is, yet all of it is significant. That's her whole. All of her expository books are about herself, without any of that egotism that you inevitably get when you start talking about yourself.

A better guide to the treasury of the Wade Collection literature could not be found than Clyde S. Kilby. For those who are just starting or who have read some and want to read more, he has these suggestions.

On Tolkien:

There's not much choice, but don't start people out on *The Silmarillion.*

On Lewis:

I always like to ask this question first, "Does the person like to read fiction?" There are, of course, people who don't. If they like to read fiction, then I suggest the space trilogy or Screwtape, of course. That's a good old standby. It normally would be understood pretty clearly. The space trilogy does have that far-off quality that we like—I mean going out in space, a science fiction quality. If they don t like fiction, I suggest *The Problem of Pain.* Here's something that's common to us all. It's short, and it covers an awful lot in addition to mere pain. He covers, for instance, that thing that Lewis talks about so much—that you can't use nature to prove anything. You can't use reason to prove anything. You can't use reason to unreason, that's a better way to say it. He says it that way in one place. If you are merely a natural product then there is no place for you to criticize yourself. Cows don't criticize, and so on.

On Williams:

I suggest the novel *Descent into Hell.* I picked that one to teach. It seemed to me that you could get some pretty clear things out of it. Here is a man who gives himself, deliberately, to hell, to the lower way. And you see him descend into hell. Then you have Pauline (and I think it's beautiful): you can see her first little phrase to suggest that she is being called of God. It is just nothing. Then you see the whole thing of her being called and coming into the light. The dead man is quite complicated, but otherwise I think it's a pretty clear novel. I don't think that you can quite recommend his nonfiction to a beginner. I think that a reader would have to get interested in Williams first. But *He Came Down from Heaven*, *The Descent of the Dove*, and probably some of his essays are your best bet with him. It was W. H. Auden who said that he read *The Descent of the Dove* for twenty-two years and still hadn't got to the bottom of it.

On Chesterton:

I would unquestionably say *Orthodoxy* and *The Everlasting Man* were good beginnings. At least, they were for me.

On Barfield:

I would certainly suggest *History in English Words*. That was his second book, I think. I told him once that his first book, which was called *Poetic Diction*, had the worst title of any book in the world. I told him that if he would change the title to *The History of Consciousness*, it would sell five times as many copies. He said, "Well, it's been on there a long time, that title."

On MacDonald:

There is no question, the children's books, any of them. They're all so beautiful, especially *The Princess and the Goblin*. In my opinion, that's the best book he wrote. *At the Back of the North Wind* is his second-best book. That book has been steadily in print for over a hundred years, which is quite something. The best thing for somebody who is thoughtful is that anthology of his [edited by Lewis], which has just been reprinted by Macmillan. It's called *An Anthology of George MacDonald*. I think that's a fabulous book. Lewis took most of the material from there out of three of MacDonald's books called *Unspoken Sermons*.

On Sayers:

The best bet with her, it seems to me, is to get the collection of her essays called *Letters to a Post-Christian World* [currently being reprinted by Macmillan under the title of *The Whimsical Christian*], that is, unless you want to put people on to her detective books. Her best book for me is *The Mind of the Maker.* I read this book long years ago. What she does there is talk about how to write, using as a model the Trinity. If there is anything bad about the book, it's that she finds too many analogies. It's a profound book.

When asked if more works by these authors would be coming out, Kilby stated that most of the fiction is already in print, and that not much more would come out until new writers start turning out books with the same mythic quality as these writers' works. We can, however, expect to see some more in print.

We have enough letters here at the Wade Collection of Lewis's to fill up two or three more volumes. There will be some more letters of his. With Tolkien, there will be a lot of publication of his scholarly articles. The only imaginative thing yet to come out will be *Mr. Bliss*, which is about thirty pages and is quite a children's story. It will come out in due course. Right now I'm evangelizing for Sheldon Vanauken's new book, *A Severe Mercy.* They told him last month that it was ready to go into a fourth edition, and before the end of the month they told him it was going into a fifth printing, which is 60,000 copies of the book since last October. I think it may still get on the best-seller list. There again you have a fine example, much like Lewis's own, of how a worldling falls into a group of people that he likes and are very intelligent. Then he finds out that they are Christian. That's exactly what Vanauken and his wife found. They became Christians—it's a great story. I've tried to get the new group of Christian filmmakers interested in the story: I think it would make a great film.

Because of the impact that the Wade Collection writers have had on Kilby and on the students who studied modern myth under him in past years, Kilby encourages aspiring authors to try their hand at myth. However, he warns:

Writing is one of the hardest jobs in the world. Nearly everybody fails as a writer. I suppose for every manuscript that gets published there are twenty that end up in attics. There is a story about Hemingway. When he was at Harvard he told a professor that he wanted to be a writer. The man said, "You'll starve." Hemingway said, "I don't care," and the professor responded, "You'll be a writer." It's all too simple, I'm sure, but that story is told.

Dr. Kilby does have some sound advice for people who want to write. He himself once desired to write one-act plays. His professor at the University of Minnesota told him that the best thing to do was to go home and read one hundred one-act plays.

I thought that was great advice. I think you must do a vast deal of reading, unless of course you're a native genius. If you want to be a writer, you have to write. I've said this to my creative writing classes for most of my teaching life. You have to quit hoping that you'll write. You have to write today, not tomorrow, today. I never had but one student that followed my advice.

Kilby tells of a well-known writers' center in southern Illinois (where the book From Here to Eternity *was written). The woman that directed the center had a unique method, in that she had everyone there, whether they had published or not, copy an entire novel word for word. Kilby modified the technique slightly, and instead he would read intently for forty-five minutes, then would go directly to writing. This he found to be very effective.*

But who knows how you learn to write? You work hard at it and you immerse yourself in it. . . . You have to keep at it. This is the worst pitfall for anybody that wants to write. You have to be unafraid of imagination. Most Christians are desperately afraid of it. You've got to be free, in the good sense of the word, not in the normal crazy sense of the word. The old thing they always say to a young writer is, "Write something you know something about." Lewis always said that you had to begin every strange story, every far-out story, with something mundane. . . . Lewis says somewhere that a man will never find anything meaningful on the moon unless he finds something meaningful in his own backyard. I think that's great stuff. I believe very much in that. Somehow, you've got to get depth. You can't just sit down and write. The British get depth, you know. They don't get as much as they used to in my opinion. They're learning too many US ways. . . . I used to tell my students in my creative writing classes, the first day and very carefully, that if they thought I could teach them to write or make better writers out of them, then they might as well quit while they could still get their money back. I told them the thing I could do for them was to make them do a lot of writing. That's about all you can ever say.

One of Kilby's current aspirations is to write a book on how the Wade Collection became the prestigious archive that it is. When he talks about the work, there is a mixture of love, humility, and excitement in his voice and manner.

You wouldn't believe what goes on here. I could tell you for twenty-four hours the things that I think are miraculous about this place. I don't know how we got this collection started with these seven authors. I just have the deep conviction that God was doing it and he keeps on doing it. We have the best collection in the world on four of the seven writers. We have people come here from Britain who knew these writers personally to use the collection. It doesn't make sense, but it's a fact. Someday I want to write the story of how a small Midwestern college became the collection where even those Britishers who were on the spot with the Inklings come for information. Writing books is a disease, you know. Once you get one written, you have two or three forever on the backburner.

Cold-blooded quoting, in the transfer from tape to print, does not always convey the qualities of the man who said the words. Lest the impression fail to come through, let it be clearly stated that Clyde S. Kilby comes across as a remarkable man—a man of God and a man of letters. He is indeed a worthy guardian of the legacy of Christian scholarship handed to us by the Wade Collection authors.

Chapter 27

MYTH: THE NOSTALGIA FOR ETERNITY

The second installment of this interview was conducted by Hal Pendergrass for the July/August 1978 issue of Arkenstone. *It deals particularly with the nature of myth and language, the relationship between the two, and some other possible sources of literary myth in contemporary literature.*

In the first part of the Kilby interview published in the May/June Arkenstone, *an attempt was made to acquaint readers with Dr. Kilby's intellectual background and present his rich insights on a variety of topics. Dr. Kilby's prolegomena to the seven authors whose writings constitute the Marion E. Wade Collection of Wheaton College (of which Dr. Kilby is the curator) and his advice to a new generation of Christian writers were included. This collection, in the span of less than fifteen years, has become an internationally known cynosure for researchers and aficionados of the literature housed there. During the course of our three-and-a-half-hour visit with him, Dr. Kilby, in his gracious and homespun manner, managed to keep two inexperienced and nervous interviewers relaxed and enthralled with his conversation. A whole new vista of Christian joy and life opened up for me within those rather humble rooms that house the Wade Collection.*

At the heart of this interview with Dr. Kilby was a discussion of the meaning and influence of myth, and the modern mythmakers. This has been an area of intense concern for Dr. Kilby in his provocative writing and his fruitful teaching career; he treats this matter more fully in earlier chapters in this collection. Indeed, his interest in myth is the golden thread that runs through all the writers whose works are represented in the Wade Collection, and is the bond linking Tolkien, Lewis, Williams, and the others as a group. Here, we break into the interview at the end of a discussion of J. R. R. Tolkien's work.

Kilby: *The Lord of the Rings* is a marvelously wonderful story—and it brings up the whole question of myth. I spend a whole quarter talking about it here [at Wheaton College], trying to get my students to see what is really meant by myth. It's not easy. They know it when they meet it, but they don't know how to talk about it. It's too much. It's beyond words.

Arkenstone: Could you talk about the relationship of myth and Tolkien's discussion of Truth with a capital *T*?

Kilby: I think the best phrase that describes it is that of Mircea Eliade. Myth is "a nostalgia for eternity." That says it about as well as anything can. The word *myth* has three meanings. Today it is used mainly in the sense of a big lie. We see this all the time in the newspapers. The second meaning of *myth* is in reference to those such as the Greek, Roman, and Norse myths. I have tried to talk about a third meaning, one that is so deep and endless that you can't ever fathom it. But fortunately, there are today good examples of myth, such as *Perelandra*, *Out of the Silent Planet*, and especially *Till We Have Faces*. And you have such writers as William Morris and Swinburne who did some mythic writing in the nineteenth century, but there are not a lot of illustrations of modern myth. Perhaps I can best allude to what my students told me on their final examinations. I would ask them, "Which of the books we read do you think is the most significant for our lives today?" They would often begin by talking about themselves and what happened to them during the course. Great basic changes had often taken place in their lives.

Ark: Is this due to the underlying Christian attitude of the writers? Is there a basic difference between a Christian work of myth and a non-Christian one?

Kilby: No question. What you are comes out in what you're writing. When teaching creative writing I once made a statement (it was probably too radical) that a novelist could hardly write one sentence that was not in some measure autobiographical. Lewis said if a Christian sits down to write a story the one thing he must not remember is that he is a Christian. He must first of all write a good story. But, says Lewis, if you are a real Christian, it will get in. He uses Aslan as a case in point, saying that he suddenly bounded in whether or no. Lewis's idea is 100 percent away from the notion of a sermon sugarcoated with fiction. Interestingly, Tolkien jumped on Lewis as too allegorical in his Narnia stories.

Ark: Other people have been critical of Lewis for being too didactic.

Kilby: Well, he certainly went as far as you can go. I think he did it successfully.

Ark: What about Charles Williams? Not all of his books are allegorical, but they explode in your face with impact and meaning.

Kilby: They're symbolic. In fact, Williams is the kind of writer that is very hard to describe. He certainly is different from either Lewis or Tolkien.

Ark: Lewis, in *That Hideous Strength* and *Till We Have Faces*, begins to have some of that same quality as Williams's works. It struck me and yet I don't know how to describe what that sameness is.

Kilby: I know what you mean. For instance, see some of the Charles Williams "flavor" when Lewis brings Merlin into *That Hideous Strength*. Almost the whole of *Till We Have Faces* is "way out" in its overtones. Every time I read it, I see more and more in it. It is by far the best book he wrote.

Ark: It seems to me that very few people are writing myth today. Would you cite any recent examples of mythic writing?

Kilby: I felt a pure mythic quality in part of *Jonathan Livingston Seagull*. But it was finally disappointing, perhaps because of a lack of ultimacy, of the genuine Christian hierarchy. I thought that was the reason. But even a partial myth made it a best-seller, and proves the power of myth to reach us at a meaningful level. It's the same thing with Peter Beagle's *The Last Unicorn*. His story is unquestionably mythic and yet somehow falls short. Ursula Le Guin is great in mythic quality but again leaves something to be desired, especially in the ultimate meaning. I felt the same way about Hermann Hesse's *Siddhartha*, which is truly mythic but with an inadequate conclusion. Much of what we call modern myth breaks down when you really examine it—or goes off into science fiction. Myth is not just story, however good; it has to be a story with a certain quality and depth to it. Lewis, Tolkien, Williams, and Sayers, in her own particular way, all wrote myth.

Ark: What is it that gives these writers that particular depth?

Kilby: The depth that you get in these people is partly owing to their knowledge of medieval history and literature. (And, of course, G. K. Chesterton and Owen Barfield are included here.) They had that background. Everyone in this collection was a student of language. Even George MacDonald in the nineteenth century did a lot of translations from the German. Lewis read Greek much as we read English. He soaked himself in Classical Greek. That is part of it, but not all of it. One must look also at their Christian convictions, their easy acceptance of the world as a genuine hierarchy—knowing that something is clearly better than something else—which is a difficult problem for so many people today, and very apparent in much of our twentieth-century writing. The seven writers in this collection never lost their sense of hierarchy. You can't read any of them without seeing that right off.

Ark: Names seem to play a particularly significant role in many of these books.

Kilby: Yes, one of the easiest ways to talk about it is by means of the names. A great many writers more or less go to the phone directory for names. (I say more or less because, obviously, it's not quite that simple.) Whereas, with Tolkien, the name makes the story, as he repeatedly said. I never felt that I completely understood what he meant. You see, he was one of the world's experts on languages and philology. He was always making up languages, even before he got through what we would call high school. He has talked about how he saw Welsh words on a coal truck. A mere list of Welsh words gave him a real emotion: it never gave me an emotion. It's that kind of quality that is built into his languages. Even the laws of change, of the evolution of words, which he knew perfectly, were built into his created languages. He once excitedly told me that at one point in doing his two Elvish languages, he suddenly found that he had, on the basis of his structural principles, devised the same word in each. He had made the discovery much as you might work out a mathematical problem. I agree with him that naming is important. He says it is *the* thing.

Ark: A great deal of modern philosophy has turned back to the analysis of language. The idea is that we use all kinds of words in common parlance that are impossible for us to define, and yet we seem to have some understanding of those things.

Kilby: Lewis sees a danger in the modern philosophical tendency to define terms to the point of thin air. The trouble is, as he says in his preface to Harding's *Hierarchy of Heaven and Earth*, that this leads you to zero eventually. I have found this out so often in public discussions. I almost want to run when you get onto the track of trying to define a word that's indefinable. I know we must always try to define, but I've seen it at times lead you out into deep water and simply drown you.

Ark: This brings us back to the point we were discussing earlier, that there is no way to define myth.

Kilby: None. Language simply fails. You can only illustrate it. Indeed, there is no way finally to define anything that really counts—love, for instance.

Ark: I think that's a statement that rationality can't be the center of our life in this world. It's part of it, but it can't be the center of it. What do you see as being the place of myth in today's culture? When you talk about the ending are you referring to what Tolkien called "eucatastrophe"?

Kilby: It's a lack of hierarchy, I think you might say—that basic thing that makes you willing, perfectly willing, to talk about truth, goodness, and beauty without any fooling around. It's just built in. The whole trouble with our century is that it has become so twisted, so egotistically twisted, that false faces are built into us, one on top of another, until you don't know where you have come. Even Christians have trouble. In college I ran into what was designated as the new critics and the new poetry, and I saw it run its course for forty years. Both the poets and critics were tremendously clever, but there was something fundamental that was missing. Of course the real place to look for signs of our decay is in television, false advertising and such.

Ark: Dr. Kilby, do you mean to make a distinction between a "myth" and the stories you've referred to as mythic?

Kilby: What one always hopes for is such a story as Lewis's *Till We Have Faces*, where the myth is total. Still one may be gratified for whatever is mythic even if incomplete. Today, with television and all, we expect everything to be explained immediately and attractively, like Post Toasties and Bayer. But if the word *myth* is not subject to that sort of thing, I do think that most people are, unconsciously perhaps, searching for it and feel a joy at any vestige of it.

I suppose it is like Lewis's search for Joy. You remember he says in his autobiography that as a little boy one day he stood by a flowering currant bush and something mysteriously flowed into him—a profundity beyond description—and filled him up and established a vast longing for more. That sounds like mysticism, but it's the kind of thing that happens to many who read Tolkien. I tried opening *The Lord of the Rings* at random to see how many sentences I had to read before I began to feel the mythic power. Generally it was less than half a page. I'm not a weepy sort of person, but genuine myth often reaches my eyes. Once I was in process of the cold-blooded business of summarizing the last part of *Perelandra*, and I sat pen in hand for perhaps two hours, weeping as I worked. What was happening? I can't tell, but it goes among the great experiences of my life. We all want life and more life. We want meaning, genuine meaning.

Ark: What about the older myths, the Arthurian tales and Greek stories?

Kilby: It is very interesting that these stories are rewritten in every generation, as in, for example, T. H. White's *The Sword in the Stone*. You see, it's permanent stuff. It seems to belong in some necessary way to humanity. Lewis, again, is a good example. In *Till We Have Faces* he takes the Cupid and Psyche myth from the ancient past and remakes it into a significant myth of his own.

Ark: How did the Greek myths, arising from totally pagan soil, get their feet so solidly upon reality, or did they not?

Kilby: Shelley, you know, said that if Plato didn't get into heaven, he didn't want to get there himself. Certainly the Greeks, and even earlier peoples, have much to say to us. Take the myth of Pygmalion and Galatea. The young sculptor Pygmalion, detesting the faults of women, nevertheless spent all his talent and energy in fashioning in marble the perfect woman. His sculpture became so beautiful that he went to one of the shrines of Venus and prayed that the sculptured figure might become a reality. He returned to find her no more than exquisite marble. Yet as he looked longingly and lovingly at her what had been stone now slowly turned into warm and delicate flesh. That's Greek and pagan, if you wish, but still it shows the longing for the ideal that is built into people. Like the Tao, it's part of the moral order. You long for the perfect way. Biblically, we must not forget that verse in the first chapter of St. John which says that Christ is the light that shines upon every man coming into the world. Every man includes Greeks and pagans. Lewis believed that at the very heart of the great myths of the ancient past we can find evidence of that light. Lewis said that the first time he even read the myth of Cupid and Psyche (and he was then an atheist) he felt there was something profound beneath the surface of the story. That's the way I see those myths. To be sure they were pagan. But that doesn't preclude them from knowing the difference between good and evil. I still have a deep recollection of my first experience in rending Plato—that wonderful account of Socrates drinking the poison, and the gloriously sane speech that he made about the world and the gods.

Afterword

BY LOREN WILKINSON

It might seem strange to conclude this volume of Clyde Kilby's writings on makers of Christian myth—which has focused mainly on Lewis and Tolkien—with a discussion of Plato and Socrates, following references to Herman Hesse, Ursula LeGuin, Peter Beagle, and Jonathan Livingston Seagull! But that strangeness echoes the gift we spoke of in the beginning, which both Kilby and the writers he championed shared: that is, to see creation itself as a source of wonder. Once again: to call the works he defended "Christian Myth" is to risk reducing their appeal to people of a particular religion (so we might imagine essays on "Buddhist," "Hindu," or "Muslim" myth).

What Kilby was defending was certainly Christian. But his genius was to help those of us who call ourselves Christians to see more of the vast scope implied by "Christian." Kilby was fond of quoting the words from the apostle Paul's Letter to the Colossians, which speak of Jesus the incarnate Word as the one in whom "all things hold together" (Col. 1:17) and, from the prologue to the Gospel of John, as "the light which lights everyone who comes into the world" (John 1:9). It is not surprising, then, that reflecting on the very metaphoric and mythic sources of language (as in Barfield) might point us toward the Incarnation; or that the myths we human sub-creators find or create reflect and refract some of that Light—the greater the story, the brighter the light (as in Tolkien). Nor is it a surprise that following to their true source the "sweet desires" aroused through pagan legend and philosophy might lead one ultimately, as in Lewis's *Pilgrim's Regress*, *Till We Have Faces*, or in the Narnia books, to the one who calls us through the door, whether that of a wardrobe or a stable, "higher up and further in." Clyde Kilby was, and—as we hope these essays have shown—continues to be, a faithful keeper of that Door.

The words of another great mythmaker, the prophet Ezekiel, bring together the metaphors of water and door. In Ezekiel's vision of the temple (which, Jesus implies in John's Gospel, is also a vision of himself) he writes, "The man brought me back to the entrance to the temple, and I saw water coming out from under the threshold of the temple." In Ezekiel's vision, the river that trickles from the door grows to a great stream, and "whereever the river flows everything will live." These writers, like Ezekiel, help us understand the true source of myth, just as Kilby has helped us understand these writers. The words of George MacDonald thus form a good conclusion to this book about a man whose "well of wonder" has been such a source, through these writers, of waters of life.

> The water itself, that dances and sings, and slakes the wonderful thirst—symbol and picture of that draught for which the woman of Samaria made her prayer to Jesus . . . this water is its own self, its own truth, and is therein a truth of God. Let him who would know the truth of the Maker, become sorely athirst and drink of the brook by the way—then lift up his heart—not at that moment to the maker of oxygen and hydrogen, but to the Inventor and mediator of thirst and water, that man might foresee a little of what his soul may find in God.[39]

39 *George MacDonald: An Anthology*, ed. C. S. Lewis (New York: Macmillan, 1960), 81.

Acknowledgments

A few notes about this book: Because these pieces are taken from various sources, written or spoken originally to a variety of audiences, they reflect varying standards of documentation. Dr. Kilby was a scholar, but his primary concern here is usually communication, not scholarly precision, and his intended audience was very broad. We have tried our best to accurately give both Dr. Kilby's words and his method of footnoting, which will thus vary in completeness from chapter to chapter. We have included here references to the books and journals where these writings first appeared. In some cases, though, these were previously unpublished pieces and have been provided through the archives of the Marion E. Wade Center at Wheaton College. All references to the letters of Lewis and others, unless otherwise noted, are from the holdings of the Wade Center.

I am very thankful to the Marion E. Wade Center, to my coeditor Keith Call, and to Mark Burrows, editor at Paraclete Press, both for their vision in finally making this material available to a wider audience and for helping to organize it. Together with the companion volume, published together with this one in the Mount Tabor Books in the Arts series—*The Arts and the Christian Imagination: Essays on Art, Literature, and Aesthetics*, edited by William Dyrness and Keith Call—we are delighted to be able to present a rich harvest of Professor Kilby's writings for a wider audience. Finally, I am deeply grateful for my assistant at Regent College, Sarah Marek, who, more than ten years ago when this project was begun, spent long months deciphering and typing often hard-to-read copies. Together we invite you to drink deeply from the stream that pours from the "well of wonder" which was the mind of Clyde S. Kilby.

—Loren Wilkinson

Sources

Among the published materials included here, these chapters first appeared, with these titles, in the following books and journals:

1 "Logic and Fantasy." *Christian Action.* January 1969.

2 "A Visit with C. S. Lewis." *Kodon.* 1953.

3 "On Scripture, Myth and Theology." Originally published under the title of "Psalms, Miracles and Orthodoxy" in *The Christian World of C.S. Lewis.* Grand Rapids, MI: Eerdmans, 1964.

4 "C. S. Lewis: Everyman's Theologian." *Christianity Today.* January 1964.

5 "C. S. Lewis and His Critics." *Christianity Today.* December 1958.

6 "The Creative Logician Speaking." In *C. S. Lewis: Speaker and Teacher,* edited by Carolyn Keefe. Grand Rapids: Zondervan, 1971.

7 "Lewis and Music." *Christian Scholar's Review.* 1974.

8 "Into the Land of the Imagination." *Christian History.* 1971.

9 "The Joy-Minded Professor." *Christian Herald.* March 1985.

10 "Holiness in the Life of C. S. Lewis." *Discipleship Journal.* July 1984.

11 "Between Heaven and Hell." *Chicago Daily News.* July 1964.

12 "Till We Have Faces." Unpublished manuscript. Kilby Papers, Box 7, Folder 1, the Marion E. Wade Center, Wheaton, IL.

13 "Kilby on J. R. R. Tolkien." *His.* 1969.

14 "Mythic and Christian Elements in *The Lord of the Rings.*" In *Myth, Allegory and Gospel.* Minneapolis: Bethany House, 1974.

15 "The Evolution of a Friendship." *Originally published as Preface, Ch. I "First Meeting" and Ch. II "Summer with Tolkien" of Tolkien and the Silmarillion.*

16 "A Brief Chronology of the Writings." Originally published as Ch. III "Chronology of Composition and Geography of Middle-earth" in *Tolkien and the Silmarillion.*

17 "The Lost Myth." *Arts in Society,* Summer-Fall 1969, 155–162.

18 "Literary Form, Biblical Narrative, and Theological Themes." Originally published as Ch. IV "Tolkien as Christian Writer" in *Tolkien and the Silmarillion.*

19 "Death and Afterlife." Originally published as Ch. VI "Postscript" to *Tolkien and the Silmarillion.*

20 "Portraits of the Unregenerate." *His.* March 1971.

21 "An Ardent Apologist." *Eternity.* November 1969.

22. "Forming of a New Friendship." Originally published as Ch. V "Tolkien, Lewis and Williams" in *Tolkien and the Silmarillion.*

23 "The Oxford Group." Transcribed lecture delivered at Gordon College, MA. Kilby Papers, the Marion E. Wade Center, Wheaton College, Wheaton, IL.

24 "Travels in England" and "The Wade Collection." Transcribed lectures delivered at Wheaton College. Kilby Papers, the Marion E. Wade Center, Wheaton College, IL.

25 "Good Books." *Christian Herald.* March 1978.

26 "On Reading and Writing Fiction." *Arkenstone.* May/June 1978.

27 "Nostalgia for Eternity." *Arkenstone.* May/June 1978.

Index to Persons

Index to Subjects

Index to Scriptures

ABOUT PARACLETE PRESS

WHO WE ARE

Paraclete Press is a publisher of books, recordings, and DVDs on Christian spirituality. Our publishing represents a full expression of Christian belief and practice—from Catholic to Evangelical, from Protestant to Orthodox.

We are the publishing arm of the Community of Jesus, an ecumenical monastic community in the Benedictine tradition. As such, we are uniquely positioned in the marketplace without connection to a large corporation and with informal relationships to many branches and denominations of faith.

WHAT WE ARE DOING

Paraclete Press Books

Paraclete publishes books that show the richness and depth of what it means to be Christian. Although Benedictine spirituality is at the heart of who we are and all that we do, we publish books that reflect the Christian experience across many cultures, time periods, and houses of worship. We publish books that nourish the vibrant life of the church and its people.

We have several different series, including the best-selling Paraclete Essentials and Paraclete Giants series of classic texts in contemporary English; Voices from the Monastery—men and women monastics writing about living a spiritual life today; our award-winning Paraclete Poetry series as well as the Mount Tabor Books on the arts; best-selling gift books for children on the occasions of baptism and first communion; and the Active Prayer Series that brings creativity and liveliness to any life of prayer.

Mount Tabor Books

Paraclete's newest series, Mount Tabor Books, focuses on the arts and literature as well as liturgical worship and spirituality, and was created in conjunction with the Mount Tabor Ecumenical Centre for Art and Spirituality in Barga, Italy.

Paraclete Recordings

From Gregorian chant to contemporary American choral works, our recordings celebrate the best of sacred choral music composed through the centuries that create a space for heaven and earth to intersect. Paraclete Recordings is the record label representing the internationally acclaimed choir Gloriæ Dei Cantores, praised for their "rapt and fathomless spiritual intensity" by *American Record Guide*; the Gloriæ Dei Cantores Schola, specializing in the study and performance of Gregorian chant; and the other instrumental artists of the Arts Empowering Life Foundation.

Paraclete Press is also privileged to be the exclusive North American distributor of the recordings of the Monastic Choir of St. Peter's Abbey in Solesmes, France, long considered to be a leading authority on Gregorian chant.

Paraclete Video

Our DVDs offer spiritual help, healing, and biblical guidance for a broad range of life issues including grief and loss, marriage, forgiveness, facing death, bullying, addictions, Alzheimer's, and spiritual formation.

SCAN TO READ MORE

Learn more about us at our website
WWW.PARACLETEPRESS.COM
In the USA phone us toll-free at 1.800.451.5006;
outside the USA phone us at +1.508.255.4685

Also available from Mount Tabor Books at Paraclete Press...

ART & PRAYER
THE BEAUTY OF TURNING TO GOD
Timothy Verdon

ISBN: 978-1-61261-572-1 | $34.99, Hardcover

In this stunningly beautiful, richly illustrated book, renowned art historian Timothy Verdon explores how sacred art can teach us to pray. "Images put before believers can in fact teach them how to turn to God in prayer. . . ." This is the "art of prayer," when faith and prayer become creative responses by which the creatures learn to relate to the Creator.

"The author, who specializes in art and spirituality, skillfully leads the reader through astute analyses of paintings and other art objects, each a puzzle to be investigated and a mystery to be pondered. Verdon's key themes unfurl through chapters on liturgical prayer, *lectio divina*, intercession, and the like, concluding with a tender reflection on prayer in the face of death. While Verdon, a long-time resident of Florence, focuses on Italian art of the Renaissance, he also considers works from other European countries and eras. Throughout he demonstrates not only mastery of his topics but also a love of great art and deep faith. The result is a visual and verbal feast for contemplation and study." —*Publishers Weekly*

VOL. 2

THE ARTS AND THE CHRISTIAN IMAGINATION: ESSAYS ON ART, LITERATURE, AND AESTHETICS

Clyde S. Kilby

ISBN: 978-1-61261-661-6 | $28.99, Hardcover

The second of two volumes that introduce readers to the reflections of the late Dr. Clyde S. Kilby, professor of English at Wheaton College. In this book, Kilby addresses topics including Christianity, the Arts and Aesthetics, the Vocation of the Artist, Faith and the Role of Imagination, Poetry, Literature and the Imagination. This book explores such questions as "Why is there inside man the desire to, even the burden to create? What is the source of this desire? What is the artist's place in the cultural life of his time?" For readers interested in the study of beauty in art and in literature, Kilby offers fascinating insights as relevant today as when they were first written.

Available from most booksellers or through Paraclete Press:
www.paracletepress.com 1-800-451-5006